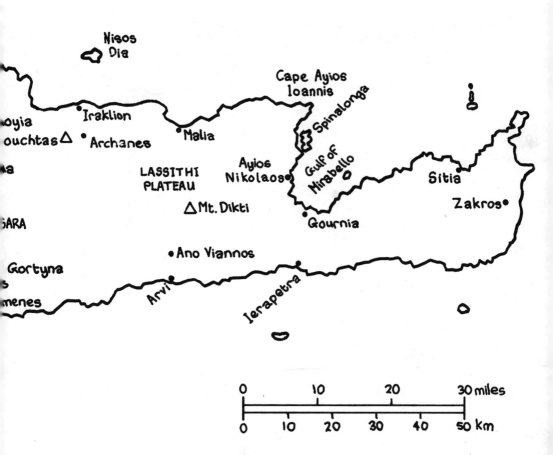

Sea of Crete

Nisos
Dia

Cape Ayios
Ioannis

oyia
ouchtas△   •Archanes   •Iraklion   •Malia   Spinalonga

Gulf of
Mirabello

a

LASSITHI
PLATEAU   Ayios
Nikolaos•

△Mt. Dikti   Sitia

GARA   Zakros•

•Ano Viannos   •Gournia

Gortyna

menes   Arvi   Ierapetra

| 0 | 10 | 20 | 30 miles |

| 0 | 10 | 20 | 30 | 40 | 50 km |

UNDER MOUNT IDA

A Journey into Crete

OLIVER BURCH

ASHFORD
Southampton

Published by Ashford
1 Church Road
Shedfield
Hampshire
SO3 2HW

British Library Cataloguing in Publication Data

Burch, Oliver
    Under Mount Ida: a journey into Crete
    1. Greece. Crete. Description & travel
    914.99'80446

ISBN 1-85253-202-5

Printed in Great Britain

Contents

Illustrations

between pages 88 and 89

The harbour at Réthymnon
The gorge of Arádena
Sfakians

between pages 120 and 121

The Minoan palace at Phaestós
Frangokástello
Kritsá

between pages 216 and 217

The isthmus of Spinalónga, near Eloúnda
Windmills on the pass above the plain of Lassíthi
Knossós: the Cupbearer Fresco in the South Propylaeum
Knossós: the west portico of the north entrance

between pages 248 and 249

View from the taverna at Sitía
The campanile of the Moní Toploú
The north-east coast near Cape Sídheros

Acknowledgements

There are many excellent books in English about Crete, from the nineteenth century onwards, and I have recommended a number in the bibliography. They are invariably written by people fortunate enough to have travelled at great length, or lived for years among the Cretans, often in remote areas, and are filled with fascinating anecdotes of customs long vanished. Other writers, qualified historians or archaeologists, impart their detailed understanding of the ancient sites. This book is not intended to compete with, or even complement this literature, but it may just interest travellers, bored with the sun and the beach and looking for a little adventure. It may, too, help them in an attempt to understand a society and a way of life that is still more distant from our Northern European world than most people would realise. I can imagine this statement offending many town-dwelling Cretans whose urban life-style (with its own Greek flavour) is really much like that of any modern city dweller. Nevertheless, there is still very little industry as such on Crete, and it is essentially a conservative society, the old ways are not readily abandoned, even by the young, and in the remote villages which no coach tour will take you to, a rural culture remains of a kind that even other Mediterranean countries have largely lost.

It would hardly be possible to mention all those to whom I owe a debt of thanks, and the many hospitable, kindly Cretans who have touched us with their warmth will probably never read this book. But I am most grateful to the Prevelakis family for their kind permission to quote from the works of the late Pandelis Prevelakis, to Faber and Faber Ltd for allowing me to quote the great Cretan writer, Nikos Kazantzakis, and also to Michael Llewellyn Smith for his translations of Cretan folk songs and poetry, published in *The Great Island*. Warm thanks are due to our travelling companion, Michael Doyle, for his photographs. Within my own family circle, I wish to thank my sons – Steven for the map, and Malcolm for his company – and my father for his proof reading. In particular, I owe a great debt to Joan, my wife, for all her advice and hard work with the manuscript.

*For Elsie Parker, Joan's mother,
who shared our first Cretan journey*

Prologue

The aircraft had begun its long throttled-back descent somewhere over Athens, gradually sliding down towards the great island at the southern rim of the Aegean. Northern Europe had been covered in a solid sheet of cloud; we had left England on a frozen grey morning, but it looked as though Greece was going to do the right thing by winter-weary travellers. Now dark blue sea showed in the afternoon sunlight and the occasional ship's wake showed up as a faint white furrow far below.

Once upon a time, the ferry from Piraeus was the standard traveller's approach to Crete; there would have been time to watch Ida and the White Mountains gradually raising their snow-covered heads above the horizon, until the long connected chain of tumbled limestone barred the way south, the towns crouching below. Today, most visitors will arrive by air, probably on a package, disgorged suddenly from a hermetically-sealed tube, a little under four hours from Luton or Gatwick or Cologne. These abrupt north–south transitions always seem to jar a little, for the Alps still separate more in Europe than the weather systems.

After six years' absence, I wondered whether perhaps our memories of a landscape sometimes harsh, sometimes beautiful, a people sometimes delightful, occasionally a little frightening, always strong meat, could somehow have been distorted or romanticised. So many English people seem to take holidays in Crete nowadays and find it pleasant but unremarkable. Last year Minorca, this year Crete, next year Corfu . . .

This time we only had a couple of weeks to travel on the Great Island, as is the case, I suppose, with most tourists. Joan and I were playing truant from running our small garage business, our young sons, Steven and Malcolm, had leave of absence from school spring term, while our friend, Michael, who had just changed his job, could hardly hope for more than a fortnight's leave. We had previously been totally enchanted by Crete, but circumstances had somehow prevented us returning since 1979. Michael had not been to Greece before and we wanted to show him as much as possible. So here we were on a two-week, two-centre package, a week in the west, a week in the east, taking advantage of every out-of-season discount available for flights, hotels, child reductions, etc. The main, fairly expensive, but essential item on the budget, was the car hire.

Anyone with a good road map (available from the Tourist Office or car rental companies) will have little difficulty in tracing our routes, bearing in mind that some of the roads and terrain described are fairly rough. You will find that a car in good mechanical order and (important this) a good ground clearance will help your peace of mind on these sections – you will not see many low-slung sports cars in local use.

We travelled in the early spring, partly because the demands of business prevented us from leaving later, and partly to avoid the summer crowds which have so increased in recent years. The mid-summer heat would in any case have precluded such an energetic trip as this promised to be. Two other advantages come to mind; one being the early season discounts on flights and hotels already mentioned, the second that the island is at its greenest and most beautiful in spring with an explosion of wild flowers after the winter rains. We had enjoyed a mild and sunny winter here before, and didn't plan to lie on the beach any more than do the Cretans themselves.

* * * *

"As a matter of interest a Boeing 767 hasn't landed at Iráklion before, so . . . er, this will be a first," was our captain's last encouraging remark before executing a series of steep lurching turns which would bring us down from the turbulent air over the mountains. Suddenly, a school of porpoises could be seen, black shapes arching, and white spray pluming up as they re-entered the water, a joyous sight. In Greece, the dolphin still means good luck and lightens the hearts of fishermen and sailors, as in the days when it was sacred to Thetis, the mother of Achilles, and the shrine at Delphi. Stories abound of their love of music and their saving of drowning men. Some sailors were once reputed to be able to call them up by name – apparently they are all called Vasili. The twenty or so 'Basils', leaping and plunging through the waves, were only in sight for a few seconds until our aircraft levelled out, but there could not have been a better omen for our journey.

CHAPTER 1

The Road to Réthymnon

The *tramountána,* the north wind, was blowing from the sea as we walked across the tarmac, cold weather by the standards of the island, although the sky remained clear and bright. The airport seemed little changed, for all the extra traffic, with coarse, scrubby grass around the runway built a few yards from a flat shore, and low dull-coloured hills visible beyond the road junctions and industrial hinterland behind. The passport and customs formalities were as slow, though polite, as ever, the baggage reclaim as frantic a scramble as before. Although we had heard that the airport had been modernised, it was rather encouraging to find the old atmosphere of cheerful Greek chaos still reigning. We were mildly surprised to find the car waiting as arranged.

Having missed the turn on to the new bypass, we found ourselves driving into the outskirts of Iráklion through dusty streets with corrugated iron shutters pulled down during the afternoon siesta. Half a million people now live on Crete and the general drift to the towns has resulted in a rapid increase in Iráklion's population since the war, something like 20 per cent every ten years. It is now the fifth largest city in all Greece. There seemed to be even more Japanese cars than before, the dust-covered lorries seemed a little less dilapidated, the shops rather better stocked and prosperity more in evidence than I remembered. At first glance Iráklion seems to be a rather ugly modern town with little of interest to a visitor; this is a misleading impression, for there is a great deal to be seen if you take the trouble to search it out – more of this later. We had no time to stop, but on a sudden whim, perhaps with Kazantzakis' old fortress-city of Megalokástro in mind, I drove up through the gap in the walls where the Gate of the Three Vaults once stood, across Freedom Square and straight through the old Turkish quarter. The traffic was light, and we were soon leaving the walled city at the Khaniá

Gate and taking the Street of the Sixty-Two Martyrs towards Réthymnon and the west.

Once clear of the city on the excellent New Road, which revolutionised the island's transport system in the 1960s and paved the way for the carefully-planned tourist boom, we found ourselves making good time past stretches of flowering shrubs with views of blue mountains to the south in the hazy sunshine. It became warm enough to wind the windows down, not as warm as Andalucia in winter, but for us, fresh from English snow and ice, it seemed pretty good for early March. Sections of the road were lined with orange sellers' stalls. I remembered the marvellous flavour of fresh Cretan oranges in winter.

At dusk we reached Réthymnon and drove through the city centre; then along the sea-shore, passing some disused factories with tall brick chimneys, to the headland on the eastern side, without finding the hotel we had booked in advance. Greece is a siesta country; shops are generally open between 8.00 am and 1.00 pm and then 5.00 pm to 8.00 pm. With the dusk, the city had come to life, and each brightly-lit shop or café interior, crowded with customers and hazy with blue tobacco smoke, appeared as a fleeting tableau framed by darkness. The old-fashioned barber shops are as much a feature of male social life as the café: all black leather, white porcelain and cut-throat razors. Greeks never really seem to like shaving themselves, and out in the countryside the peasants tend to leave it to a weekly visit to the barber on a Saturday, making a social occasion out of it.

Turning back into the city, I parked across the street from a small building marked "Tourist Information". The distorted sound of a Cretan lyre blasted raucously into the street from a loudspeaker, making it just as noisy inside as out. Eventually, after I had called out a few times, a short middle-aged man emerged from the back room, his hands encased in shiny red rubber gloves and exuding a strong smell of alcohol.

"Good evening," I began, "I wonder if you would kindly tell me . . ."

"English?" he shouted above the music, "I like all English people – my brother!"

"Oh how kind. I wonder . . ."

"My name is Kostas." My new friend struggled to remove the rubber gloves and shake hands. "Who are you?"

"How do you do, my name is Oliver." In Greece nobody bothers much with surnames, which establishes a pleasant informality at the very beginning of relationships.

"Are you staying in a hotel in Réthymnon?"

"Well hopefully, yes. What I wanted to ask . . ."

"Here is a list of Réthymnon hotels. Some not open yet. Early season. Did you come on the bus?"

"No," I said, deciding to swim with the tide for a bit, "we hired a car at the airport."

"Who from?"

"From Avis actually; look couldn't we turn this music down a bit?"

"Don't you like Cretan music?" He looked put out, but nevertheless turned down the volume a fraction.

"Oh yes, very much," I assured him while he gathered up various brochures from piles on the counter and thrust them towards me.

"Have you the *Travellers' Guide to Crete*?" he demanded, indicating a copy of the book.

"Well yes, I think we have it in the car."

"My name is in the front of that book. I am an international person. Tourists arrive and ask for me by name."

"Such is fame, I suppose."

We mused together silently for a moment on the burden of being in constant international demand.

"Just by the way," I ventured again, "You couldn't tell me where the Rethymna Beach Hotel is by any chance?"

"Didn't you drive past it on the way here?"

"Well I didn't see it. Never mind, we'll go back and look. Thank you for your help."

"Goodbye my friend. Anything you want, come to me. My name is Kostas."

As I reached the car, the lyre was wailing across the street again. Later on in the evening I looked in John Bowman's excellent *Travellers' Guide to Crete* and, sure enough, found an acknowledgement to "Kostas Pallierakis, the extraordinary operator of the Tourist Information Office in Réthymnon".

Turning back towards Iráklion, this time on the old road, we found our hotel a couple of miles out of town, thankfully unloaded the car and headed up towards hot baths. The Rethymna Beach might, I suppose, be accused of being as bland in character as any big hotel, but it does run like a well-oiled machine and must be one of the most comfortable hostelries in Greece. The cooking is surprisingly good too and particularly strong on local dishes. As this was the first day of the new tourist season, we found a party in progress when we came downstairs after unpacking: free ouzo and a series of speeches by local dignitaries and the hotel manager. When all were done, a *lýra* and *lúta* struck up in a series of folk tunes, sometimes wistful, sometimes wild and stirring. The *lýra* is a uniquely Cretan instrument, though not directly related to the ancient lyre which was made with a tortoise-shell for a sounding box. The lyre of Crete is a three-stringed viol, adorned with small bells on the neck, which is held upright on the knee and played with a bow. Its origin is mediaeval, and possibly Venetian, but the sound is strident and oriental in character. Many foreigners find the harsh sound irritating, others find it irresistibly compelling, as do the Cretans who love music, dancing and song above all things. The *lúta* is best described as a type of mandolin. Incidentally, the *bazoúkoi,* which is heard so much in Greek music and frequently in Crete nowadays, is a relatively recent arrival, having been brought out of Asia Minor by the refugees from Smyrna in 1923. Similarly the *santoúri,* which Zorba the Greek was famous for playing, a kind of zither struck with little mallets, is an instrument from northern Greece, as befitting a Macedonian. Popular Greek music is quite a jumble of styles today and on Crete you are as likely to hear the music for the mainland *hasápiko,* the butchers' dance, as for the graceful *sýrtos* of Asia Minor or the *pentozáli,* the five steps, the dramatic warriors' dance of Crete which the Cretans themselves claim came from the Curétes. The cheering part is that they like their own tunes so much, for I can't think of anywhere in Europe where so little imported rock music is played on the radio. Accompanying the band was a dance group of young people in traditional dress; the girls' proud and watchful parents, moustachioed fathers in polished boots and riding breeches, mothers in their best black coats and shoes, sat on a row of wooden chairs drawn up behind. It was a contrived affair for the tourists of course, not a real *glóndi* or party like a wedding or a name day. But as they went through their repertoire, sometimes dignified and stately in the circling *sýrtos,* sometimes wild with the tall young men kicking high in the air and slapping their boot heels in the *pentozáli,* there was a surprising lack of showy or contrived gesture. Sadly, most of the foreign guests applauded half-heartedly and went in early for dinner. No plates were broken.

It was warm enough for a few cicadas to be heard from the balcony that night over the sound of the sea, in spite of the steady on-shore wind. We slept with the door open.

CHAPTER 2

The Roots

Réthymnon was bustling soon after breakfast the next day. Work begins early here, and the gendarme in Martyr's Square was already struggling to control the morning rush hour. We turned left off the coastal highway on to the old road, through the small villages of Prinés and Goniá with their tiled, pitched roofs. After the bleakness and dull cold of the English winter which we had left behind, the lush green vegetation under the olive trees, sprinkled with wild flowers, seemed almost miraculous. February had been wetter than usual, and the resulting rush of growth and bright colours in the clear spring light made us stop the car time after time to wander in the groves among anemones coloured red, white and mauve, carpets of crown daisies and yellow *ranunculus asiaticus,* the turban buttercup. Great iris tubers somehow pushed their way through the tumbled rocks, with promises of even richer colours in the weeks to follow. The outlandish stems of the century plants tilted rakishly high over the road, the huge leaves writhing like snakes upon the verge. In their native Mexico, these plants are used by peasants who ferment the sap, but here razor strops are made from the trunks.

As we wound through the gentle sunlit countryside, the massive presence of the Lefká Ori to the south gradually became apparent, with snow-covered peaks seeming to jostle closer and closer to the road. These White Mountains are named, not for the snow, which disappears between June and October, but for the curiously white colour of the bare limestone summits in the hot sun of midsummer. The highest peak, Páchnes, is at 2,453 metres, just slightly lower than Mount Ida, Crete's highest point. I once heard of a group of shepherds who decided that a few days' work piling up the loose rocks around the summit should easily produce a cairn tall enough to overtake Mount Ida's extra 3 metres, and claim the honour for their own mountain of the west. The job must have turned out to be harder than it appeared because it never has been completed. Apart from Páchnes, there are many crests over 2,000 metres in the White Mountains and one only has to look at the map to see that this intractable, roadless terrain is the wildest part of the island, rising straight up from the depths of the Libyan Sea to the south, to a central massif which looks impassable to all but the omnipresent eagles tracing slow circles around the crags.

These foothills and villages to the north of the White Mountains are known as the *ríza,* the roots, and are the traditional home of the island ballads known as *rizítika,* or songs from the roots. The songs of Crete, like the dances, are of several quite formal styles. The *amanádes* are wistful Turkish songs of passion and love, usually ending in the phrase *Amán! Amán!* (Alas! Alas!). The *mantinádes,* a word of Venetian origin, are rhyming couplets, often composed on the spot and sung round the company line by line as a sort of competition in quick-witted invention. Often satirical, like a kind of limerick, they can be serious too, and apart from the spontaneous composition, there is a vast repertoire of famous *mantinádes.* A couplet which reflects the fatalistic and familiar attitude to death in Crete, so different from our own, goes: "The world's a tree and we the produce of it, And Charos is the reaper and takes the fruit of it."

Charon, the silent ferryman of the dead over the River Styx in the old Greek legends, has in Cretan folklore become transformed into Charos, the Angel of Death himself and ruler of Hades. Charos, as the Horseman of the Apocalypse, rides out to ensnare souls, young and old, and take them down to his own grey kingdom. Curiously, for a Christian people, there is little mention in the folklore of a paradise after death.

> A slender girl met me on the three steps of Hades
> And I thought she would ask me of her mother
> Her brother or her sister or her first cousins;
> But she did not ask me of her mother
> Her brother or her sister or her first cousins,
> But she sat down and asked me of the upper world.
> – Does the sky still hold up, does the upper world
>   stand?
> Do brave young men and women still get married?
> Do they build churches, do they build monasteries?
> Do they baptise children?

> (Trs. Michael Llewellyn Smith, *The Great Island)*

The *rizítika* are more balladic in style, often rather monotonous and dirge-like in their harsh musical accompaniment from the lyre. They tend to be sung at weddings and some are known as *Songs of the Road,* to be sung when the bridegroom's party travels to fetch the bride from her father's house, others as *Songs of the Table* for the feast afterwards. The subjects are dramatic and emotional, songs of war and rebellion, songs of slavery, songs of *xenitiá* or exile, and always that Cretan fascination for death as in the *Soldier's Farewell:*

> Mother, if my friends should come,
> If our own people come,
> Don't tell them what has become of me.
> Say nothing about me, or where I am,
> To make their hearts heavy.
> Lay the table for them to eat,
> Lay out the sleeping benches,
> Find a place for their arms,
> Let them sleep till morning.
> And when they take their leave,
> Tell them how and where I lie . . .

Probably the most often quoted and certainly the most popular in the west of the island, is *The Rebel,* which immortalises the Christian freedom fighter longing for the fine weather of spring to come so that he can go to war against the infidel Turks, turn wives into widows and children into orphans.

> When will the sky grow clear?
> When will spring come round?
> So I can take my gun again,
> (My beautiful patroness)
> And go down to the Omalós
> And the paths of the Mousouri . . .

Long after the Turks had left, this song was adopted by the Venizelist party of the west, as containing sentiments guaranteed to stir any Cretan worth his salt.

* * * *

The green meadows beside the roads were scattered with beehives, and every few yards it seemed, we came on a little painted roadside shrine, sometimes built at the site of accidents, and all requiring the sign of the cross from the more devout passers-by. The shrines contain olive oil lamps and votive offerings of silver arms, legs and eyes dangling before the icon. These represent the afflicted part of the body for which the supplicant wishes to pray, or cajole the chosen saint into providing a cure. Sometimes one sees whole silver babies and wonders what story of heartache or tragedy lies behind the little moulded figurine. The practice is an old one, for similar figures have been excavated at an ancient shrine of the healer Asclepios.

Turning closer under the mountains and past the village of Kournás, we came to the only freshwater lake on Crete, for the porous limestone rocks of the island do not normally allow water to collect. The difficulty of constructing storage dams for rainwater has long been a hindrance to agriculture here. Lake Kournás is a mysterious stretch of water, about 150 acres in size, with steep bare hillsides to the west and south. The clear waters are obviously very deep; of course, local legend claims it to be bottomless. In fact the depth was plumbed in 1949, and found to be 64 metres, but the level varies with the season. Springs of cold water well up in the south-west corner, with an inexplicable surge and increase in flow every five years. There is an old story that a village once stood here, and that the lake is haunted by the ghost of a young girl raped by her father; also that if a gun is fired across the water, the bullet will never reach the far side.

On the road down to the reed beds by the shore, we passed a man in a rough sheepskin jacket, gun slung over his shoulder and dog at his heel. The little *kafeneíon* at the water's edge was shut for the season, so we wandered along the margin among bushes and flowers by a muddy path. Lizards lay out warming themselves in the morning sun, some small, agile, brown and white-spotted, others larger, slower and green coloured, some 12 to 15 inches long. Michael found a locust in a bush; dazed and sluggish it sat on his hand to be photographed. Wild duck started up from the reeds as we passed and winged away towards the dark hills across the lake. We could see nothing alive in the clear, sterile-looking water, although there is supposed to be a kind of freshwater crab. At the end of the lake is a man-made channel and a system of sluices to irrigate the plain of Drámia below and towards the sea. Inland, beyond the spur of the hill behind the lake, lies the strange ruined village of Mathés, with a fourteenth-century church tangled in the roots of a giant carob tree.

Descending towards the plain and crossing the New Road, we came to Georgioúpolis, situated on the coast by the mouth of a little river with areas of reedy brackish swamp behind, which gave the area a bad name for malaria before the war. This quiet little fishing port has its connection with history, being named after Prince George, High Commissioner of Crete, who at the end of the last century planted the fine eucalyptus trees which are its main feature. In the pleasant central square, old men sat on chairs pulled out into the sunshine, in front of whitewashed houses with wrought-iron balconies and pots of geraniums and basil under twisted shade vines and fig trees. We walked down to the fish dock in the river mouth, where fishermen were working on their boats, and beyond to a wide sandy beach fringed with yellow sea medick. In spite of the stiff on-shore breeze, the boys wanted to swim, and Joan stayed with them while Michael and I picked our way along a low breakwater of tumbled rocks to the fishermen's chapel far out from the river mouth. From here, we could see the wild cliffs of Cape Drépanon, the Sickle Cape, jutting out to the west, and look back at the little town nestling among its great shady trees with the foothills of the White Mountains looming behind. The tiny figures of the boys could just be discerned cavorting along the sweep of sand in front of a flock of grazing sheep.

The story of Prince George is rather sad; he arrived in Crete amidst scenes of wild enthusiasm and yet retired seven years later, eclipsed by a more vigorous political force beyond his power to resist. In 1898, after an incident involving the death of a number of British troops stationed in Candia (Iráklion), the Great Powers of England, France, Italy and Russia combined to force the Turks to leave Crete at last, after so many years of rebellion and bloodshed. The island was granted autonomous status, although still nominally under the suzerainty of the Ottoman Empire. Prince George, the younger son of the King of Greece, landed at Soúda Bay on 21 December amidst extraordinary rejoicing to become High Commissioner. Nikos Kazantzakis, described the scene :

When the royal ship arrived all decked up with flags, and they began to fire off rounds from the guns, and the Prince set foot on Cretan soil . . . Have you ever seen a whole people gone mad because they've seen their liberty? No? Ah, boss, then blind you were born and blind you'll die. If I live a thousand years, even if all that remains of me is a morsel of living flesh, what I saw that day I'll never forget! And if each of us could choose his paradise in the sky, according to his taste . . . I'd say to the Almighty: "Lord let my paradise be a Crete decked with myrtle and flags and let the minute when Prince George set foot on Cretan soil last for centuries!"

(Nikos Kazantzakis, *Zorba the Greek*)

The Prince governed from Khaniá over an island with its own flag and currency, and introduced a number of much needed reforms. However, a large faction among Cretans desired *énosis,* full union with Greece, in spite of the political embarrassment this would cause to Greece itself. In 1905 there was an unsuccessful and bloodless revolt led by the young lawyer, Eleftherios Venizelos, which nevertheless resulted in the retirement of Prince George. The union of Crete with Greece finally became officially recognised in 1913 – after Venizelos, now Prime Minister of Greece itself, had defeated Turkey and Bulgaria in the Balkan Wars.

We walked back to the *kafeneíon* under the first trees of the village and ordered cold German beers, sitting on rickety cane chairs in a big courtyard under a corrugated iron roof. The beer came in large bottles covered with condensation and the proprietor and his wife stayed to pass the time of day. In Greece, the land of leisured conversation, a stranger is virtually duty-bound to pay his way with some information about himself or the outside world.

Two more customers arrived on a small rusty tractor, which they left amongst the tables, and began to play cards in the Cretan manner, every card slapped noisily on to the table with immense bravado and much dramatic gesture. We stretched our feet out on the chairs in front of us and sipped our beer. Joan and the boys were still distant figures out by the sea. We were definitely beginning to unwind, to slow down in tune with our surroundings. When there is work to be done on the land here, the people work hard, none harder. But they are mercifully spared our northern work ethic and they have no belief in the innate value of work for its own sake. If the olive trees are in good order, the sheep are safe, the nets are mended, they can happily relax for hours in the café, with no sense of guilt. *Isichía* is their word for peace and tranquillity.

Musing on these things, we were almost asleep by the time Joan and the boys came up from the sea for their drinks. Georgioúpolis seems an idyllic spot, at odds with its unhealthy reputation and the swamps of giant reed behind. In much of Greece, malaria was eradicated by the introduction of a little creature called the Central American mosquito fish, which eats the deadly anopheles larvae – a neat solution compared to the alternative of extensive DDT spraying. A smell of barbecued meat from somewhere up the street put us in mind of lunch and so we reluctantly returned to the car and set off for Vríses.

On a flat section of road through gardens of orange trees, we passed a man swinging a plastic bag of the fruit. Remembering the orange sellers of the previous evening on the new road outside Iráklion, we stopped to buy some.

"Good morning," I began uncertainly in my phrase book Greek, "How much are the oranges, please?" *Portokália* is the word for oranges, the first having been introduced from Portugal long ago.

He smiled to show he had understood, a brown weather-beaten face, taking in our pale, northern complexions, cameras and Avis hired car.

"Deutsches?" he asked politely, for the English and German accents sound very similar.

"No, English," we replied, the first of many times, and his smile grew broader as he unlocked an old wrought-iron gate into a grove beside a white chapel and climbed up into the nearest tree. I stood beneath with the boys, ankle-deep in a pile of discarded rotting oranges as he selected the best of the rich globes, glowing like lanterns among the dark green leaves, and threw them down to us till our hands and pockets were all filled with large sweet, juicy fruits; 3 or 4 kilos and we cried out to him to stop. I asked him how much they were, although we had guessed the answer already.

"Ochi, nix drachmes!" he said, waving his hands and accepted our profuse thanks with gracious courtesy – it was his moment of triumph. This was just one of many examples of hospitality and also a lesson that here the greatest favour you can show a man is to accept his gifts with gratitude. *Philoxenía,* or generosity toward strangers, is a matter of great tradition and pride, while meanness is a shameful thing to Cretans; this in an island where quite serious crimes, even of violence, tend to be seen as all part of life's rich pattern. The northern habit of dividing restaurant bills, for instance, is regarded with abhorrence – if you eat with a Cretan you will invariably find that he has slipped out and quietly paid the bill before the end of the meal. The passion for *philoxenía* can be at its most embarrassing in a small village, when people you are sure possess a mere fraction of your own worldly wealth insist on buying all your drinks. There is no solution to this problem in a country where you don't need money to have style. They have a word for this philosophy too – *levendía,* the gallant attitude to life – and its application is a great compliment to anyone.

Vríses, The Fountains, with its memorial to the 1898 rising, is a village with an air of the mountains about it, lying as it does at the junction of the old Réthymnon–Khaniá road with the route south across the White Mountain passes to the wild province of Sfakiá. In the spring, the melting snows above make the little stream running through the centre of the village chatter over its stones, while ducks and geese squabble around the pools. Like nearby Lake Kournás, this is a rare pleasure in this dry, thirsty land. Once, when Crete was covered with great cypress forests, water was abundant. Even in the nineteenth century, travellers reported plentiful water supplies in areas where today there are long droughts and wells dry up. Now the trees are gone and the water with them, while the goats steadily attack the remaining maquis and phrygana year by year.

As in so much of the west, many of the men here still wear the traditional mountaineers' dress of high leather boots and the *kefalomándilo,* a black-fringed headcloth, sometimes looking a little like a turban. The embroidered jacket, sash and enormously baggy *vrákes* (breeches) affectionately known as crap catchers, are only worn by very old men now, the younger generations tending to wear smartly cut riding breeches with their boots. Once the outfit would have been topped by a red-lined cloak for special occasions; these too have disappeared, although shepherds often wear a cloak of thick white or brown wool against the cold air of the high pastures. The women for their part, unless young, tend to be dressed in traditional black with their heads and lower faces wrapped in Arabic fashion as they work in the fields or wash clothes in the stream. There is no hard and fast rule that married women should wear black clothes, but mourning for any relative normally lasts at least two years, for a husband or son probably for life, and so the opportunity to wear bright colours is restricted. Incidentally, there is virtually no divorce in the villages and even widows tend not to remarry. In some areas, there is an inhibition among the older women about showing their teeth – hence the scarves wrapped around the chin – which must date back to Turkish times or even to the old Arab belief that an evil spirit could enter through an open mouth. There is no doubt that traditional rural society was totally male-orientated and the flamboyant dress of the men, contrasted with the rather quiet, retiring appearance of the women, illustrates the point perfectly.

In the centre of the village, we chose one of several *tavérnas* under the large plane trees. Picking a table on the balcony, we sat watching the ducks in the stream, the air filled with the sound of water. There is an old story that for one hour every night, even such sparkling water as this sleeps and flows slowly and quietly. You must dip and drink the water gently at this time, or it will send you mad. Freshwater springs and streams are supposed to be haunted by the nereids, strange beautiful ghosts who swim in the water at night and bewitch mortal men.

We were soon served with stewed lamb, fried potatoes and Greek salad with *féta* cheese, bread fetched from the bakery across the street by the daughter of the owner and a jug of the local brown-coloured wine. The famous, or notorious *retsína,* according to taste, belongs to the mainland, although it is becoming more popular here. Resin is not normally added to Cretan wine, but it often has a sharp acidic tang which makes a good contrast to the olive oil in the food, "cuts the oil" as they always say of *retsína.* (I once heard that thyme branches are put in the bottom of the vat in which the grapes are pressed.) The great plates of creamy ewes' milk yoghurt and honey which followed were a revelation. Delicious as it was, we could barely eat half of it, so liberal were the portions. We eventually became totally addicted to this Cretan delicacy, to which the cows' milk product cannot compare, even if the cholesterol level would horrify a dietician.

Evidently, our own concern about travelling during the forty days of Lent, a fast which is taken seriously, was unfounded. Many Cretans will still not touch meat, eggs, fish or milk during these days, and towards the end they even give up wine. This virtually involves living on potatoes, beans, pulses and *hórta,* salads made from various wild plants which are popular here. It is permitted to eat the snails which everybody turns out to collect on a wet evening. In the midst of all this self-denial, the *tavérnas* usually seem to be able to produce chicken, lamb, or an omelette for travellers. I sometimes wondered if the fragrant smell of roasting meat and herbs drifting down the street was not causing anguish to the more devout.

Vríses is regularly visited by coachloads of tourists in the summer as was made plain by the bill for lunch, which, although reasonable by English standards, was pretty steep by those of Crete. Across the street, we found a souvenir and fancy goods store where I picked up a string of *kombolóyia.* Every Greek man has a set of these amber worry beads to pass the time in the *kafeneíon,* or on the street corner. They look like rosaries, but have no religious significance and there are all sorts of dexterous games that can be played with them, flicking the beads along the thong one or two at a time, or swinging the whole set around the palm of the hand. The habit is believed to have originated in India and China, made its way westward and reached Greece with the Turks. The number of beads varies, but it always appears to be an odd number. The Turkish *tespi* rosary, by contrast, has 99 beads, one for each of the 99 names of Allah. Cretans would hate to admit it, but this is just one of a number of little customs the Turks left behind. The fez, the flywhisk and the long *chibouk* pipes may have gone now, but very occasionally one sees an old *nargileh* coiled up in the corner of a *kafeneíon,* and the eastern habit of growing a fingernail long to demonstrate that one is above manual labour still exists.

Joan went to use the lavatory below the *tavérna* before leaving, but confined her visit to a very brief inspection. In a sort of open cavern by the stream was a nice example of a hole with two foot pads in the best French tradition and apparently not cleaned for years. If you wish to travel in the countryside here you must either get accustomed to these, or use the deserted hillside as discreetly as possible.

The New Road west from Vríses winds through rocky valleys behind Cape Drépanon, newly planted with conifers in an attempt at reafforestation. The great forests of cypress and cedar trees which covered ancient Crete were a major source of shipbuilding timber throughout the Mediterranean. Now, after so many centuries of felling, charcoal burning and grazing, little proper woodland remains, although there are a few notable exceptions and examples of fine individual trees remaining. The Gorge of Samariá has groves of the original cypresses, giant in stature, some of them over 100 feet tall, and too inaccessible to be felled; these are now carefully preserved. When Cretans talk of a fine figure of a man, they still say "tall like a cypress tree". There are many small ilex and oaks in parts of central Crete, with occasional big chestnuts and planes, especially near water. The Amári Valley, high up in the foothills of Mount Ida, also has some fine trees left. Man has tried to compensate to some extent by planting olives, figs, quince, pomegranates, medlars and almonds since ancient times. Prickly pear and the aloe form his hedges. Oriental planes spread over the village squares, and in the streets are white mulberries and the china berry tree. There are sometimes long lines of eucalyptus to shade the traveller on the road and, where water is plentiful, groves of orange and lemon. But once the villages and the irrigated gardens are left behind, in the main, the limestone skeleton of the land lies exposed to the elements, covered by no more than low, thorny spurge bushes.

After passing the old Turkish fort above the road at Kalámi, now used as a prison, we were confronted by the broad sweep of Soúda Bay, the finest natural deep-water anchorage in the Mediterranean, some 12 kilometres long and 3 or 4 kilometres across to the Akrotíri Peninsula on the far side. The Greek word *soúda* means trench and exactly describes this deep inlet, which can accommodate the largest ships. Soúda Bay is an important base for NATO and the Greek Navy. Allied shipping used it in the Great War, and during periods when Greece has tended towards a more neutral stance in East-West affairs, the Russians have been anxious to obtain its facilities for their warships. The entrance to the Bay is commanded by Soúda Island, where the Venetians built one of three island forts along the

16

north coast. Although the Turks had captured the mainland of Crete by 1669, this strategic outpost held out until 1715 in Venetian hands. During the occupation by the Great Powers after 1898, British soldiers were posted on Nísos Soúda.

The Bay is the more remarkable as Crete is otherwise notorious for its lack of secure harbours. The entire southern coast is unsafe for any ship to lie off, except in fair weather, and there is no port for vessels of any size. Before the Second World War, big ships had to lie off Iráklion, Réthymnon and Khaniá for passengers to be ferried to and fro by rowing boats – a more or less frightening experience, depending on the weather. Although the harbours at Khaniá and Réthymnon remain inaccessible, except to tiny coasters, the big car ferries from Piraeus come in now to Iráklion and the modern port facilities at the head of Soúda Bay, and have had a marked effect on the economy of the island. The great peninsula of Akrotíri, which protects the Bay from the north, was famous for its monasteries, isolated villages and rare wild flowers – and vampires. Some of the land is high, over 500 metres. The building of a NATO missile base some 20 years ago, with consequent restrictions on movement and, more recently, the new airport for Khaniá, have considerably detracted from its charm.

Following the German invasion of mainland Greece in April 1941, this area was strongly defended, together with the vital airfield at Máleme, further west beyond the city of Khaniá. The Greek prime minister, the Réthymniot Emanuel Tsouderos (his predecessor having committed suicide after surrendering Athens), the cabinet and the King himself were in Khaniá. The little agrarian country of Greece had fought back against the Axis Powers with more success than any other nation on mainland Europe, totally blocking the Italian advance through Albania until Mussolini was rescued by Hitler's intervention. For tactical and moral reasons, Churchill was absolutely determined to hold Crete at least, whatever the cost. This determination and conviction does not appear to have been shared to the same extent by local commanders. Moreover, the garrison, mainly Australian and New Zealand troops evacuated from the mainland, were exhausted and, in some cases, demoralised. As the Luftwaffe, with almost total air superiority, and using advanced bases in southern Greece, began a relentless series of air attacks on Allied shipping in Soúda Bay, a sense of foreboding and oppression began to settle on the defenders.

On 20 May, the invasion began, parachutes opening like coloured flowers and falling gently through the early morning skies. The German paratroopers' main objective was the airfield at Máleme.

On the first day they got in 7,000 men by parachute and glider, but their casualties were horrific and on a scale which no German forces had yet experienced in the war. An invasion by sea was turned back by the Royal Navy, although two cruisers and four destroyers were lost in the process. Nevertheless, the airborne attack continued against fierce resistance until a force of 20,000 German troops with their equipment had been built up. Once Máleme airfield had fallen and German transport aircraft could land, the writing was on the wall. Réthymnon and Iráklion had been taken by further detachments of paratroopers, and on 28 May the Italians landed to take Sitía, which was not defended. Most Cretans of military age were away in Albania, but the remainder, old men, women and children, defended their villages with old shotguns, rusty sickles and whatever makeshift weapons they could lay their hands on. Both the Allies and the Germans were somewhat appalled by their ferocity in defence of their home soil – particularly the Germans, who for some extraordinary reason had been briefed to expect a friendly local population.

Eventually, the majority of the remaining Allied troops were moved south through the White Mountains and evacuated by sea from Chóra Sfakíon; some 14,000 men escaped, 13,000 had been killed or captured. The Australian Sixth Division alone lost three battalions. German losses were 12,000 to 15,000 men from some of their most prized units. The terrain of Crete is such that it could not be completely occupied in the manner of a northern European country, and the Germans effectively held the lowlands and key roads only. So began four years of fierce resistance by Cretan *andártes,* or partisans, aided by Allied agents, with consequent savage reprisals against village populations. There is now an Allied war cemetery near the shore of Soúda Bay and its German counterpart is at Máleme.

On the day of our visit, a row of dull grey destroyers barely showed against the Akrotíri mountains across the deep blue waters of the Bay. There are signs warning against photography at intervals along the road and white leather-coated motor cycle policemen enforce this rule with regular patrols. After leaving the modern port and naval base of Soúda to the right, we were soon in the outskirts of Khaniá, set across the neck of the peninsula on the Bay of Kydonía.

CHAPTER 3

Khaniá and Venizelos

Khaniá, administrative capital of Crete until 1971, when it was superseded by Iráklion, is still the dominant business and marketing centre for the whole west of the island. Although a large, thriving city, it somehow has a provincial air and lacks the metropolitan flavour of Iráklion, which has a touch of Athenian *chic* about it. Known in ancient times as Kydonía, after King Kydon, son of Apollo, the area has been continuously inhabited since the Neolithic period. The name Kydonía was found on Linear B tablets unearthed at Knossós. From the Post-Minoan to the early Byzantine era, this ancient city played a more or less influential part in the politics of the area, but fell into stagnation when the Arabs took it in the ninth century. In the later Byzantine period its influence revived, until Venice acquired Crete in the thirteenth century. After 23 years in Genoese hands, Khaniá was retaken and ruled by Venice until 1645.

The city was known at that time as the "Venice of the East". The famous military engineer, Sanmicheli, constructed the great wall with four bastions around the harbour, much of which still remains, together with houses, palazzos, and, despite severe bombing during the Second World War, no less than 23 churches. The Venetians energetically colonised and profited from the resources of their island possession, which they named *Candia*. In spite of periodic and violent uprisings, savagely suppressed, they in many ways established a mutually profitable relationship with the Cretans, who managed to retain their Byzantine culture and traditions. The importance of Crete as a naval base to secure the eastern trade on which the prosperity of the Venetian Republic was founded is obvious, but the island itself was developed and exploited. Ports were deepened and improved, while the more important roads were stone-paved for heavy cart traffic. (It has been suggested that not until the road construction programme after the last war did the island's infrastructure reach an equivalent level again.) Venetian ships loaded up with shipbuilding timber from the remaining forests, tar for caulking, olive oil, cheeses, grain from the plain of Messará, cotton, silk, sugar cane and great quantities of the famous Malevesi wine. Venetian administration was immensely complex, but efficient – in times of crisis a special envoy would be sent from Venice known as the Proveditore Generali, who would be endowed with extraordinary and indeed virtually unlimited powers to cut through red tape. Some of these were men of exceptional ability.

For many years Turkish pirates had raided the coast, but in 1645 a great invasion fleet arrived to besiege Khaniá, which, in spite of Sanmicheli's fine defences, fell in two months. A year later they had taken Réthymnon, although Iráklion proved a tougher nut to crack.

Curiously, in view of their long and relatively recent occupation, the Turks have made only a modest impact on the architecture of Khaniá. The handful of mosques are converted to other uses now – delicate minarets against the sky, now more than sixty years since the muezzin last called the Faithful to pray. One suspects that somehow the Khaniots have managed to minimise or ignore the remnants of Islam in their midst, without any acts of conscious vandalism. If you ask the way to a mosque by name, you are likely to be answered by a look of blank incomprehension. We saw old Turkish buildings in use as stores or garages and the base of one minaret filled with lace-making machinery. Perhaps this is connected with a fact that Cretans would prefer to forget; this is the one part of Greece where conversion to Islam took place to any great extent. In the eighteenth century, more than two-thirds of the population had renounced the Christian faith and turned Muslim.

On reflection, this conversion was probably superficial and a typical example of Cretan deviousness. It has to be admitted that the Turks had no intention of directly persecuting Christians. Indeed, the metropolitans were able to continue in their traditional role as religious and secular leaders and this initially made their new masters seem preferable, in some Cretans' eyes, to the Venetians, who had made some attempts to press Catholicism on their subjects. Nevertheless, it soon became clear to the Christians that there were very positive financial advantages in turning Muslim. Heavy taxes were imposed on Christian merchants and all Christians had to pay the *kharatch*, or capitation tax, literally "to keep their heads on their shoulders", as the grim joke went. As more and more Cretans embraced Islam in order to avoid these burdens, some of the renegades joined less scrupulous Turks in preying on the *rayahs*, or cattle, as the Christian subjects were known. It will be seen that this system eventually became self-defeating as the taxable Christian minority dwindled in size. The lasting result was the implantation of a deep-seated hatred of the Turks and renegades in the Christian Greek's soul, a series of bloody uprisings, and prejudices which last to this day.

These circumstances produced a curious phenomenon: the crypto-Christians, of whom the most famous were the Kurmulidhes, a powerful family of the rich wheat-growing area of the Messará. For generations, this clan adopted Muslim first names and prayed publicly at the mosque. They were highly regarded by the Pasha, and used their influence to mediate between the Turks and their fellow Greeks. But, in fact, they remained faithful Christians, being baptised and married secretly by Orthodox priests smuggled into their houses at night. Eventually, their consciences troubling them, they sought the counsel of the Bishop of Jerusalem, who confirmed their worst fears. They could not expect to enter the Kingdom of Heaven unless they openly declared their faith. Following a family conference, some thirty determined to confess to the Pasha, knowing that it would almost certainly result in their martyrdom. The Metropolitan of Iráklion managed to deter them, pointing out that the confession would result in the deaths of the priests who had ministered to the family.

The Kurmulidhes achieved their martyrdom at last. In the great uprising of 1821, during which Crete lost half its population and extreme cruelty was shown by both sides, the family openly declared their faith and fought with the Christians. Three of them who were captured and condemned to death could have saved themselves by turning Muslim, but would not do so. By the end of the uprising in 1824, Crete now being a land of burned out villages with starving widows and orphaned children crouching among the ruins, only two out of the sixty-four men of the Kurmulidhes had survived.

Under the Pashas, Crete gradually declined. Unlike the Venetians, the Turks did not colonise at first and their administration was generally characterised by a lack of vigour and imagination. The Ottoman Empire was already old (Crete was the last conquest) and their system had only really worked during the period of expansion. The Turks had proved themselves the finest soldiers of their time, but their nomadic warrior background ill-suited them to peace-time rule and they considered themselves above trade. As time went by, Greeks acquired a prominent position in the foreign trade and administration of the Empire, some rising to high office in the Sublime Porte.

In Crete, the Turks ruled in the towns, while outside the walls, the population was largely left to its own devices, with the exception of the heavy taxation embodied in the *kharatch*. The Cretans received little or nothing in return for their payments as ports silted up and roads fell into disrepair. Agriculture and local commerce were neglected, as noted by the Frenchman, De Tournefort, who remarked on the sad condition of the once famous orchards of Khaniá. The Cretans had at first quite cheerfully watched the Turks defeat their old Venetian masters, but, burdened by taxation and divided by apostasy, they soon became embittered. A further imposition was the tribute of children. Christian families would provide a son to be inducted into the *Yenicheri*, Janissaries or New Force. It must be admitted that this was an élite corps of the Empire's army and initially some pride attached to the loss of a son in this way. It was, after all, the only possible escape from poverty for the son of a peasant. Similarly, a well-favoured daughter might with honour become an odalisque in a Turkish harem. The Janissaries stationed in Crete, however, became an embarrassment to the Turks, being quite beyond the control of the Pashas and Constantinople. These unruly mercenaries behaved much as brigands, blackmailing and extorting from the Christians as they wished. The Janissary tribute was withdrawn after 1821.

As the residence of the Pasha, Khaniá in the nineteenth century must have seemed distinctly colourful and exotic, with officials and troops from various parts of the Ottoman Empire stationed in the city. Travellers described Dervishes in long green shirts and tall hats, some thousands of Bedouins from Egypt and Cyrenaica encamped in tents, and the green flag of the Prophet waving over the citadel in the Kastélli quarter near the harbour. Today, the minarets are the most obvious reminder of Turkish days.

The wind was blowing hard on-shore as we parked by the inner end of the harbour, affectionately known as the *mándraki,* or "little sheepfold", and only good for fair weather. The Aegean Sea, now a dull matt blue under a cloudy sky, was piling up against the Venetian breakwater and tumbling into white foam at the outer entrance under the tall slender stone lighthouse. The Turks used the breakwater as a place of execution and, during their brief occupation in the 1830s, the Egyptians reconstructed part of it as a small ship-building yard. Now only political slogans can be seen, sprayed on to the long wall. Against the quays, lines of fishing caiques, a few yachts of those rich enough to idle away the winter around the Mediterranean and an old sailing schooner rolled and tugged on their mooring ropes, the rigging clattering and vibrating in the breeze. The suddenly cold afternoon had moved most of the customers inside the *kafeneíons* and *tavérnas* which line the harbour.

These restaurants are famous for their seafood: calamares, octopus, red mullet and particularly sea urchins, eaten with lemon, olive oil and bread. Some of them are situated in great vaulted archways which run far back under the houses, not unlike the little businesses one sees under London railway arches. These are the remains of the Venetian *arsenali*, strong enough to withstand cannon fire, into which the galleys were brought for repair during the winter and where new ships would be built in summer. There were once nineteen of these in a row.

The eastern basin, although shallow, has some protection from the mole, whereas the western basin lies open to northerly storms. At the junction between the two, we turned the corner and the town appeared as a low mass of closely-stacked buildings across the disturbed waters, a curious mixture of Venetian and Turkish architecture, shades of red and ochre with gaping windows and arched doorways.

The Mosque of the Janissaries, built immediately after the Turkish conquest, has been clumsily converted into a tourist information office and the streets behind are now filled with gift shops. Nevertheless, some of their wares seemed well worth inspection, particularly the ceramics and woollens. Many of the old buildings of the inner walled city were destroyed by the bombing of 1941, but as we wandered deeper into the Kastélli quarter, we came to carved wooden doors in narrow winding streets of Turkish houses. Overhead are the balconies where Turkish women could lie unseen and watch the street. Here are the traditional trades: carpenters and cabinet makers, manufacturers and repairers of steel pans, workers in wrought iron, saddlers and, in Skridlóf Street, a row of cobblers' workshops. Practitioners of the same trade still gather together here in the oriental tradition. In Skridlóf Street, you can have a pair of mountain boots made to measure for about 6,000 drachmes, a treat we have promised ourselves on another trip, for no ordinary boots will stand up to Crete's thorn-bush covered highlands. Khaniá is a market centre for mountain people, and the shops contain the implements mountaineers come to buy: mule saddles, shotguns, binoculars, water bottles in leather carriers and, of course, boots. Elsewhere, in the maze of little streets, we came across cavernous junk shops with such objects as hookahs, ornate muzzle-loading *kariofílis* rifles and silver-handled Albanian pistols to remind one of an exotic past. Unfortunately, these last are likely to be fakes, as the once famous gunsmiths of Khaniá have now turned their hand to producing skilful replicas of the old weapons of the independence fighters. "Khaniá for arms . . ." begins the old saying.

23

The best Venetian houses are in the Topána quarter to the west of the harbour, and in some cases the original owners' coats of arms with Latin inscriptions can be seen on the walls. There is a naval museum here where I left the others to keep an appointment on Sfakianáki Street. I met them later in 1821 Square, where a great plane tree stands, shading tables and chairs where men sit for hours over a tiny cup of coffee and a glass of water. (We know it as Turkish coffee, but here they insist on calling it "Hellenic coffee".)

After the great uprising of March 1821 on the Greek mainland, the Muslims massacred thirty Christians in Khaniá, dragging Bishop Melchisedek of Kissámos through the streets by his beard and hanging him from this same tree by their favourite coffee house, as a stone tablet records. Not far away, at the head of 1866 Square, there now stands a statue of the Kydonían leader, Hadzimichalis Iannaris, one of the heroes of the Great Revolt of 1866. He is in appearance everything that a Cretan freedom fighter or *pallikáre* should be. Magnificently moustachioed, his figure is festooned with great pistols, fork-handled dagger and sword, and hung about with cartridge cases.

The word *pallikáre* requires some amplification. Originally they were mediaeval foot soldiers, but the expression in Greece today refers to all the traditional male virtues of courage and strength: "a fine figure of a man," "a devil of a fellow". In the Crete of the nineteenth century, indeed later, the word implied a fanatical desire for freedom, an almost foolhardy, suicidal courage and a capacity for acts of extreme cruelty. The cult of the *pallikária* is the real legacy of the Turks.

To the east of the old city lie the neo-classical mansions of the district known as Khalépa, a quarter settled by wealthy Greeks in the late nineteenth century. In 1878, the famous Pact of Khalépa was signed in the house of the Mitsotakis family, giving wide-ranging guarantees of civil rights to the Christian population. Mr Sandwith, the British Consul, played a prominent part in mediating between the two parties. In the event, most of the Turkish promises were broken.

When Prince George arrived in 1898 to take over the administration, he chose to live in this rather elegant suburb with his court. The original arrangement was that Prince George was to hold the office of High Commissioner, under the suzerainty of the Sultan, for three years. The ships of the Great Powers withdrew at once from Soúda Bay, but the troops remained to enforce order. The Great Powers also met much of the cost of the new administration. The following year, an "Assembly of Autonomous Crete", 138 Christians and 50 Muslims, met for the first time and a constitution was drawn up.

Crete had achieved freedom in everything but name. The Turkish troops had left, except for a tiny garrison on Soúda Island, and the nominal Ottoman suzerainty was obviously no more than a device to save face. However, as the initial euphoria dissipated, a deep sense of dissatisfaction took its place. The Christian Cretans totally identified themselves with Greece, and only *énosis*, complete union with the mother country and the severing of the connection with the hated Turks would satisfy them.

Greece itself, a small, weak nation, holding very much less territory than it does today, had been involved in a disastrous war with Turkey in 1897 over the Cretan issue. Prince George's father, a prudent man in an uncertain position (it is said that he kept a portmanteau packed at all times, although he eventually ruled for fifty years as George I, King of the Hellenes), no doubt emphasised to his son the difficulties that *énosis* would cause.

By March the following year, the lawyer Eleftherios Venizelos, the leader of the *énosis* faction, realised that their goal would not be achieved without drastic action. His party retired from the Assembly to his home village of Thérisso, high in the White Mountains above Khaniá. Here they took up arms, declared a Provisional National Assembly of Crete, and proclaimed *énosis* with Greece. For many amongst them, it must have seemed quite like old times. Fortunately, this revolt was really a symbolic gesture and no blood was shed. When the winter came, Venizelos surrendered to the Consuls of the Great Powers and no reprisals were taken. Prince George resigned in favour of the universally respected Alexander Zaimis, previously Prime Minister of Greece. With Crete in a state of peace, by the summer of 1908 the Great Powers felt able to withdraw their troops.

In the same year, the balance of power in the Balkans shifted drastically. The Young Turks' revolution of army officers, which resulted in the abdication of the Red Sultan, "Abdul the Damned", set off a series of opportunist reactions from the nations on the border of the Empire. It seemed to the Cretans that with Turkey in confusion, the time must surely be ripe for union, and once more they proclaimed *énosis*. Again, the administration in Athens disowned them, and within a month the forces of the Great Powers had returned to cut down the Greek flag flying over Khaniá.

Finally, it was the exasperation of the Greek mainland population which came to the aid of Crete. Since the founding of their state, Greeks had always subscribed to the *Megáli Idéa,* the Great Idea of expanding their boundaries to include their fellow Hellenes who suffered under foreign rule. It should be remembered that at this time Greece consisted of the Peloponnese, Central Greece, Thessaly, a small part of Epirus, the Ionian islands (which had been ceded by Britain in the nineteenth century), and some of the islands of the Aegean. More than half of the peoples who, through language, culture and religion could only be defined as Greek, still lived outside these borders. The Great Idea of including these Greeks of the *diasporá* was ambitious indeed, for over the centuries of oppression, the Greeks, like the Jews, had wandered far and wide. It had always been accepted as a sacred duty to gain Crete, Epirus and Macedonia. Thrace, the remainder of the Aegean islands, Cyprus and the Dodecanese might be hoped for. Greeks had colonised the coast of Asia Minor itself since ancient times and formed a series of settlements around their city of Smyrna, cheek by jowl with the Turkish homeland. What dare they think of Constantinople itself, the lost City enshrined in every Greek heart, which the infidel Turks ruled as Istanbul? What of the Greeks of the Black Sea, from the Caucasus, from Russia and Trebizond? With these prospects before their eyes, the inaction and vacillation of their government at a time of Turkish weakness was too much to bear. The army and navy mutinied, the government fell and Athens was in an uproar. King George retained his throne with difficulty. The only obvious choice to form a government and restore order was . . . the Cretan, Venizelos.

Venizelos began his administration in October 1910 and, from the first, demonstrated the highest qualities of statesmanship and sheer nerve. After two years, on 14 October 1912, he admitted the Cretan Deputies and proclaimed that the Chamber was now the sole legislative body of Greece and Crete. Four days later, he declared war on Turkey in a Balkan alliance with Serbia and Bulgaria. The campaign was rapidly and successfully prosecuted, and at the end of the First Balkan War, Greece had acquired the remainder of Epirus, Macedonia and further islands in the Aegean, including Lesbos and Chios. Unfortunately, Article 4 of the Treaty of London, which ended the war, laid down that Crete should be ceded by Turkey to the Balkan Allies, but through an oversight did not specifically name Greece. A second Balkan War broke out, this time between Bulgaria and a Greek/Serbian alliance, with Bulgaria amazingly claiming a right to Crete. The Treaty of Bucharest at the end of these hostilities, which can only have benefited Turkey, dismissed this pretence out of hand.

On 14 November 1913 a treaty was signed between Greece and Turkey in which the frontiers were defined, and Crete formally included within Greece. King George I had been assassinated, but a month later his elder son and grandson, King Constantine I of the

Hellenes and Crown Prince George, accompanied Eleftherios Venizelos to Crete. At the place known as the *Fírkas,* by the old Venetian wall in the Topánas quarter of Khaniá, they hoisted the Greek flag on a pole, which still stands and is revered to this day.

The political career of Venizelos continued as stormily as ever. He was fundamentally opposed to the new King Constantine over the issue of neutrality during the Great War. Eventually he lost patience, his revolutionary background asserted its influence, and in September 1916 he sailed for his power base in Crete again, accompanied by Admiral Koundouriotis, the pro-British Commander-in-Chief of the Navy. Once established at Khalépa, he proclaimed a revolution and called on all patriotic Greeks to enter the war against Bulgaria, Turkey and the Central Powers. While the forces in Athens remained loyal to the King, Venizelist elements in Thessalonika began to prepare an "Army of National Defence" to join the Allies on the Macedonian front. The Allies responded by blockading Greece and King Constantine was forced to leave, upon which Venizelos returned to Athens and Greece entered the war. Greek troops made a significant contribution in the Balkan theatre during the last year of the war and took part in the triumphal entry into Constantinople. But the rift between Venizelos and the King penetrated all levels of Greek civil and military society. The political division into Venizelist/Republican and Royalist camps has bedevilled Greek politics through most of the twentieth century.

At the Treaty of Sèvres in 1920, Greece was awarded Northern Epirus, Thrace and a mandate over Smyrna. These territories represent the high watermark of Greek expansion. The international standing of Venizelos was now high. He had impressed Lloyd George, possibly the most powerful man in Europe at that time, by his pro-British stance during the Great War. Venizelos was perhaps too much influenced by this connection; with the Black Sea Greeks of the *diasporá* in mind, he committed Greek troops to the combined invasion of Communist Russia – a serious error. Meanwhile Greece's old enemy, Turkey, was recovering from defeat under their great leader, Mustapha Kemal, who was working steadily to restore the former Empire's shattered armies.

Venizelos now evolved the most audacious plan of all, in which he was encouraged by Lloyd George and Constantine (who had regained his throne). This was a direct frontal attack on Turkey through the Smyrna enclave, with the aim of annexing by force all Greek-populated areas of Asia Minor and finally Constantinople itself. The success of this plan would be the climax to the Great Idea and the culmination of all the hopes of Greek patriots over the years – except perhaps for the question of Cyprus.

In fact, for the first time Venizelos had severely miscalculated the feelings of the Greek population. Exhausted by ten years of mobilisation, poverty and the neglect of internal problems during the concentration on foreign affairs, they voted him out of office. Nevertheless, King Constantine and the General Staff carried on with the planned attack, and what became known as the "Asia Minor Disaster" resulted. Mustapha Kemal, who had commanded the Turkish troops at Gallipoli, decisively defeated the Greek expeditionary forces. A dreadful massacre took place as the Turks took Smyrna, with countless incidents of looting and rape, the city being almost entirely burned to the ground. Greece was totally demoralised and shattered. It was perhaps fortunate for Venizelos and his government that they had lost power at the beginning of the campaign. A shameful trial of responsible ministers was held, resulting in executions. King Constantine, who perhaps took more than his share of the blame, was deposed for a second time in favour of his eldest son, who was persuaded to accept the crown as George II.

The Treaty of Lausanne in 1923 was designed to end the Great Idea once and for all as a source of conflict in the Balkans. Greece formally lost Smyrna, together with the eastern part of Thrace bordering on "Turkey-in-Europe". A massive exchange of populations was decreed to ensure that no further territorial conflicts could take place on ethnic grounds. More than a million Greeks arrived from Asia Minor, having lost everything but what they could carry. Some 360,000 more came from Bulgaria and eastern Thrace to join the refugees from Communist Russia and the Caucasus. Bulgarians were forced to leave their villages in Macedonia and move back across the frontier, while 360,000 Turks were expelled from the Greek mainland. The remaining 25,000 Turks in Crete were exchanged for a similar number of Asia Minor Greeks. The human misery caused by these exchanges is incalculable and for many years the shanty towns remained around Athens and other large cities as Greece strove to absorb this dramatic increase in population.

The country remained in confusion. The armed forces deposed the new king and declared a republic on 25 March 1924. Though Venizelos was in and out of favour for some years, once again his genius for foreign policy showed itself and he determined to build permanent bridges between the war-torn nations of the Balkans. In 1930, the "Year of Miracles", he managed to negotiate a complicated but long-lasting peace with Greece's neighbours and even to reach an accommodation with Kemal's Turkey, which, in spite of their many differences, remains to this day as a sort of uneasy *modus vivendi,* with periods of varying tension. In his effort to improve the domestic economy he was less successful, and in 1933 he lost office again.

When, in March 1935, the royalist faction proposed to restore the monarchy once more, Venizelos and his Liberal party supported an attempt at a military coup by General Plastiras. Although the army was divided and indecisive, the Greek navy sided with the rebellion and the fleet sailed from Salamís with Venizelos on board the *Averoff,* a second-hand Italian heavy cruiser that a Greek millionaire had bought for his country. Following the plan of action which had worked so successfully on two previous occasions, Venizelos made for Soúda Bay and his native Crete, where an oil tanker owned by a member of the Venizelos family was to meet them and keep the warships refuelled. The situation had its elements of comedy and the newspapers referred to the *Averoff* as a "floating taverna". Nevertheless, a squadron of Hawker Harts from the Hellenic Air Force, which had remained loyal, carried out an attack, causing bomb damage to one of the forward guns of the flagship.

The rebellion on the mainland collapsed, and Venizelos with the senior officers of the fleet escaped to Rhodes. He was later condemned to death in his absence. Nevertheless, when George II was once more restored to the throne, he declared an amnesty in which Venizelos, now dying, was included – though many of the officers who had supported him were not. In a final statement, Venizelos urged all Greeks to mend their differences and support the restoration of the monarchy. At the last, he displayed the generosity of spirit of a great patriot and statesman, a giant figure against whom all subsequent Greek politicians have been measured. Crete is immensely proud of him.

The great consulates and embassies of Khalépa now lie quietly sleeping behind their overgrown gardens and palm trees, the heady days of power politics long forgotten. Venizelos and his son, Sophocles, are buried on the Hill of the Prophet Elías, further along the road to Akrotíri and overlooking the city. This is the spot where Cretan rebels, including Venizelos, first raised the Greek flag in 1897.

Later, on the New Road, we passed an encampment of the gipsies who winter in Crete at the edge of the city, the smoke of their cooking fires blowing through their lines of tents in the gale. As we drove along the miles of straight sandy beach to the east of Georgioúpolis, the white horses on the windswept sea marched towards the tamarisk-bordered land in regular lines as far as the eye could see.

CHAPTER 4

Sfakiá

In the early morning, before breakfast, Michael and I strolled on the long sandy beach at Réthymnon, jacketed against the cold *tramountána,* watching workmen moving driftwood and debris, then piling more clean sand between the breakwaters with a small bulldozer. No doubt when the season really got under way, this stretch would be lined with umbrellas and tanning bodies, the shallows filled with swimmers and windsurfers while the ski-boats would drone up and down. What do the older Cretans make of it all, who only swim when they have to and carefully cover themselves from the sun? In the midsummer heat, this cool north wind is welcomed as the *meltémi,* the honey wind (*beltempo* to the Venetians) even when it blusters enough to be dangerous to small boats in the Aegean. Today, the cloud cover was solid and the light grey and bleak.

Over a breakfast consisting of large quantities of yoghurt and honey, we decided to change our plans and bring forward our visit to the remote district of Sfakiá on the south coast. Joan and I had previously learned that the climate of Crete, like that of most mountainous islands, is localised and liable to rapid change. If the north coast is cloudy and dull, there is a fair chance that the far side of the mountains, thirty miles away, may be bathed in sunshine.

The conversation came round to Crete's one famous animal, *capra aegagrus creticus,* or the Cretan ibex. Locally known as the *agrími,* the wild beast, or *kri-kri,* it is really a kind of of wild goat with close relations in Pakistan, Afghanistan, Iran, the Caucasus and the Taurus Mountains of Asia Minor, but quite unique in Europe. It can be assumed to have made its way here along the Dinaric mountain chain from Central Asia, before the rising of the Mediterranean marooned it on the island of Crete. There are beautiful Minoan sealstones depicting the *agrími,* and in the last century it was present on Mount Ida, also on Antímilos in the Cyclades. In spite of its legendary agility and elusiveness, the *agrími* has been so depleted by hunting that it only survives in any numbers in the White Mountains of Sfakiá and Sélinos, particularly in the Gorge of Samariá. Here, they have been strictly protected by law for many years, although in view of the mountaineers' expertise with firearms and general contempt for outside regulation and interference, I doubt whether it enjoys total immunity even today. There are also sanctuaries on three small uninhabited islets: Nísos Ayii Theódori near Khaniá, Nísos Día near Iráklion, and Nísos Ayii Pántes in the Gulf of Mirabéllo. The population on Nísos Día has, in fact, thrived so well that hunting licences have been issued in recent years, albeit for prohibitive prices.

We had never seen an *agrími* and it seemed unlikely that we ever would while walking casually in the mountains, but Malcolm said, "I've seen an animal like that here," and led me away to a partly fenced-off area in the garden where the hotel was obviously in the process of assembling a little zoo. There, surrounded by domestic goats, sheep and turkeys, were a pair of *agrímia*, staring with hard yellow eyes at us through the wire. I hadn't appreciated their sheer size; the long scimitar-like horns reached above eye level and the heavy-boned muscular bodies made their agility among the crags seem all the more impressive.

The prehistoric bones of elephant and pigmy hippo have been found on Crete; it seems that the Minoans were able to hunt deer, wild boar, hares and various wildfowl, besides the ibex. Today, the deer and wild boar, together with Greece's remaining bears and wolves are confined to remote parts of the mainland. There is plenty of small game in the Cretan hills: partridge, quail, turtle doves, duck in places, and any number of hares. Otherwise, the mammals are unexceptional, wild cats, badgers, martens and weasels all being fairly common. The mountains are very well populated with birds of prey, however, and Crete's position as a staging post between Europe and Africa has resulted in flocks of migrant ornithologists visiting the island in spring and autumn to observe the large numbers of winged visitors.

We turned off the new road at the sign for Vríses, underneath which someone had scratched "Sfakiá" through the paint. A whiff of woodsmoke from the stoves came through the vents as we drove through the village, and then we began a steady winding climb into the White Mountains, overtaking the peasants riding their mules up to the olive groves, who invariably acknowledged our greetings with a friendly wave and a smile. We passed the Ravine of Katrái, where,

31

in the 1821 uprising, a large party of Turkish soldiers were trapped and massacred by the mountaineers. Again, in the Great Rising of 1866, Turkish troops who took part in the famous Arkádi Monastery siege made the same mistake in the same place and were slaughtered by Cretans seeking vengeance. The road climbs very rapidly now and the vegetation changes to a bleaker, northern European type; the aloes and Arabian figs of the Mediterranean disappear from the roadside, giving way to the tumbled stones and harsh *phrýgana* of the mountains. There are no trees or large shrubs here, but all the aromatics which can withstand the blazing hot sun of summer, and winter's cold winds, with little soil to nourish them: rosemary, lavender, thyme, marjoram, basil, savory and mint, thorny burnet and spurge bushes. The smell as these plants are crushed underfoot, or just from the wind blowing across the hillside, is indescribably delightful.

We began to notice that every metal road sign, an obvious and tempting target, is more or less riddled with bullet holes. Mountaineers, especially the Sfakians, have a long tradition of bearing firearms, and are almost invariably very good shots. The police rather frown nowadays on the carrying of slung rifles in the towns, but men here often carry a pistol in their pockets and the mountains still sometimes echo with the sound of a shepherd blazing away at a distant stone in sheer *joie de vivre*. It is traditional to greet visiting friends with volleys of shots in the mountain air and once no wedding was complete without gunfire, no party without a few bullets lodged in the ceiling. There is a delightful tale from the end of the last war, at the time when the German forces only held the district around Khaniá, the rest of Crete having been liberated. A British bomber pilot returned from an attack on Khaniá to report that he had been amazed to encounter anti-aircraft fire on his way home over a supposedly liberated and friendly Iráklion. Investigation revealed that he had flown over a rather enthusiastic wedding party.

After passing the turn to Alíkampos, there are few signs of human influence on the scenery. The road now becomes a series of second-gear hairpin turns cut through steep cliffs, screes and narrow defiles. Here we began to approach the cloud base. The land is desolate and barren, nothing but loose boulders and stunted thorn bushes. At one point, however, the way descends slightly to a lonely valley, with a few cultivated fields clustered around a white farmhouse far below.

We stopped for a moment to stretch our legs. Shepherds and their flocks were moving on the slopes, and so enclosed was the place by the mountain walls, that they could call to each other without difficulty through the vast intervening space of the natural amphitheatre. The tinkling sounds of the sheep bells constantly floated up to us. Above and behind, the stony screes swept up to disappear in the clouds. Only the shepherds live in the high mountains during the summer, camping for weeks on end by the rough stone sheepfolds built by their ancestors, crouching over their fires against the nights which, even in high summer, are as cold as ice. They spend their time making cheeses, and to stabilise the temperature store them in black slate-roofed huts like beehives. In times of war and rebellion, the Cretan *pallikária* have always retreated to these fastnesses from which no regular army has ever quite managed to dislodge them. Ancient walls and fortifications are scattered about as a reminder of countless grim and bloody little actions which no history book records: struggles with Venetians, Turks and Germans in which no quarter was asked or given. In times of peace, the shepherds remain, spinning out their simple, lonely existence with no comforts that will not travel up the mountainside in a mule pack. In the winter, there is nobody here, only the snow and the constant scouring winds.

Higher up the road, we began to reach drifts of snow packed in hollows and streaming down gullies from the snowline proper, which, in a hard winter, comes down to about 600 metres. Wisps and ragged streaks of cloud were now pouring south with the wind through the valley below us. Quite suddenly, as we swung round yet another bend, we realised that we had reached the head of the pass at 867 metres. The view had opened out to disclose a curious plain surrounded by conical hills, on the nearest of which stands the ruin of a grim-looking tower guarding the pass. These upland plateaux, which geologists call *poljas,* are a common feature of the Dinaric limestone, the Plain of Askýfou being one of a number on Crete, usually fertile and well-watered, and the more unexpected because of their surroundings of rugged, barren hillsides. The Plain stands at about 700 metres and supports a number of scattered hamlets and the village of Askýfou itself by the road, although it must be a hard living in the cold winds and mists of winter.

This is not one of the "white" limewashed villages of the lowlands, and there are no pretty flower gardens and potted geraniums to be seen here. The rough grey stone houses seem to crouch for protection against the weather under the 2,200 metre peaks of Kástro and Kakovolí to the west. Isolated farmhouses, inhabited all through the year, are very unusual in Crete, for the people have always formed close communities for mutual support and assistance. But there are now a large number of mountain villages with less than twenty families; indeed I can think of a number with only two or three families remaining, and a good many more which are totally abandoned. The authorities have a deliberate policy of encouraging mountaineers to move down into larger rural communities where services can more easily be provided.

Two old men were standing outside the tiny coffee house as we drove through; they broke off their conversation to first stare and then wave to us, leaving a brief impression of aquiline noses and bristling waxed moustaches. More bleak, stony land leads up again to the little village of Imbros, and then the road runs along the side of a deep ravine which eventually grows to become a gorge of great depth, running south like a knife-cut through the mountains. At the same time, the barren rocks give way to occasional cypress trees which finally turn to a forest, one of the last remaining, clinging to the precipitous cliffs. The effect of this vast gorge is to funnel the cold wind blowing from the north Aegean into a powerful gale shrieking through the gap towards the southern coast. We saw that writhing clouds were being blown along below us, faster than the car itself was moving.

When we pulled off the road to look down into the depths below the blast of air nearly pulled the car door from its hinges. We had to brace ourselves against rocks and trees to take photographs while the tree-tops thrashed frantically below us. There seem to be two kinds of cypress; those which grow up tall and straight and those which spread their branches out; in Crete they call them male and female. The trees of the Imbros Gorge are nothing to the giants of Samariá, but they make a fine sight after so many miles of bare land. The motor road was built during the 1930s; before that the only way into Chóra Sfakíon was the mule track which runs along the bottom of the canyon. The gorge is one of the places where the obscure *chasmophytes* of Crete can be found, those strangest of rare plants which hide away from the sun and grazing animals in the crevices of these dark cliffs.

In spite of the cold wind, a watery sunlight was occasionally breaking through from above, and the sky ahead looked brighter. High as we were, we had reached the southern slopes of the White Mountains, and the numerous alpine flowers, irises and tubers, pushing their way through the rocky soil against the rich dark green background of the cypresses, indicated a kinder climate. In a few kilometres more, we were suddenly out into bright, clear sunshine, the clouds miraculously evaporating as they rolled over the edge of a vast and dramatic ramp of land falling in a single sweep from our feet to the Libyan Sea, some thousands of feet below. The scale of the view made us feel like insects crawling on the rim of some great tawny-coloured sand pit, the mountain spurs, miles away in the distance, fading to paler shades of blue and the sea a strong violet below. The mouth of the gorge behind us seemed like a great cauldron overflowing with steam which evaporated in the sunlight. The gale of wind issuing from it still made it difficult to stand steadily, and below us the road could be seen snaking to and fro down the slopes, bare now, although they are pink with oleander blossom later. The only man-made thing is the road and there is not a tree to be seen on the slopes.

Descending so rapidly that our ears popped with the increasing pressure, we passed the turning to Komitádes, Frangokástello and the eastern part of Sfakiá, and shortly arrived in Chóra Sfakíon, the "Place of the Sfakians", and the capital of the district. From this description, one might expect a substantial town, but we had pulled up in the dusty square of a tiny fishing village where the remaining population live in cottages nestling behind a minuscule harbour, enclosed by steep cliffs. Ruined walls can be glimpsed, half-hidden by the olive trees on the terraces above. Somewhere up the hill is the remains of the "Castel Sfacchia", built by the Venetians. The most prominent buildings are a strong, fortified blockhouse of a police station by the square and a short line of *tavérnas* above the sea wall. Tables and chairs were now ranged out in the hot sunshine; only a handful of clients whiled away the morning as if waiting for the activity to come, when the summer tourists arrive in boat-loads from Ayía Roúmeli at the foot of Samariá to the west. A few men worked desultorily on boats and fishing gear in a corner of the harbour wall. The wind, which had been so penetrating high above, was now no more than a warm breath, scented by the herbs of the mountain, and we began to peel off the layers of pullovers and jackets in which we had encased ourselves. A gendarme, sitting outside his narrow-windowed concrete fortress, told us that there was no petrol in Chóra Sfakíon; we would have to go back and turn east to Komitádes, the only village in the whole eparchy of Sfakiá with a filling station. Leaving the problem for the moment, we were soon sitting outside the first *kafeneíon* before delicious fresh orange juice and cold glasses of *Fix* beer, while Steven and Malcolm clambered over the rocks by the tiny beach. *Fix* was for years an institution in Greece, though the word results from the hellenising of the German name "Fuchs". When Otho, son of King Ludwig of Bavaria, accepted the crown of the new Greek state at the invitation of the Protecting Powers, he and his court took along Herr Fuchs, the brewer, in order to assure themselves of supplies of good German beer. Beer has been a popular drink in Greece ever since, though the *Fix* brewery, sadly, has recently closed.

Two hundred years ago, Chóra Sfakíon was the largest town on the south coast, and the traveller Robert Pashley, who was here in 1837, believed that there had been 12,000 inhabitants. It was the busy centre of a rich and thriving district, famous for its hundred churches and chapels, now mostly ruined or disappeared. Even what little remains is largely rebuilt, for Chóra Sfakíon was bombed almost to destruction in 1941. The town has declined as the population of the whole province has declined, there being only some 3,000 souls left in the whole of Sfakiá today.

It is often said that the men of Crete are more typically Greek than those of the mainland, and that the men of Sfakiá are the most typically Cretan of all. It is inevitable that the blood of modern mainland Greeks must be intermingled with that of the Goths, Slavs, Turks, Vlachs, Armenians, Albanians and others who have come and gone over the centuries. Here, at this remote outpost of the Balkan peninsula, one might logically expect to find an older, purer racial type, but so famous and legendary has the independence and character of these people become, that it is hard to separate fact from fiction. It is often claimed that the Sfakians are the racially pure descendants of the northern Dorian tribes who invaded Crete after, or during, the collapse of the Minoan or Minoan/Mycenaean empire – with the assistance of Theseus of Athens according to the legends. Others say that they are descended from the Saracens who held Crete briefly in the ninth century. It is certainly true that, whereas most Cretans have what might be described as a typically Mediterranean appearance, tending to wiry physiques, middle height and dark complexions, the Sfakians are often quite distinct. The men tend to be tall and broad-shouldered, often well over six feet, frequently with abundant curly brown hair and occasionally quite fair complexions. Even fair hair and blue eyes are not unknown. In character, they are more reserved than most Cretans, not unfriendly or any less hospitable, but more conscious of their own dignity. The Greek word *philótimo,* which can be translated as a combination of honour, status and courage, springs to mind. The main impression gained during conversation is of quiet self-assurance and competence in their own environment.

Just as the racial origins of the Sfakians have been lost among the myths and legends, so we cannot learn the answer to the question which has occurred to many travellers: is their independence and self-reliance the result of many centuries winning a living from the extraordinarily rugged and tough terrain of the White Mountains, or did they choose the land to suit themselves? Their overriding desire through history appears to have been to be left to their own devices;

external interference and regulation of their affairs, taxation and general conformity to central authority being anathema to them. Their mountain stronghold has always been their greatest ally in preserving them from the bureaucratic restrictions under which most of us live. It must be stated in fairness too, that their desire for isolation never prevented them from indulging their flair for piracy, brigandage and generally helping themselves to the flocks and produce of weaker neighbours. But then herdsmen have always been more aggressive than cultivators and without the courage of the *kléphts*, the brigands of the mainland who rose against the Turks, there would be no modern Greece.

It is said that the Romans left Sfakiá virtually undisturbed during their occupation and that this freedom continued during the Byzantine and Arabic periods. The Venetians certainly made a number of attempts to subdue the region, but found the experience highly unprofitable, and for the most part the Sfakian autonomy continued, despite various uprisings. Sfakians were in the forefront of most of the revolts against the Turks, who also found this rebellious and warlike race impossible to control. Indeed, other Cretans suffered for them, as Sfakians would carry out guerrilla raids and then retreat into their mountains, leaving villages in the foothills to bear the brunt of the reprisals. Nevertheless, although the Turks never broke their spirit, it was in these revolts that the flower of Sfakian manhood expended itself, and their population and wealth never recovered. Again, during the Second World War, after most of the Allied troops had been evacuated through the Imbros Gorge, and taken off from Chóra Sfakíon by destroyer, the men of Sfakiá took up their abandoned weapons and the area became one of the focal points of the resistance. They proved a constant and aggressive thorn in the side of the German administration – as did Cretans from many other districts – and their series of ambushes and surprise attacks were undeterred by mass civilian executions and the burning of villages in reprisal. In this way, the *andártes,* or partisans of the mountains, frequently incurred the enmity of more peaceable Cretans who were prepared to compromise with the conquerors to some extent.

Apart from their love of freedom and admirable resistance to foreign tyranny, there is a darker side to the Sfakian character. I have already mentioned that their disregard for the law has, in the past, led to a certain amount of piracy and the brigandage which has been a failing of many mountain peoples. Smuggling and sheep stealing are activities which might be added to this list. But the Sfakians are notorious throughout Greece, even more than other

Cretans, for their addiction to the blood feud or vendetta. Much as in those other Mediterranean islands of Sicily and Corsica, what are known in Crete as *oikoyeneiaká,* or "family problems", were resolved with a rifle on the hillside rather than in the courts, and disputes between families over complex grazing rights, or the theft of sheep, would last for generations and result in numerous deaths out of all proportion to the original offence. It seems generally agreed that more Sfakians have lost their lives in blood feuds than were ever killed by the Turks or Germans. Perhaps the comparison with the Sicilian vendetta is misleading; I should emphasise that these are considered to be affairs of honour involving only the participants, there is no criminal society here and the blood-letting does not appear to be exported abroad. Many Sfakians have left for the east of Crete, other parts of Greece, Australia or America, rather than remain in their own village with the constant threat of sudden death by ambush. Some of these enforced exiles have occurred quite recently and the blood feud is not entirely a thing of the past.

The authorities have been relatively unsuccessful in controlling this violence, given the lack of co-operation from the Sfakian communities. The gendarmes – invariably drafted from other parts of Greece – have had a thankless task, and usually resort to deporting the more persistent and dangerous feuders to distant parts of Crete or other islands. One can imagine the feelings of the more peaceful inhabitants as these truculent and blood-stained characters arrive to settle among them. David MacNeil Doren, in his excellent *Winds of Crete,* written in the 1960s, describes meeting shepherds armed with machine guns against their enemies and, in particular, an encounter with one man reputed to have taken more than fifty lives. Foreigners were at that time advised by the police against travelling alone in Sfakiá, and during the 1920s Robert Byron was provided with a file of policemen to escort him through the area – quite illogical this, as whatever their internal quarrels, few Sfakians would abuse the tradition of hospitality towards a peaceful stranger.

The Sfakians were known for their vendettas even in Venetian times. The Proveditore, Foscarini, wrote that when a Sfakian felt that honour required vengeance, he would put on a black shirt and never remove it until the debt was paid in blood – the "sacrifice a murdered man needs most". Many years ago, people from this part of Crete emigrated to the dry hills of that strange peninsula of the Peloponnese known as the Deep Máni, the "Land of Evil Council", a fascinating corner of Greece whose people are said to have originated from Sparta, and to have remained pagan until the ninth century. There, no songs were sung except the *miralóyia,* "words of destiny", dirges for the dead, and the birth of a son, or new "gun", would be greeted with a fusillade of rifle shots. Feuding in the Máni was developed to an art form, each family building separate stone towers armed with long cannon so that they could blast away at each other from one end of the street to the other. The newly arrived Sfakians must have felt entirely at home, and the Cretan surname ending "akis" (it simply means "son of", as does the ending "opou-los" in the Morea) is still common in the Máni.

Even today, the police in Sfakiá maintain a surprisingly strong presence for such small villages. The bloodshed died out for a while after *énosis* with Greece, presumably overwhelmed by the general euphoria brought by freedom. It flared up again during the Second World War, due to sheep stealing and fuelled, no doubt, by the large quantities of captured arms which found their way up into the hills – and intermittently since that time. There are a number of other hints of the dangers of the past to be seen here. The houses in a Sfakian village are rarely adjoining, as is usual in Crete, but each stands alone. An alert and aggressive guard dog is chained by almost every house – it is impossible to approach nearer than a hundred yards or so without a cacophony of barking announcing your presence.

Strangest of all, now that the Sfakians have gained their freedom from oppression and, with the exception of approximate conformity with the laws of modern Greece, have effectively retained their independence, their population (though not their culture) is declin-ing as never before. Perhaps they thrived on conflict, and peace has only led to a dwindling of their spirit. The constraints of the land-scape ensure that their economy must always be pastoral, as opposed to agricultural, traditionally producing cheeses and yoghurts to market in Khaniá. The fishing in this part of the Mediterranean is poor and the illegal use of dynamite has damaged stocks further. Sfakians have mainly produced for their own needs, eaten their own lambs, made their own bread, drunk their own wine and smoked their own tobacco. There does not seem much opportunity for the growth of a cash economy, even if this conservatively-minded people were disposed to exploit it. Money-making does not seem to be uppermost in their minds anyway. Rebellions, blood feuds, deportation and emigration have left a tiny fraction of the original population of this once busy landscape filled with ghosts of the past, empty, ruined houses and deserted villages. Do the remainder feel the weight of all those blood-stained ancestors, those powder-blackened *pallikária,* leaning over their shoulders, dogging their footsteps and sapping their strength?

Recently, the new factor of tourism has emerged, which may have a drastic effect on the economy of the area after all. Now, thousands of visitors to the west of Sfakiá make the walk down the Gorge of Samariá every summer, and are then ferried by small boats to Chóra Sfakíon, to be collected by coaches and returned to the resorts of the north coast. A steadily increasing number of visitors, many Germans curiously, come to stay in the district, to walk, live in the villagers' houses and make contact with people of a fast-disappearing breed, or just to escape from the modern world in a land almost without roads. I would not care to predict the eventual result of the tourist influx; as a welcome source of revenue it is halting the rate of emigration among a population who, for the most part, retain their traditional, courteous welcome to strangers. One would like to think that all tourists will behave as well in a country where good manners are taken very seriously; many Cretans on the north coast have been disillusioned by the unseemly behaviour of their foreign guests. Exposure to mass tourism, if such it becomes, usually rapidly changes the character and way of life in rural communities. In the case of Sfakiá, I suspect it may not. One has the feeling that they have had a look at the modern world and are not entirely impressed. Old customs are not abandoned here without good reason and this applies to the young as well as to the old.

Perhaps it is the roads which make the greatest changes after all; the last section of the road down from Imbros to Chóra Sfakíon was only completed in the 1950s, and the White Mountain passes are often closed by snow in winter. The only other way in, a long winding road along the coast from the east, is even more recent. Both roads are impressive feats of engineering, and it seems unlikely that much extension of them will ever be possible.

There is a road up to Anópolis, however, the village high in the mountains along the coast to the west of Chóra Sfakíon. It is a fairly good dirt road which winds up a series of switch-back hairpins, leaving a view of the sea below to make one dizzy. Against the horizon, 37 kilometres to the south of Chóra Sfakíon, lies the steep rocky island of Gávdos accompanied by little Gavdopoúla, the "Chick of Gávdos". I have never been there, but I believe that about 150 people still live on Gávdos, though some villages have apparently been abandoned for lack of water. There is something romantic about names on a map from such a lonely place; it would be an adventure to take the boat which visits from Chóra Sfakíon when the weather is calm and see for ourselves. There was a German garrison on Gávdos during the Second World War and a number of Allied soldiers landed on it while desperately trying to reach Egypt in leaking rowing boats, even makeshift rafts.

Some 600 metres above the sea, we reached a *kafeneíon* on the outskirts of Anópolis and I went in to ask the way. The cool, dark interior was crowded with customers and noisy with the conversation of card players sitting by tiny cups of coffee, glasses of water and arrack, the atmosphere wreathed in tobacco smoke. The noise stopped momentarily as I walked in and a score of bright, hawk-like eyes swung round curiously. Anópolis is the stepping-off point for the high Madará of the White Mountains and in summer the flocks, on which the village depends, are moved up to graze the uppermost pastures between the great peaks. In the spring, the men of the village, who will later have to live for long weeks away from their families in the stone *mitátoi,* or cheese-making huts, have some leisure to enjoy company and conversation. The proprietress made a half-hearted attempt to show me some admittedly very good handmade lace, and then with a graceful and hospitable air, offered me a glass of clear cold water, poured from a gourd behind her. Cretans are proud of the water from their own springs and like to be complimented on its quality.

I thanked her for the water and her directions, and we drove on the unpaved track through the large sprawling village until we reached the statue of Daskaloyiannis or "Teacher John", a native of Anópolis, and one of Crete's greatest heroes. Daskaloyiannis belonged to the time of Sfakiá's wealth and power in the late eighteenth century, having been a respected *kapetánios,* or leader, head of one of the noblest families of the province. The captains of Sfakiá and their loyal families and adherents at this time have been compared to the clan system of Scotland before the '45 rebellion. Having survived the Venetian occupation with their system relatively intact, the Sfakians profited initially by the Turks' disdain for trade. This allowed Greeks to control much of the Empire's mercantile activity. At this time Sfakiá possessed a fleet of forty ships, apart from her rich flocks.

"Teacher John" – the epithet is a tribute to a man of education, rather than to be taken literally – was a wealthy merchant and shipowner, widely travelled and with the habit of dressing in Frankish clothes. While on a voyage to the Black Sea, he met the Russian brothers, Gregorei and Alexei Orlov, who had been instructed by Catherine the Great to foment unrest and rebellion in Turkey's Mediterranean possessions. Greeks at this time looked to the rising star of Imperial Russia to free them from Muslim tyranny; the Orthodox Eastern Church was still cherished and protected in Russia. The religious links were strong. Did not the double-headed eagle of Byzantium live on in the arms of the Emperors of Russia, since the Palaeologue princess, Anastasia, had married Ivan the Terrible?

Daskaloyiannis allowed himself to be persuaded to begin an uprising in Crete simultaneously with one which the Orlovs had arranged in the Peloponnese. A Russian fleet would come with a great army to complete the destruction of the Turks in Greece. The insurgent leaders of the Peloponnese had been promised 10,000 Russian troops; when they were disembarked, the fleet would come to the aid of the Sfakians and drive the Turks out of Crete. As planned, Daskaloyiannis led 800 *pallikária* down from the White Mountains in 1770 and took the Turks by surprise. He rapidly gained control of the west and penned the Turks inside the walls of Khaniá. There was no question of taking the heavily fortified town with such a small force; daily, and with growing anxiety, the Sfakians watched for the arrival of the Russian ships. When the Turks counter-attacked with an immensely superior force, they were gradually forced to retreat before them into the White Mountains, and finally to the very borders of Sfakiá itself. Still they hoped the Russians would arrive and turn the odds in their favour.

In fact, the Russian fleet consisted of four ships which had sailed round from the Baltic and landed a few hundred soldiers in the Peloponnese. Combined Russian/Greek forces did manage to capture the town of Navaríno, and there was a successful naval action against Turkish ships off the island of Chíos. However, the rebels were defeated at Trípolitsa shortly afterwards by Albanian troops and the revolt petered out. No Russian ships approached Crete – they had never intended to, merely wishing to arrange a diversion from their action on the mainland. Daskaloyiannis had been duped, and the Sfakians, although they did not know it, were alone. The Pasha sent a letter, offering to discuss terms for a surrender, but the Sfakians fought on through the rocks and gorges, delaying the Turkish army at every cheese-hut and sheepfold. One story tells that the last line of defence was the great ravine at Arádena, only a few kilometres from Anópolis, and that a Sfakian traitor sold the secret of the only path to the Turks.

Daskaloyiannis, feeling deeply his responsibility for the destruction around him, received a letter from his captured brother, Nickolas, begging him to accept the Pasha's offer to discuss honourable terms and thus end the bloodshed. Nickolas assured Daskaloyiannis that he would not be harmed if he gave himself up to parley – but he signed his letter with three capital 'M's, a code previously arranged between the brothers to warn of treachery. In spite of this, and the advice of his lieutenants, Daskaloyiannis complied with the letter and surrendered himself to the Turks. It is said that Teacher John was received courteously by the Pasha, given fine food and a *chibouk* to smoke.

"The people of Sfakiá are rich and privileged," said the Pasha, "so why are you rebelling?" When he heard that freedom from tyranny was the heartfelt desire of all Cretans, he flew into a terrible rage. Having refused, even under torture, to sign a surrender, Daskaloyiannis was taken out and flayed alive in the market place at Iráklion, without uttering a sound if the story is to be believed. The tale has been kept alive down the years by the *Ballad of Daskaloyiannis,* a long poem alleged to have been composed by an illiterate cheesemaker called Barba Pantzelio. Some years after, at a sheepfold high in the White Mountains, he recited his poem, with tears in his eyes, to a shepherd with the old Byzantine name of Skordylis, who wrote it down. This scene may sound unlikely, but in fact it is very typically Cretan or Greek. There is a great love of poetry and language among the mountain people, and a tradition of composing *mantinádes* and *rizítikas.* This love of the spoken word is often common among people who in the past were mainly illiterate. It is still true that many of the older people of the Cretan countryside cannot read or write, yet they have a larger vocabulary and more skill in its use than their English equivalents. There are many who can recite the *Ballad of Daskaloyiannis* by heart, and at parties and celebrations they never tire of the old stories and the old songs. This is the tradition of the mediaeval ballad singer or the bard, honoured guest in the king's hall, and it lingers on in these hills.

Sfakiá never recovered its wealth or its population. The Turks now treated them as the rest of the island, with heavy taxes and numerous petty restrictions. It was forbidden to build a house of more than one storey. Permission had to be granted for the building or even repairing of a church. The ships were lost and the villages were in ruins. The great aristocratic families had nearly been wiped out, and the system of clans, each loyal to its *Kapetánios,* was broken. Many Sfakians emigrated, a movement which has continued to the present day, with additional waves after the revolts of 1821 and 1866. "Where are you now?" asks the *Ballad of Daskaloyiannis,* naming the old families one by one, some of which dated back to Byzantium. No longer were there any "silver-haired old men to sit by the table, to eat and drink, to sing with strong voices, and tell of heroic deeds and the woes of war, and the tables to echo from one side to another."

"Teacher John" is enshrined as a national hero, and his portrait is on every schoolroom wall. From Chóra Sfakíon they will take you by boat to a cave away to the west where the rebels of 1770 assembled and minted their own coinage. The statue at Anópolis, though ferociously armed and terrifying of demeanour, now stands pleasantly surrounded by whitewashed houses, olive trees and foraging chickens. One would have expected to find the Russians totally discredited in Crete, but the faith that salvation would eventually come from that quarter continued through the nineteenth century, fanned by the conflict between Russia and Turkey. Cretans would sing the *Moscow Song* to infuriate their Turkish overlords. In *Freedom and Death,* the Cretan author, Kazantzakis, writes of Captain Michales' grandfather, a character probably based on one of his own ancestors:

> ... his fear-inspiring grandfather, "Mad Michales" rose up in flesh and blood to his inward eye. How could he die, who had so many children and grandchildren? Far and wide, the old people still remembered him, the way he used to gaze along the coast of Crete, shading his eyes with his paw. He was looking to see if the Muscovite ships were coming out of the sea and sky. He tilted his fez awry, sauntered up and down the walls of Megalokástro, bowed before that accursed *koúles* and sang in the Turks' face "The Muscovites are coming!" His hair and his beard were long, his boots high and hitched to his belt and never – it was said – did he take them off. He wore too, a long black shirt, for enslaved Crete wore mourning, and every Sunday after Mass he used to swagger along with *his* grandfather's bow over his shoulder and a quiver full of arrows as well.

> (Nikos Kazantzakis, *Freedom and Death*)

One could speculate as to the possible consequences for Crete if Sfakiá had kept her fleet until the revolt of 1821. The shipowners of Hýdra and Spétses made fortunes during the Napoleonic Wars by carrying Russian wheat from the Black Sea and running the English blockade into France, Spain and Italy. At this time, Greek merchant ships sailed, by treaty, under the Russian flag. The barren little island of Kássos possessed a fleet out of all proportion to its size and was famous for the skill of its seamen. When De Lesseps opened his canal at Suez, he insisted on using Kassiot pilots to navigate the ships through the narrow waterway. There are millionaires today in London, New York and Athens who owe the foundation of their family fortunes to these early fleets which did incalculable service to the Greek cause in the War of Independence.

CHAPTER 5

A Village without Roads

A smaller *kafeneíon,* with a terraced roof, stands, together with the police station, among the scattered olives at the far end of Anópolis. Three or four tall, booted, young men sat on a bench in the sun outside and responded politely to our "Good morning". The Cretans have curious customs concerned with the order of greetings: a man on foot speaks first to a man seated, the native of a village waits for the stranger to speak first and so on. Our way to Arádena lay straight on, and we bumped in the car up a stony track leading on to bare and rocky uplands.

After a short while, the rough road comes to a sudden end for no apparent reason in a maze of dry boulders and thorns. Leaving the car, we walked a few yards to the right and suddenly found ourselves at the brink of a great gash through the reddish coloured rock, stretching as far as we could see in both directions and putting paid to any possibility of extending the road. In places the cliff is bare, and elsewhere bushes and scrub pine hang over the edge of the dark chasm. The place has a sinister and forbidding air. On the far side stands the almost empty village of Arádena, reached by an extraordinary stone staircase which seems as old as the rocks of the gorge, zigzagging first down one precipice and then up the other, passing the gaping mouth of a cave at the bottom. Was this the path betrayed to the Turks in 1770? As we descended the stairway, a pair of mules could be seen winding laboriously up towards us. The first was laden with two milk churns lashed to the wooden saddle and led by a cheerily grinning small boy in a tattered blue sweater. The second was ridden by a huge barrel-chested man, about 40 years old, curly-haired and unshaven. He was dressed in a black pullover and breeches above stout mountain boots, a leather holster was slung on a strap over his shoulder and a chequered headcloth was tied around his brow. He held a shepherd's crook across the pommel of the saddle, and urged the animal upwards with curses and blows of his fist. He was clearly in a filthy temper. Frankly, I have never met anybody more like a brigand in appearance. It was rather like meeting Carver Doone during a walk on Exmoor. He wouldn't reply to our "Good morning", or speak to us at all, studiously ignoring us as he cursed and swore his way upwards. Such discourtesy is so exceptional in Crete, we wondered how we might have offended him. Had we been mistaken for Germans, something which had caused us problems on one or two occasions in villages with long memories? Perhaps he was just sick of being stared at by tourists and, after all, the ride across and up that path would put a saint out of temper.

A little further on, a dog came running down the far side of the gorge to meet us, its barks echoing among the rocks and answered by another, unseen, animal, somewhere among the ruined houses of the village. As it approached, snarling and showing its teeth, with the hackles straight upright on its back, Joan began to show a quite sensible concern. I picked up a couple of rocks.

"Don't worry," I said, with an assurance I didn't really feel, "It's only bluffing; if I throw a stone, it will back down."

"I understand rabies is rife in the Balkans," Michael remarked helpfully. It didn't seem the time to argue about whether this was part of the Balkans.

In the event, we stood in a group very still on one side of the narrow path, while the dog, of indeterminate breed and unpleasant appearance, circled warily around us with a permanent low growl in the back of its throat and the lips wrinkled back from its canines. When I involuntarily moved my hand a fraction, it jumped straight into the air about three feet and raced on up the path.

"There you are," said Michael, "much more afraid than we are."

The dog's owner was following on about 100 yards behind, again with a mule and milk churns. This was a smaller man, in ordinary European dress, who seemed somehow nervous, although he did rather reluctantly consent to talk and give a few directions. I remember he reckoned journey times in cigarettes, for in this rough country, scored with impassable ravines and beset with detours, time is more relevant than actual distance. His second dog, as edgy and aggressive as the first, took the rearguard about another 100 yards behind him. We speculated at some length as to why a man would find it necessary to train his dogs to travel in that manner.

Most of the houses in Arádena stand as empty shells, the bare windows seeming like eye sockets in a skull. The men of Arádena have a particularly bad reputation for the vendetta, and since the Second World War the village has been virtually emptied by blood feuds and deportations. A few still remain, and the tiny Byzantine Church of the Archangel Michael at the edge of the gorge has been recently whitewashed. Close by are the ruins of ancient Aradín, a Phoenician settlement, while further into the mountains lies the even more isolated village of Ayios Ioánnis on a precipitous path down to the foot of the Samariá Gorge.

On the road back to Anópolis we passed the surly muleteer again and then, some while later, as we entered the village, we were amazed to find him trotting through the outskirts ahead of us. He had somehow cut across a loop of the road over what appeared to be a sheer cliff, 100 metres high. As I parked the car in the shade of a tree, I noticed that nobody spoke as he rode past the line of men still sitting on the bench outside the *kafeneíon*. They stared at his broad retreating back while the tall, booted proprietor muttered something as he got up to go inside. There was no sign of the small boy; perhaps he had gone into the Anópolis school.

The interior of the *kafeneíon* reminded me of little *fondas* in the high sierras of Spain. The usual cast-iron stove stood in the centre, with a long horizontal pipe led out through a missing window pane, in defiance of all normal recommendations for obtaining a good draught. A stuffed eagle with wings spread wide was mounted high on the wall and beneath it hung an old curved black Turkish sword and a bayonet. One or two faded photographs of heavily-armed men in black-fringed headcloths were pinned up, while a shotgun and a dead marten hung from a nail. A long shepherd's crook of twisted olive wood was thrown in a corner. A few tables and chairs were scattered about on the concrete floor.

The owner, a man of considerable dignity and charm, with curly, grizzled hair and a fine moustache, served us beer and soft drinks and then an excellent omelette and Greek salad with *féta* cheese and olives, together with a big copper measure of sharp brown-coloured wine. He seemed pleased to find that we were English and chatted to us about life in the village. There was a bus standing outside, which I think he said went down to Chóra Sfakíon and then over the mountains to Khaniá and back once a day. The wine was their own, from the small vineyards scattered around the village. The eagle on the wall prompted us to ask if they were much threat to the lambs, and he explained that yes, they took many lambs, but the moment when a raptor swung heavily down on to the flock was the best chance to shoot it if your rifle was accurate. Despite the ecological implications of this remark, we were rather impressed. "My God," Michael whispered to me, "when did you last meet a man who shoots eagles?"

The importance of the sheep flocks to the people of the mountains cannot be over-emphasised. More than half of Crete is so rugged that it cannot be cultivated, and is let to graziers. All the grazing rights belong to someone; the system of rents and agreements is extremely complicated and quarrels over rights of pasturage have added to the tensions between different villages and families. An official, known as the *agrophylakas,* or country warden, arbitrates in these matters. There are about 750,000 sheep in Crete, of which roughly a third are kept near the villages as home flocks. The remaining two-thirds are constantly in the care of their shepherds, and make the trans-humance with the seasons between the winter pastures in the foot-hills or on the plain and the high mountain pastures of summer. There is no supplementary fodder available, and by the end of the long, dry summer the animals are lean and the milk yields are low. Each of the main mountain ranges has its own breed – the *Lassíthi, Psilorítis* and *Sfakiá;* this last is claimed to be the largest, with the best milk yield. Although traditionally the cheese and yoghurt is made on the spot by the shepherds, there is a tendency, now that transport is not quite so difficult, to send the milk into dairies in Khaniá and Réthymnon for processing. Sheep in Sfakiá mean wealth, and the temptation has always been strong to rustle badly guarded animals from a district just sufficiently far from home to avoid detection. Besides, the nature of the enterprise appeals to the Cretan's swashbuckling sense of adventure. When there is a wedding in Sfakiá, they used to say, everybody steals sheep to give to the bride.

The path up to the summer pastures of the Anópolis flocks is also the route to the summit of Páchnes, although it is a long, stiff climb and the round trip takes two days. The way leads to the north out of the village through pine woods up to the Ammoutyra cistern at about 1,850 metres, where you can sleep – if you can keep warm enough. The next day, with an early start, it is possible to follow the path between the Troháris and Kakovolí peaks to come upon Páchnes ahead and to the west. The path carries on to the Madará pasturage and the shepherds' summer quarters, all the surrounding peaks being over 2,000 metres. Given enough time, food and water, and a guide to show the path, a fit walker can eventually cross this harsh landscape of chipped limestone, ancient huts and caves, to descend into the Apokorónas villages on the northern side. From the top of Páchnes, it is just practical to walk back to Anópolis in the same day.

Feeling replete, and a little guilty after our fine meal, we com-miserated with the proprietor over the trials of Lent.

"Forty days," he muttered gloomily.

The early spring is a busy time for festivals in Crete. The extensive New Year celebrations are followed by the Feast of Epiphany, when the bishop of seaside towns throws a symbolic cross into the harbour to bring luck. Carnival time, or *Apocriés,* involves a long round of parties with a great deal of eating and drinking in preparation for the hard days ahead. Stuffed vine leaves, pasta and macaroni, stewed chickens and hares are all served, together with those peculiarly Cretan delicacies: sheep's heads, goats' hooves cooked in egg and lemon sauce, guts, genitals and eyeballs. The first day of Lent is *Kathará Deftéra,* Clean Monday, a day of ritual purification when pans are scoured out with ashes. It is also a day for picnics out of doors to welcome the spring, for flying kites and baking loaves covered with sesame seeds.

After coffees, when paying the extremely reasonable bill, we made the mistake of rounding up the amount by only a few drachmes and declining the change. The owner was not offended, but this was obviously a matter of honour; in a moment a lemonade bottle of colourless liquid and four glasses were whisked from under the counter, and a generous measure set in front of each of us.

"Ah, *rakí?*" we asked in pleasurable anticipation.

He frowned slightly. "No, don't say *rakí,* that is Turkic word. We say *tsikoudiá.*"

Greeks like to clink glasses and drink toasts, but our host obviously felt that the usual "*stiniyássas*" (your health) or "*pánta yiá*" (may you be for ever happy) were inadequate.

"Thatcher," he proposed proudly, "we drink to Thatcher, right?"

As socialists, we had a problem here and I wasn't at all sure that Andreas Papandreou would fill the bill, having seen the large number of posters for Mitsotakis' New Democracy Party scattered around the village.

"Kinnock," I countered, raising my glass.

"Nice chap," said Michael, "he's just been over here talking to Melina Mercouri. He wants to give the Elgin Marbles back."

"Key-nock?" said our friend, looking slightly puzzled, but he drank all the same.

Michael and I were aware that we were expected to knock it back in a single swallow and, indeed, I have come to the conclusion that this is the best way to deal with *tsikoudiá* or *rakí,* call it what you will. Made by distilling the grape-mash left in the press after the wine juice has been run off, and drunk at any time after it has cooled down, it has a raw but clean taste with a kick and an after-glow like Polish vodka. In Crete, it is often drunk as an early morning pick-me-up, as the Spanish peasant takes an *anis* against the morning cold. I had heard that the drink known as *rakí* all over Greece and Turkey was called *tsikoudiá* in parts of western Crete – but I hadn't known why.

We found later that the word was used in the White Mountains and various salients and minor ranges, as far as Ano Viánnos, for instance, under the Dictaean Mountains, but was unknown elsewhere. What a wonderful time one could have researching the exact territory of this obscure piece of nomenclature!

A fairly merry party spilled outside some time later, handing around cigars from a tin in the car. The proprietor directed us through the village and over the hill to Loutró.

"How far?" we asked him.

"About one hour. Just follow the telephone wire."

"And to come back?"

"Maybe two hours."

We took the indicated path, between flat-roofed houses with arched doorways, past chained and barking watchdogs, little byres and scratching chickens. Most of the work of the house seemed to be carried out in the yards, which are provided with chairs and tables underneath gnarled vine branches. Women sat in the sun preparing salads, sewing and gossiping with their neighbours, while toddlers played in the dust around their feet. The interiors of village houses are often very simple, being little more than secure stores for agricultural produce and a refuge from the night and bad weather. Smiling, shy children with large dark eyes showed us the way when we were uncertain, until we began to climb the steep hill above the village to the south towards a white chapel.

On pausing for breath, the flat roofs and white houses of Anópolis and various smaller hamlets clustering on this little plateau made a fine sight. Small patches of vines, orchards and a few fields surround the village, the bright green of the irrigated land rapidly fading into the dull greys and khakis of the *phrýgana*-covered mountains. Although Anópolis has a cheery, robust feel to it, there cannot be more than a thousand or so inhabitants, whereas 70,000 may have lived on this plain in the Roman and Byzantine period. Protected from sea raiders by its surrounding mountains, yet supplied by its port at Phoenix below, it thrived long before Chóra Sfakíon's heyday. The remains of crude defensive walls and ancient buildings can still be seen.

The row of posts with its twin telephone wires marched up the hillside until, suddenly, underneath the white walls of the chapel, we crested the ridge and could look down to the sea more than 600 metres below. The slope sweeps straight down at an angle of about thirty degrees without a respite. An uncertain-looking path, occasionally reinforced with loose boulders, disappears out of sight, somewhere below and to the right. The mountains plunge straight into the sea at all points except for a single peninsula of low land, on one side of which a tiny cluster of white buildings could just be made out around a curved beach. This cape is called Moúros, and is the only safe winter mooring on the whole south coast.

Walking downhill often seems harder than walking up, and the loose, ankle-wrenching stones and penetrating, knee-high bushes of wire-netting spurge were soon playing havoc with ordinary rubber and canvas trainer shoes. I began to wish I had bought a pair of high leather Cretan boots from the cobblers in Khaniá. Even British army boots didn't stand up to this garrigue for long. During the Second World War, when Royal Navy MTBs used to come nosing into this lonely coast on dark nights, to land fresh agents and take others back to Egypt for leave, a curious little ceremony would take place on the beach. The *andártes* and British officers, about to quit the island, would take off their boots, leave them for those who remained, and embark in their socks for the fleshpots of Cairo.

After thirty minutes' steady descent, we were streaming with sweat in the hot sun, but when we stopped, the peninsula seemed as far below as ever. I seemed to be carrying everybody's jackets. Looking up, we could see a pair of eagles tracing long circles in the sky by the cliffs above. We passed an iron-covered cistern let into the slope, surrounded by yards of red dust, trodden down by goats. Lower down, odd groups of sheep moved off along intersecting paths ahead of us, their bells tinkling and clanking among the reddish-brown stones. We once heard that a good shepherd will take the trouble to tune the bells of his flock, and so make the whole landscape melodious for himself and passers-by.

After twenty minutes more, the village did look nearer, but we were beginning to be concerned about the time. If it was going to take one and a half hours to descend, would it take us three hours to climb back? The afternoon was now well advanced, and we didn't relish the thought of trying to find the path up the mountain in the dark. The sight of the telephone wire was somehow encouraging. The yellow offices of the OTE (the Greek telephone company) are often found in the remotest villages as a reassuring link with civilisation.

The *tsikoudiá* having now worn off, we virtually force-marched the last section, in spite of the heat, and arrived almost on top of the roofs of Loutró, "the bathing place", or "hot springs", just one hour and ten minutes after leaving Anópolis. Scrambling between the whitewashed walls of deserted houses, we found ourselves standing on a little crescent of beach next to a *kafeneíon*. A group of white-haired and ancient men sat in a circle around a table, crooked sticks at their elbows, shaded by a tamarisk tree. A pair of small, brightly-painted rowing boats lay motionless in the water, as if embedded in a sheet of crystal.

All over Greece these pensioners sit in the sunshine, their friends of many years at their side, the village they have known all their lives in front of them. For long hours they will sit over a single cup of sweet coffee and a glass of water – or no drink at all, a chair by the *kafeneíon* being the inalienable right of every village elder. Conversation is desultory, minutes pass without a word spoken, yet no face looks bored or frustrated. They seem able now to look back on a lifetime of toil and poverty, the emigration of their children, even the slow death of their village, with a fatalistic calm and content. Many seem to live to a great age. One cannot help but think of the "senior citizens" of Britain: lonely flats in unfriendly cities, television warnings of hypothermia during every frosty spell, day centres and meals-on-wheels, "visit a lonely elderly person at Christmas", and all the casualties of a mobile population in a cold climate. I sometimes wonder if there will be a place in the sun for us in our declining years. An old lady served us with Coca-Colas, smiling shyly, while we sat on a wall to ease our aching calf muscles. The boys, for all their lack of size and stride, didn't seem unduly affected by the exertion and soon wandered off beachcombing.

The little peninsula of relatively low-lying land, on the east side of which the present village nestles, is covered with traces of earlier civilisations: Hellenistic, Roman, Byzantine and Venetian. On the west was the ancient port of Phoenix, which served Anópolis above. It was mentioned by the geographer, Strabo, and in the New Testament as "Phenice". It is said that a diver can trace the remains of walls and masonry under the sea. The Church of Christ the Saviour contains Byzantine frescoes, and one can also see the building known as the Chancellery, where the council of the 1821 revolutionaries met.

We talked to a young German couple who were drinking coffee in the shade, their towels and swimming costumes drying on the wall before them.

What did they do all day?

"Oh, we follow the little goat paths; there are tiny beaches along the shore where we swim in the mornings. In the afternoons we just sit here in the sun."

"How do the people here live, surely not by fishing?" I asked, looking at the tiny boats.

"No, from tourism!" she laughed. "They take tourists along the coast by boat, to Chóra Sfakíon and Ayía Roúmeli. When I first came here the place was dying, only old people. Now there is work in the summer for the young men; they do not need to emigrate. It is better that the old people can see their grandchildren growing up. In some of the other villages, people are still leaving. In Ayios Ioánnis, there are only two families left now."

They, at least, seemed to have overcome the Cretan mountaineers' antipathy to German people. This prejudice, which varies from area to area and village to village, is unfortunate because many German tourists visit the island, making earnest efforts to meet and understand the people – rather more than the average British holidaymaker, in fact, who usually won't make the effort to learn even a few words of Greek. On the whole, Cretans now seem slightly more prepared to let old wounds heal, especially when the visitors concerned could not even have been born during the war. Nevertheless, there are a few villages whose reception of German tourists ranges from coldly polite to actively hostile.

As we turned back to the awesome slope, we were confused by the many winding and indistinct paths around trees and boulders. When we did emerge on the hill, we eventually found ourselves on the wrong track as we were gradually working back down towards the sea to the east. Ten minutes were lost in returning to the village and identifying various landmarks from our descent before we were properly under way, keeping a careful eye on the telephone lines. In fact, we made better time uphill than expected, while the sun had lost its earlier heat as it sank down towards the hazy western horizon. We rested under the final cliffs of the ridge, where the eagles still swung slowly around, though keeping a respectable distance away from us. Looking down at the calm sea stretching away into the mists of the evening, it was hard to believe that this is such a dangerous place for small boats, notorious for sudden squalls.

A boy with a satchel gave us a cheerful "Kalispéra" as he came down the slope after school in Anópolis. Some schools in Greece work two "shifts" and finish late. Scorning the path, he trotted straight down the loose scree towards Loutró far below.

Finally, we climbed up and found the right path through the upper cliffs and down into Anópolis, one hour and thirty minutes after leaving the coast, and safely in daylight. As we walked through the outskirts of the village, men and women were sitting outside their houses, after their day's work in the fields, sharing bread and garlic from a common dish. I watched one old man spill a libation of wine from his glass on to the earth before he drank. There are some odd customs and beliefs in Sfakiá, quite apart from those of other Cretans. If you wash in company with a Sfakian, he will not hand the soap directly to you, lest it wash the friendship away.

The mules plodding home from the fields were laden with pruned olive wood for the stoves. Once or twice we saw the ornately embroidered knapsack called *sakoúli,* covered in brightly coloured designs. It is said that one can tell a man's village by the patterns on his *sakoúli.*

We came to a group of old men seated on a bench, dressed in white cloaks and headcloths wrapped around exactly as a Turkish turban, with purple sashes over voluminous knee breeches and boots. There is an extraordinary story about these baggy *vrákes;* it involves the literal interpretation of the Orthodox belief that a new Saviour will be born of man – therefore, anally. The enormous amount of space within the breeches is said to be designed to allow the newborn infant room to emerge.

Back at the *kafeneíon,* the proprietor was slicing tomatoes with a fearsome-looking knife about fifteen inches long. His cold beer was very welcome, but he wouldn't have one himself.

"Too much yeast," he said, looking regretfully at his ample waist. He passed round a tin of Greek cigarettes and fed more wood into the stove in the centre of the room, for it had turned chilly. Tired as we were, we considered staying to eat, but it is a long road back to Réthymnon late at night and so we made our farewells, promised to return another year, and left just as the light faded.

The bends of the mountain road seemed interminable in the dark. It was so late when we arrived back at our hotel that we decided to go straight in to dinner, dusty and dishevelled as we were, assuming that there was any dinner left. It was being served in the night club, this being the weekly cabaret evening. Every other guest seemed to have bathed and dressed with meticulous care. As we walked in, a somewhat oily young man in a blue blazer, open-necked shirt and cream-coloured flared slacks was on the stage with a microphone, working hard at injecting some party spirit. We might have been in Athens, or Benidorm, or a northern English club for that matter. His eye lit on me for some sadistic reason and he minced over to the edge of the stage.

"This gentleman will judge our dancing competition," he said.

So, as we made the best meal we could, thinking of hot baths and soft beds, we conferred to award points out of ten as elderly couples waltzed, quick-stepped and tangoed in front of us. The worst moment was provided later by a slightly drunken woman with a strong Midlands accent, who insisted on taking the microphone to sing Theodorakis' *Those were the Days.* The band, to their credit, managed to keep straight faces. Our boys, who should have been exhausted, seemed to have found a second wind and were fascinated. The whole ritual was the strangest thing they had seen all day.

CHAPTER 6

The Monastery of Arkádi

Nikos, our waiter, smiled when he saw the outsize plates of yoghurt and honey Michael and I helped ourselves to at breakfast.

"Don't English people like cornflakes any more?"

Nikos reminded us in character and appearance of a very likeable, but somewhat feckless and irresponsible lad we had once worked with. The similarity was such that the two became somehow confused in our minds. Although Nikos was an excellent waiter, he also conveyed an impression of being helpless in the grip of superior forces. He took very little seriously, and was a master of the eloquent shoulder shrug, while his quintessentially Greek lifting of the eyes to heaven was a wonder to behold. When we told him of his similarity to our old friend, he seemed slightly disappointed and remarked that most people thought he looked like Paul McCartney.

"Do you not think so?" he said, standing in the light of the window, "Only I have not his money . . ."

The man who runs the little garage and *kafeneíon* towards Réthymnon insisted on checking the oil and tyres after filling our fuel tank. At the same time, he kept up a running badinage with friends passing up and down the road on little motorcycles and those curious three-wheeled pick-ups so beloved of Mediterranean farmers, and known here as *mikanís,* or the "machine". These have a tiny fibre-glass cab and a remarkably noisy and smoky little engine. Some are in the most amazing mechanical condition, their doors tied shut with pieces of string and worn steering joints causing the front wheel to vibrate and wander alarmingly. Their flat-out maximum speed of thirty miles per hour or so is something of a blessing in the circumstances.

There is a smaller, even stranger device which is a common sight wherever there is any cultivated land. This is the single-axle tractor or *fréya,* which, when seen at work in the open fields or loosening the soil between the vine roots, looks rather like the "'rotivator" that English market gardeners use. It is a machine equipped with long handlebars for the operator to guide it, and a single-cylinder two-stroke engine which drives a set of blades to loosen and turn over the soil. But the *fréya* shows its true versatility when the farmer wants to go to town. Off come the rotivator blades and on go a pair of rubber-tyred road wheels. A sort of trailer with seats is attached into which he squeezes himself, his wife, the children, her mother, and away they go, puttering along slowly but surely and trailing blue smoke. Cheap loans are available from the Agricultural Bank to buy these, and they must have been many Greeks' first introduction to motoring.

Once, a large proportion of the private cars in Crete seemed to be basic derivatives of small Fiats and Renaults and particularly the Citroen 2CV. There are less of these to be seen now, as the market has become more sophisticated and their place is being taken by Japanese pick-ups and saloons.

We crossed under the new road at Plataniés and plunged into the arcadian countryside behind Réthymnon: no harsh rock here, but green grass and wild flowers under gnarled olive trees. The groves on either side were busy with workers, occasionally with nets spread under the trees to catch the fruit gently knocked from the branches with long poles. There are many different varieties of olives and skilled cross-grafting is used in order to keep trees fully productive. The different strains crop at different times, but the harvest begins around Christmas-time and continues through the spring. Olives tend to be processed locally and are carried off to the *fábrica,* or press, by donkey or mule. Nothing is wasted even after the oil is extracted; the crushed stones make a fuel known as *pyrína,* which is burned in stoves and braziers.

We passed through a procession of pretty villages: Adele, Pigí, Ayios Dimítrios, Loútra, Kiriána and Amnátos, leaving a brief impression of courtyards bedecked with pots of flowers and luxuriant creepers. The wooded hills gradually increase in size and grandeur until, at last, the road follows a bare yellow rock gorge, densely treed at the base. A little later, the road swings sharply to the left and here we stopped before the most famous monastery of Crete, the Moní Arkadíou. A large expanse of stony flat land, like a parade ground, stretches between the lip of the gorge and the sandy-coloured outer walls of the building, battered and blackened in places, as well they might be. We parked under a great cypress tree and stood for a moment admiring the fresh green of the fields and wooded hills beyond.

The monastery was probably founded in the fifth century by the Byzantine emperor, Arkadius, and a few traces of the early building remain in the grounds. A fourteenth-century inscription has been found, referring to the original monastery church, which was dedicated to St Constantine:

"I am called Arkádi. Here I have the apostolic Emperor Constantine's church."

The majority of the present building, however, together with the beautiful Venetian-style church dates from 1587. In the sixteenth century, Arkádi had a reputation for the hand-copying of religious manuscripts, most of which are now sadly destroyed. During the early part of the Turkish occupation, an accommodation seems to have been reached with the ruling authorities and the monastery was granted a number of privileges. However, it later became closely involved with the liberation movement, this support leading to the "holocaust" of 1866, and in the Second World War, the monastery helped the resistance on numerous occasions. But the events of 1866 resulted in Arkádi's particularly honoured place in Cretan history. Indeed, it has been said that Arkádi is to the Cretans as Masada is to the Jews.

The "Great Revolt", or the "66" as it became known, began on 1 May of that year, when some 1,500 leading men of the Christian community met on the Plateau of Omalós, high among the White Mountains. They formed a National Committee under the leadership of Hadzimichalis Iannaris, the Kydonian chief whose statue now stands in Khaniá. (The prefix "Hadzi", quite common among Cretans of the period, indicates that a pilgrimage had been made to Jerusalem). Sub-committees were chosen for the various provinces, and Gabriel Marinakis, Abbot of Arkádi, was elected President of the Réthymnon Committee. When Turkish troops were sent to the Omalós to arrest the rebels, they were fired upon and driven back.

The Sultan despatched Egyptian troops to put down the uprising, much as in 1821, and proposed to the National Committee that if they would lay down their arms and submit to rule from Egypt, a number of reforms would be instituted to the Christians' advantage. Meanwhile, in Réthymnon, Ismael Pasha had become aware of the Abbot's involvement in the revolt and sent word to Arkádi that if they would not reject the Committee and abstain from all revolutionary activity, the monastery would be destroyed. In July, a force of soldiers was sent up to the monastery, but the monks and the members of the Réthymnon Committee had taken to the hills. The Turkish troops retired empty-handed, after causing a certain amount of damage within the church.

In September, a General Assembly of Crete met at Chóra Sfakíon and rejected the Sultan's offer. The Assembly proclaimed *énosis* with

Greece and immediately appealed to the Great Powers for protection against Turkey. Almost at once volunteers began to pour into the island from the mainland, but King George I of the Hellenes and his Prime Minister, Koumoundouros, remained cautious. Greece adopted a carefully neutral stance while awaiting the decision of the Great Powers. France and Russia both favoured *énosis,* but the British Government was opposed and it became plain that Crete could expect no assistance from abroad.

The tempo of events began to quicken. Turkey imposed a naval blockade and prepared to attack the insurgents in force. The Cretans, for their part, began to realise that they could not expect foreign assistance beyond the individual volunteers from Greece and grimly prepared to fight it out, gripped by a patriotic fervour of almost religious intensity. A final warning was received from Ismael Pasha – the monastery would be completely destroyed if the rebellious activity of the Réthymnon Committee did not cease. The decision to defy the warning is said to have been taken under the great oak tree which stands in the monastery fields. Preparations to fortify the building were begun immediately under the direction of Panos Koroneos, a volunteer from the mainland, who nevertheless could see that Arkádi would not withstand a sustained attack by superior forces. It seemed to him that the Cretans' best hope lay in their traditional tactics of guerrilla warfare from the hills, and he strongly advised the Abbot and his companions that an attempt to withstand a siege would be disastrous. But Arkádi had achieved a symbolic importance in the minds of the rebels beyond ordinary military logic, and they insisted that nothing would move them from their chosen ground.

"I came to offer my life for my country but not to be caught alive in here," Koroneos is understandably reported to have said, and left with his own forces in an attempt to divert the Turks. Ioannis Dimakopoulos, a young Peloponnesian volunteer, remained behind as garrison commander. By this time, apart from 287 armed men, including the monks, the monastery contained about 700 women and children, some the wives and families of rebels, others having taken refuge from the surrounding villages. There seemed to have been no doubt in the minds of the defenders that resistance would be suicidal, but all were in the throes of a passionate and typically Cretan determination to sell their lives dearly for the cause. The watchword at Arkádi was "Freedom or Death", a saying on the island to this day.

On the night of 7 November, a Turkish regular army of 15,000, including Egyptian Coptic Christians and 30 cannon, left Réthymnon in two columns and by the next morning had encircled the monastery. The Turkish commander, Suleiman Bey, called on the Cretans to surrender, but they replied by opening fire. A massive bombardment of the monastery began and continued all through the day, with the Turks gradually capturing various outbuildings and attempting to destroy the gate. During the following night, two heavy artillery pieces were brought up from Réthymnon and positioned in the stables to bear on the main compound. Meanwhile, the Abbot administered the last sacrament to every soul in the monastery. The battle began again at daybreak on the 9th and the walls were battered by artillery until the western gate collapsed. The defenders were running short of ammunition and, as the Turks forced their way into the compound, hand-to-hand fighting with swords and bayonets became general.

It is said that the Abbot Gabriel Marinakis himself called for those left alive to retreat to the powder magazine and blow it up, rather than fall into the hands of the enemy. During the mêlée, with groups of rebels defending various stairs and passageways, and with darkness falling, a large number of women and children and some of the surviving fighters gathered in the powder store, originally a wine cellar, at the corner of the outer wall. While the Turks strove to force the door, Konstantinos Giaboudakis, from the nearby village of Adele, drew his pistol and fired it into the powder barrels; the resultant explosion killed several hundred Turks as well as the Cretans in the magazine. Some say that a tiny baby miraculously survived.

The besieging Turks now went beserk with rage against the "Christian giaours", slaughtering indiscriminately. Thirty-six men caught without ammunition in the refectory were beheaded. At the end, 114 Cretan prisoners were taken, 864 having died in the battle, together with almost 1,500 Turks. The compound of the monastery was strewn with corpses and the whole area was littered with bones for years afterwards. The severed head of the Abbot Gabriel Marinakis was carried on a sword back into Réthymnon.

There is a strange story that, after the battle, the positions of the Egyptian Coptic troops on the surrounding hills were found to be covered with discarded bullets. They had pulled the lead from their cartridges and fired them off as blanks, being unwilling to take the lives of fellow Christians.

* * * *

The main gate of the monastery was rebuilt after 1866. Perhaps the most striking view, and one which appears on many postcards, is that of the church façade, seen across the rough flags of the compound from within the arch of the entrance. The three doors, of which the centre one is bricked up, the Corinthian columns and high campanile with three bells make a fine sight. Although the soft stone is heavily damaged and pockmarked, it is possibly the finest example of Venetian architecture remaining in Crete.

A young monk hurried across the courtyard, long dark oiled hair and beard curling over his black cowl (Orthodox clergy are not permitted to shave or cut their hair). We walked over the mossy stones and into the dark interior of the basilica, where the air was cold and smelled sharply of incense and olive oil. Candles were flickering in their tall holders, the wax dripping in great stalactites to the floor. The watch lamps glowed and guttered before the icons. The interior of the church was burned out during the massacre and so the cypress wood altar screen and most of the icons are relatively modern. A taxi driver from Réthymnon was showing round a party of Americans. Their whispering voices hissed through the gloom and the silence.

Outside, in the warmer air and occasional watery sunlight, we inspected an ancient cypress tree, battered by cannon fire, in the branches of which a rebel fighter had managed to hide and survive the slaughter. We passed through a massive arched door into the kitchen and bakery, still in use today. I noticed an old handmill for grinding flour, great iron pots on the ashes of an open wood fire and a sink carved from a solid block of stone. There appears to be no running water and the floor is made of rough cobbles. A dead rat lay in a corner of the passage, presumably killed by one of the many cats which prowl the corridors. All these rooms had the darkness and chill resulting from immensely thick stone walls and tiny windows.

The refectory is a great barrel-vaulted chamber, illuminated by light pouring dramatically through a high circular window, for all the world like a still from *Citizen Kane*. The door is still marked and peppered with bullet holes and the long benches and tables are notched with sword cuts. The powder magazine must once have been a similar room, but the roof has been neatly, almost surgically, removed by the explosion and we stood on a carpet of grass looking up at the sky. There is an inscription on the wall:

"The flame that was lighted in this crypt, and which shone on glorious Crete from end to end, was God's fire, the holocaust in which Cretans died for liberty."

There was once a plan to put up another inscription at Arkádi, in honour of the Cretans and British who fought together in 1941–45. This project was rather sadly dropped in 1959 in the midst of the Cyprus troubles.

We climbed to the parapet of the wall, lined by terraces and monks' cells facing inwards. Rows of potted plants and drying washing gave a pleasant feeling of comfort and domesticity after the spartan gloom of the kitchens. From here, we could look down on the courtyard and a laden orange tree by the church. I noticed the *semántron* bell, the strange curved piece of iron (sometimes wood) which is hung from two cords in Greek monasteries, and struck with a hammer to call the monks to meals and prayer. The church bells are conventional, of course, although almost always external and rung from outside the building with ropes which are fastened to the wall when not in use. When a real gale blows, a wind which will set the heavy bell swinging and clanging in the tower without human agency, people speak of a "bell wind".

The sun came clearly out from the clouds at last to illuminate the view inland: green monastery fields and vineyards giving way to oak trees and rolling hills behind. In the far distance, the higher mountains around Mount Ida were just visible. The cloisters below were cluttered with odd agricultural implements, sections of bee-hives, hoes and spades, sacks and wooden boxes.

A monk led us up a short stairway and unlocked the museum, waiting patiently but uncommunicatively, as we walked past rows of black-framed portraits of the dead heroes, all "bristling like lobsters" with weapons, some with moustaches nearly reaching their shoulders. Some of their firearms are on display, a curious mixture of the ancient and modern guns which circulated in the nineteenth-century Levant: British carbines, American breechloaders modified to take Cretan muzzle-loading cartridges, "Lazarina" flintlocks, "Brahim Pasha" carbines and "Bernadakis" rifles from Russia. The strangely Arabic-looking *kariofílis* muzzle-loaders, with their immensely long barrels and silver-plated butts, were the most valued for mountain warfare. The name is a corruption of "Carlos e figlis", famous Italian gunsmiths, who sold these rifles all over the Levant. They were extremely accurate over long distances in spite of their weight and the time required to recharge them – "stand still Turk, while I reload!"

Many embroidered religious vestments from the seventeenth and eighteenth centuries are displayed in glass cabinets, rich with crimson and gold thread. In pride of place is Arkádi's banner, showing the Metamorphosis of Christ, which flew during the battle. Riddled with bullet holes, it was returned to the monastery, together with the bell, in 1870 by a sympathetic Turkish officer. A number of sacred relics were hidden in a cave after the holocaust, and later returned to be displayed here, together with garments and personal possessions of the Abbot Gabriel.

Outside the gateway, the taxi driver was leaning against his Mercedes, smoking a cigarette, while his Americans looked around the curious dome-shaped building at the edge of the gorge. Once a windmill, this has been converted to an ossuary for the bones of the victims. Many of the skulls in the glass cases bear the gruesome marks of sword cuts and bullet holes. Here, too, is an inscription:

"Nothing is more noble and glorious than to die for one's country. Fire, the sword and all else is defied for its sake."

The date 9 November is now a public holiday in Crete, and anniversary ceremonies are held at the monastery which has become a potent and emotional symbol of the island's freedom.

What did Arkádi achieve? The Turks eventually suppressed the '66 as they had each preceding rebellion. The holocaust seems at first sight to have been a futile, if heroic, stand, a bull-headed display of misplaced courage. In fact, Arkádi pushed the Cretan issue firmly into the limelight. Turkey had not realised that the world had become a much smaller place since the revolts of 1770, 1821 and 1828. The massacre was widely reported by the foreign press; both Europeans and Americans were shocked by an episode of barbarity which seemed to belong more to the Middle Ages than to the second half of the nineteenth century. Garibaldi sent a message from Italy to the "brave children of Ida". Victor Hugo spoke on the Cretans' behalf, the American senate officially sympathised, while Moscow sent money to aid the cause. A Cretan Committee was set up on Sýra. The *Panhellion* began to run the Turkish blockade, while Philo-Cretan societies, organised by expatriate Greeks in England, bought a paddle-steamer built for blockade running in the American Civil War. Renamed the *Arkadi* in 1867, and crewed by British engineers well paid for their risks, she ran more than twenty cargoes of arms and ammunition into Crete before a Turkish warship forced her on to the rocks at Cape Kriós at the south-west of the island.

As the fires of rebellion gradually died down, it became clear that the prestige of the Ottoman Empire had suffered a severe blow. Pressure of public opinion now forced European governments to face a problem which it had previously been more convenient to ignore. The Great Powers considered the matter of Crete, largely in ignorance of the island and its people, in the context of the general security of the Mediterranean and their own interests. Russia, linked by religion and other historic bonds to the Greek cause, was for *énosis*; France believed Turkey to be now incapable of governing Crete effectively and similarly favoured *énosis*, for reasons of basic justice as well as wider political considerations. The British, however, in the person of Lord Stanley, the Tory Foreign Minister, were mindful of the Suez Canal about to open and concerned for the security of the route to India. The British view was that the Ottoman Empire, crumbling as it plainly was, should be supported in the interests of security in the Levant and to counteract Russian influence. Thus, Britain's veto delayed *énosis* by 47 years.

Turkey made a number of concessions to Christians embodied in the Pact of Khalépa of 1878, but few of the promised reforms materialised. In 1896 a further revolt broke out, with bloodshed in Khaniá between Christians and Muslims. The Great Powers brought pressure to bear on the Sultan to renew the Pact of Khalépa, call a National Assembly of Cretans and to declare a general amnesty for all combatants. Nevertheless, by February 1897 a civil war between Christians and Muslims had broken out again in the west of Crete.

When the Christians proclaimed *énosis* on this occasion, Greece was unable to hold back. A Greek army landed near Khaniá to claim the island. The Greeks immediately found themselves embroiled in a further war with Turkey and the situation became rapidly chaotic. The Great Powers (Great Britain, France, Italy and Russia) felt themselves compelled to intervene, and sent a joint force to occupy Soúda Bay and Khaniá, forcibly separating the warring factions. The rebel forces were established on the neck of the Akrotíri Peninsula, the young Eleftherios Venizelos being amongst them. At one point, the warships of the Great Powers bombarded the Cretans for raising the Greek flag here. There is a story that when the flagpole was broken by a shell, one of the Cretans stood up, holding the flag in his own hands. The sailors of the fleet are said to have ceased serving the guns and cheered him.

It was decided that while the island should officially remain under Turkish sovereignty, full autonomy should be granted the Cretans and a High Commissioner appointed. All four Powers would hold Khaniá, while the combined fleet in Soúda Bay would be commanded by the Italian Admiral Canevaro. The Turkish troops and Muslim population were effectively confined to the towns.

But selecting a suitable High Commissioner proved a lengthy task. Administrators from Switzerland, Luxembourg and Montenegro all turned the post down. During these deliberations, on 6 September 1898, a riot broke out in Iráklion; the Muslims ran amok and indulged in a general slaughter in which nineteen British sailors and the British Vice-Consul were killed. On hearing of this, Admiral Noel, the commander of the British iron-clads in the harbour, took prompt action. The guns were swung round to bombard the city and the rioters given ten minutes to surrender – a classic example of gunboat diplomacy! Britain had run out of patience and the ring-leaders were hanged, while all Turkish troops were ordered to leave the island. After so many years and so much bloodshed, the long sad story came to an end. Three months later, Prince George arrived as High Commissioner, to herald in a new and unfamiliar era of freedom and self-government.

* * * *

After leaving Arkádi and taking the road towards the coast, we pulled up at the village of Amnátos, with its church precariously built on a steep little knoll above the houses and orange orchards. Walking up the circular concrete path around its base, we passed a tethered mule and entered the churchyard, wandering among the tombs and vaults. Most are well tended with photographs of the dead in glass cases, vases of flowers and burning watch lamps, the little saucers of olive oil with a strip of thread for a wick, which are exactly as the ancient Greeks made them. Reading the inscriptions, we were impressed by the generous lifespans some of the villagers seem to achieve, for, wars and feuds apart, the Cretan diet and climate is healthy. A few of the vaults are so broken and neglected as to allow the bones and skulls to spill out of the cracked stonework. But Greeks treat death more familiarly than we; it is a well-known enemy to be cheated if possible, but no mystery is attached to it. Coffins remain open until burial so that the mourners may kiss the corpse, which will be interred with a coin for the ferryman and sometimes the marriage crown, carefully preserved. The men will stay silent, perhaps mutter a valediction – "let the earth rest lightly on him" – but the women will have stayed up through the night, keening and singing dirges, and the vocal expression of their grief will continue to the graveside. Mourning is a matter for women, it is they who will wear the black, perhaps for the rest of their lives. There was a time when men would show their grief by growing a beard, once a rare thing here, although every adult male had a moustache. Ashes are put on the grave 40 days after the death, and again, on the Feast of All Souls, cedar wood is burned in remembrance. The cemeteries do not occupy much of the scarce land, because after three years the bones are removed from the earth and put into a charnel house, piled with those of their ancestors.

Most peasants are fatalistic, and the old Cretan countryman talks of Cháros, the reaper rather than the ferryman, as a familiar adversary who has been bested till now, but to whom he must succumb sooner or later. But Cháros can be tricked, delayed for a while at least. Patrick Leigh Fermor, travelling in the Máni, came across a strange superstition:

> When a woman has lost a male child (a "gun"), she carries her next-born son out into the street in her apron shouting, "A lamb for sale. Who'll buy a lamb?" "I will," says the first passer-by. He pays a small sum, stands godfather to him at the font, then hands the lamb back to its mother. It is a ruse to cheat Cháron by confusing the familiar track with a false scent.
>
> (Patrick Leigh Fermor, *Máni*)

A few years ago, even stranger and more sinister superstitions lurked in these Cretan hills. It is not generally realised that Greek folklore is full of stories of the *vrykólakas,* or vampire, who once seems to have thrived in this part of the Balkans. In all Greece, the islands of Crete and Santoríni were the most notorious for this phenomenon (sometimes known as the *katáchanas,* the fiend, on Crete), which haunted and plagued lonely mountain communities. A stillborn or unbaptised child, an ex-communicate, a suicide, a corpse buried without religious rites, in particular a murdered man un-avenged – all these might become a vampire. The belief goes back for a thousand years and extended almost into modern times, for corpses have been exhumed and staked within living memory in some remote areas. The Orthodox Church maintains an ambivalent atti-tude to the matter, rather as the Church of England does towards the service of exorcism. Sudden death was common enough in western Crete and the vampire legend multiplied and grew. The Akrotíri Peninsula was once particularly plagued by this curse. The Holy Trinity Monastery became immensely wealthy by offering to rebury suspect corpses with full religious rites and thus exorcise the demon.

The nineteenth-century explorer, Pashley, was told the following story in Kallikrátis, an isolated village in the mountains of eastern Sfakiá. A vampire had terrorised this village for many months, killing children and even grown men by night. No one knew who the creature was, or where he came from. One day a shepherd of the village was pasturing his sheep near the Church of St George when it began to rain, and the man went into the graveyard to take shelter. One of the graves was covered by an arch and, as this was a snug, dry place, he lay down for a rest, taking off his weapons and placing them on the tombstone. In time, he fell asleep.

The grave was that of the shepherd's *sýnteknos,* or godbrother. This is a peculiarly Greek relationship which requires some explana-tion. When a child is baptised, a godfather stands with the parents at the font, and this ceremony binds him to both parents and the child with ties as strong as blood. Similarly, the sponsor of a young couple at their wedding, in the fashion of the English "best man", becomes a friend, patron and adviser to the newly-weds and their children for life. These connections are taken very seriously today as a formal way of cementing friendships and, in the past, were an important way of contracting alliances and patching up feuds. *Sýnteknos* is a Cretan expression, the more general word is *koumbáros*. One of the hazards of modern Greek political life is the large number of these relationships any successful politician is obliged to enter into, and maintain, in order to secure his local power base – the equivalent of a good English constituency MP.

To return to our shepherd and the vampire; when dusk fell, he was awakened by a voice from the earth beneath him: "Sýnteknos, get up hence, for I have some business which requires me to come out."

The shepherd realised the ghastly truth, that the vampire was the buried corpse of his own godbrother. He continued to lie silently on the grave while the voice from the earth repeated its demand. Eventually, he replied that he would not do so, for fear of his own safety. But if his godbrother would swear by his winding sheet to do him no harm, only then would he get up and allow him out.

The vampire argued, but eventually, finding his godbrother to be resolute, swore the oath by his winding sheet, the only vow sacred to a *vrykólakas*. Then the shepherd arose and picked up his arms, which he had laid down by chance in the pattern of a cross. Thus the vampire was able to emerge from his tomb, and he told the shepherd to wait in the churchyard for him. When the vampire eventually reappeared, his hands were bloody and he was carrying a human liver, having killed a young couple ten miles away. His horrified godbrother watched him blow into the liver to increase its size, as a butcher does. The vampire asked him to share in the grisly meal, but, fearful of contamination by the same terrible curse, he only pretended to eat. As the vampire returned to his tomb, he instructed his godbrother to tell no one, "For if you do, my twenty nails will be fixed in your children and yourself."

In the event, the shepherd went to the village priest with the whole story. The priest organised a band of villagers to dig up the corpse and the shepherd's story was confirmed when the body was found to be in a state of perfect preservation. The corpse was burned on a pyre to destroy the power of the undead. When the shepherd arrived to join the group, a single drop of the vampire's blood fell on to his foot and burned into his flesh with an agonising pain. On raking through the ashes, a little finger nail was found to have survived the fire and it was not until this was destroyed that the village was finally free of the unholy creature.

Whatever strange ghosts haunt the lonely canyons and gorges on dark nights, this was too pretty a place and the sun was now too bright to dwell on these gloomy tales for long. Michael and I leaned over the railings, watching a farmer filling the panniers of his mule in the orange grove before leading it towards the village on our right.

"Kaliméra, good morning," we shouted down to him.

"Kaliméra, where do you come from?"

"From England."

"Oh, my friends!" He picked an orange from the pannier and with shrugged shoulders made a pantomime that it was too far to throw. Then he thought again, slapped the mule on the rump to make its own way home and came some distance up towards us. With a mighty throw, he sent the orange sailing over the railing and, by a fluke, I caught it.

"Go to the good!"

"Efkaristó!" We waved our thanks as he followed his mule down the path to the village. It had been a truly remarkable throw. Did they play cricket? Only in Corfu. We sat eating the orange by the locked door of the church, peering through a broken pane into the gloom within, bright colours showing only where a ray of light from a window fell upon the iconostasis.

We strolled around the village ourselves, talking to the children enjoying their Saturday's freedom from school. Everyone was smiling, wanting to meet the strangers. George Seferis, the poet, said: "Wherever you go in Greece, the people open up like flowers." It seemed a prosperous little place, with tractors scattered about the street, piped water and irrigation systems everywhere and concrete roadways running out to the fields, laid over the old stone flags and cobbles.

A dark-haired girl of about twelve, holding two smaller children by the hands, started at hearing our foreign accent and then asked in English: "Hey, are you tourists?"

"Why yes."

"Are you Americans?" Her own transatlantic accent was fairly strong.

"No, we're from England. Do you come from this village?"

"From Canada. But my parents came from this village."

"Have you been here long?" we asked.

"About six months."

"Are your family just visiting their old home?" But she did not seem to know the answer to this; perhaps they were back for good.

"How do you like living here?"

She made a wry face; she must have been missing her school friends and the bustle of Toronto. She directed us to a *tavérna* down on the main road where we could find some lunch, then, leading her two small charges away, she said goodbye with a Greek's natural courtesy and charm, seeming somehow old for her years.

In the event, we drove further on down the valley until we came to a little roadside *tavérna* with delightfully misspelt signs in English outside. We sometimes felt it would be kind to correct these for the owners, but always feared to hurt their feelings. Other signs were probably best left: "meat with balls" was one favourite of mine.

The owners of this establishment rushed up on seeing us as if nobody had been in for months. Maybe no one had, for there were no other customers on this particular day. A bottle of *retsína* was brought, together with fresh bread and the usual Greek salad with *féta* cheese, while the proprietor cooked *souvlákia,* or lamb kebabs, over a wood fire outside. He was quite happy to chat to us over a glass of wine as he did so, rather like a barbecue party at home. The food was simple but excellent and we did it justice, following it up with fresh fruit and Greek coffee.

The word *tsikoudiá* was not understood here, but *rakí* certainly was, and we ordered an extra glass for our host. After drinking everybody's health, the inn-keeper insisted on circulating the un-marked bottle of clear spirit several more times. Now, virtually adopted by the family, we all pulled our chairs round in a semi-circle before the television and watched the news from Athens, a film on cave exploration in the Peloponnese and, finally, *White Fang* with Greek sub-titles. The proprietor sat contentedly puffing at one of our duty-free cigars, occasionally pushing more wood into the stove, while his wife brewed another pot of sweet black coffee.

CHAPTER 7

Réthymnon

It was well into the afternoon when we finally set off to drive back into Réthymnon. The early morning bustle of the town might never have been. Later in the evening, families and friends would stroll or promenade up and down in the *vólta,* the walk, a social occasion of urban Greece rather akin to the Spanish *paseo,* but now the streets were sunk in the lethargy of a Saturday afternoon. We parked on Venizélou, by a long, curved, sandy beach and walked around to a Venetian lighthouse on the mole, which guards a little port very similar to the one at Khaniá. There is the same mixture of Venetian and Turkish architecture, perhaps on a smaller scale: arches and shutters, iron balconies and richly-coloured façades crowding closely to the water. Along the quay are old iron lamp posts like those of Victorian London.

The new outer harbour at Réthymnon was a commercial disaster, for it filled with sand and silt as soon as it was built and resists all attempts at dredging. Only ships small enough to use the inner, Venetian port can come into Réthymnon, which seems to have been in gradual, genteel decline ever since the Venetians left. "Khaniá for arms, Réthymnon for book learning . . ." Réthymnon has always been a town of the middle class, and perhaps the upper class in straitened circumstances. A town of lawyers and doctors, men of education and culture, it is famous throughout Greece for its writers and poets to this day. The writer, Pandelis Prevelakis wrote a delightful description of life here in the early years of the century, *The Tale of a Town,* which is now regarded as an important contribution to modern Greek literature. It is a charming book, wryly acknowledging the bourgeois values and limitations of this little provincial community, yet somehow bursting with affection at the same time. Read it before you visit Réthymnon and you will be able to amuse yourself looking for evidence, in odd corners, of that town of seventy years ago. Here by the harbour was the coffee house which the Turks frequented, the *nargilehs* bubbling and fuming as they sat listening to the story-teller. The Arrimondi fountain, built by the Venetian Rector in 1623, still stands at the junction of Thessaloníki and Paleológou Streets, but the *kiatib*, the public letter-writer, no longer sits there with his box of parchment and pens. This narrow crescent-shaped street behind the harbour, and now named Arkadíou, must have been the old "Tsar Street", once famous for its drapers and gunsmiths who traded all over the Near East. Here, at the castle walls, the Turkish landowners could have been seen every evening, riding their fine Arab horses into the city from their country estates before the great gate was closed for the night. The triple-balconied minaret of the Nerantziá Mosque still soars over the rooftops, while on the headland the *Fortezza,* the largest single fortress Venice ever built, glowers at the sea like a couched lion.

The name Réthymnon means a stream of water, and a settlement existed from the late-Minoan period, though little is known of its history, even into mediaeval times. The Venetians made the town into an important trading post for the export of wine and oil, and in the sixteenth century built the great castle on the promontory. This massive citadel was thought to be impregnable, earlier fortifications having been damaged by pirates. Nevertheless, the Turks took it in 1646 with less difficulty than they were to encounter at Candia, while the Rector and his entourage were evacuated by galley. The cathedral and palace within the walls fell into ruins during the Turkish occupation. Although the Russians cleared and tidied the park within the fortress during the occupation of the Great Powers, further damage occurred through bombing during the Second World War. There is still an impressive mosque in the compound, however.

We walked under the jutting rocks on the seaward side of the *Fortezza,* the high walls overhead grown with moss and patches of grass, but virtually undamaged. The road along the sea wall was deserted, except for a pair of Alsatian dogs chained to trees outside a locked *kafeneíon,* constantly barking and wearing circular paths in the dust at the radius of their restraints. Clambering around the steep grassy cobbles under the ramparts inland, we gained a view of red-tiled roofs, whitewashed houses and that incongruous Nerantziá minaret against the distant mountains. Almost every building in this part of the town seems to be crumbling.

Apart from its intellectuals, Réthymnon is famous for cakes and honey pastries, mulberry *rakí* and pork cooked with fennel. Like all regional specialities, they never seem to be available when you are actually on the spot, but I mention them in a spirit of hopefulness.

The town also has a reputation as the home of some of the oldest families in Crete. Prevelakis mentions the Byzantine names of Melissinos, Vlastos, Kallergis, Gavalas, Skordylis, Varoukhis, Kalaphatis and Daphomilis, together with the Venetian Dandolos, Damolinos, Moatsos, Saounatsos, Venieris and Bernados. As no archives or parish records were kept during the Turkish occupation, it is often very difficult to trace family histories and there is usually no more evidence of ancestry than an ancient name and local tradition.

Behind the *Fortezza* lies Smyrna Street, one of many in the towns of Greece, and a reminder of the one and a half million "oriental" Greeks who once had their home in Asia Minor. A reminder too of a dream which still remains somewhere deep in the Greek psyche. Today, the word for essential Greekness is *Romiosíni* and Greeks are traditionally *Romioí,* literally "citizens of Rome", and referring more precisely to East Rome or Constantinople. Though the last emperor is long dead and Constantinople fell to the Turks in 1453, the Cretans, as all Greeks, regard it as their spiritual capital, referring to it only as "The City". Down the centuries, the dream of redeeming the City has been nurtured in the innermost soul of the Greek people: "over the years, in time, she'll be ours once again."

When Greece's policy of irredentism climaxed in the direct attack on Turkey through the Greek enclave of Smyrna in 1922, the subsequent defeat by Kemal Ataturk was a stupendous and demoralising blow. As the Turkish army captured the city of Smyrna, an orgy of killing, looting and rape took place and the majority of the city burned to the ground. Incidentally, a relative of mine was once aboard a ship which docked at the Turkish port of Marmaris when a reunion of mountaineers, veterans of this campaign, took place. Ancient as they were by then, she described them as absolutely terrifying, a Turkish version of the Cretan *pallikária.*

The subsequent Treaty of Lausanne decreed an inhuman exchange of populations, some one and a half million Greeks living in Turkey to be evacuated (the entire population of Greece was then only five and a half million) and 400,000 Turks to leave Greece. The 30,000 Turks who remained in Crete after 1898 regarded it as their home and, despite their Muslim religion, lived happily with their lowland Christian neighbours, if not the mountaineers. "Me too, my guts are Cretan", they used to say, with some justification after many generations of settlement. There is overwhelming evidence of the peaceful co-existence of the two races here, in Asia Minor and indeed in Cyprus. But in Crete, in Asia Minor and, above all, in Cyprus, this village-level common-sense was submerged by wider political issues and misplaced patriotism. The compulsory population exchange

devastated the Turks of Crete who lost land, homes and property –
farms and vineyards which had occupied a lifetime's toil.

Prevelakis describes how, as a boy, he watched the Turks in
anguish destroy the shutters and doors of the homes they were
leaving behind. The Greek refugees from Smyrna, waiting to move
into these same houses, began a riot which had to be quelled by the
militia. Prevelakis' account of the departure should be compulsory
reading for any politician who suggests this solution for problems of
race and frontier:

The Army formed a cordon round the Turkish quarter, occupied
the approaches to the harbour and finally called on the Turks to
cross the area one by one and embark. It was a black moment and
seemed as endless as the night. People fainted with emotion. At last
the Turks moved to go down into the ships. They went in with their
clothes torn, their hands dripping blood. The women had lost their
veils. They went by in single file between a double line of soldiers,
like thieves caught stealing other folk's belongings, looking askance,
red-eyed, their teeth clenched with rage. They embarked, the port
authorities loaded their baggage in order and stowed it on board the
steamers. Night fell and day dawned and still the work went on. At
noon next day we heard the steamers hoot three times, the noise of
the anchor chains resounding along the shore. And then there came a
single cry from thousands of throats, from men, women and children,
a cry which God in His mercy grant you never hear, savage yet
imploring, full of misery and fear. The wind caught it up and bore it
to us in snatches.

(Pandelis Prevelakis, *The Tale of a Town*)

There used to be a Turkish cemetery in Réthymnon. The graves
faced east towards Mecca, surmounted by stone turbans and fezzes.
After the Turks left, it was broken up and then turned into a pretty
little park.

I once saw a few feet of old documentary film showing the Smyrna
Greeks departing for the ships. They seemed an exotic, eastern
people, all their household goods loaded on to trains of camels.
Many of them actually opted to settle in Crete, bringing new
customs and songs, the art of growing raisins and fishing from boats
equipped with acetylene lamps. Others, less fortunate, lived for years
in the slums and shanty towns around Athens until they were
assimilated. These refugees came to be a fertile recruiting ground
for the Communist Party.

This afternoon the gate to the *Fortezza* was closed so we walked back to the harbour. The inner, Venetian, port contained only a few fishing caiques, while the silted outer anchorage was totally deserted. During one of the dredging attempts, Venetian cannon and a three-masted ship full of marble were found in the sand. They say that ships' masters would see the lighthouse and the great fortress on a stormy night, thankfully turn into an apparently safe haven and find themselves firmly gripped in the suction of the mud. As the Réthymniots welcomed the sailors safely ashore, they would be mentally totting up the salvage value of the accessible timbers and cargo.

The population were now appearing and strolling along the waterfront, men deep in conversation, fingering their strings of worry beads, youths in groups cat-calling the girls or gathered around small motorcycles pulled up on the kerb. As we drove back to the hotel, we suddenly became embroiled in an extraordinary procession of vehicles, some adorned with the green flag of PASOK, Papandreou's Pan-Hellenic Socialist Party. Every driver, his headlamps blazing, was blowing his horn frantically and waving encouragement. Constantly, more cars and motorcycles from the other direction turned round to join the demonstration until the streets were choked. Such a good time was had by all, in fact, that when the far end of the town was reached, a congested and confused U-turn took place, flags waving dangerously out of windows, and the whole parade was noisily repeated. Farmers, waiters, mechanics, workers from the cheese factory, all were overwhelmed by their enthusiasm for democratic republicanism: "This is a time when captains are sailors, and sailors are captains . . ." Pedestrians applauded as happily as if the circus had come to town, while New Democracy supporters were presumably keeping quiet until their day came. The elections were not far off. (This was the time of Papandreou's ousting of Karamanlis from the presidency. A typically Greek political crisis had been provoked by the refusal of Constantine Mitsotakis, the Cretan who succeeded Karamanlis as leader of New Democracy, to accept the presidency of Sartzetakis, PASOK's preferred candidate. In the event, PASOK won the subsequent elections convincingly, and Sartzetakis was recognised as president by New Democracy.)

Greeks must be the most enthusiastically political race in the world, perhaps because self-determination has been denied them for so much of their history, and perhaps also because of their natural gift for conspiracy and readiness to attribute base motives to their opponents. The sympathies of most towns and villages can be quickly deduced from the green, blue, or, more rarely, the red Communist

KKE slogans painted on every wall, almost as many as in Portugal, which must lead the world in political grafitti. Politics, both domestic and foreign, are undoubtedly the main topic of café conversations and quite simple country people often surprise the visitor by asking astute questions about English affairs which demonstrate a considerable insight. This political awareness is perhaps in surprising contrast to the fact that Greek administration is extremely centralised, Crete's four administrative prefects, police, taxation and education authorities being appointed by Athens. The exception is the Church, which has direct access to the Patriarch of Constantinople to this day.

At the grassroots, politics in Greece is still more concerned with personalities than with issues. How often does one hear in the coffee shop that there are "no great men today", no Venizelos, no Churchill, no Roosevelt, no Kennedy. In Crete, the influence of the Venizelos family lingers on even now, the allegiance felt towards the famous Eleftherios Venizelos having been transferred to his son, Sophocles, until his death in 1964, and then through the Centre Union Party to the Papandreous, father and son. Of course, this is a sweeping generalisation; elements in Crete have supported the royalist right, and indeed the Communists. Nevertheless, it is broadly true to state that Crete, especially the west, is a firm base for radical republicanism. Incidentally, the royalist issue is not entirely a thing of the past, even now. It should be remembered that in 1981 Karamanlis felt unable to attend the Prince of Wales' wedding in London, having learned that Constantine was to be officially present as King of the Hellenes.

Foreigners tend to scoff at the instability of Greek governments. In 1971, Karamanlis himself wrote that Greece had only functioned properly as a democracy on three occasions: during the Trikoupis administration of the nineteenth century; from 1910–15, during Venizelos' first period of office; and under Karamanlis himself. Having held power for eight peaceful years from 1955 to 1963, there having been fifteen governments during the post-war decade, he had a right to make this boast. If Venizelos was the political giant of the early twentieth century, Karamanlis has been the dominant figure through the later years. The young Karamanlis, a Macedonian born under Ottoman rule, son of an irregular fighter against the Bulgarian *comitadjis,* began his political career as a royalist, just as that of the republican Venizelos ended. They were at opposite ends of the political spectrum, yet Karamanlis' admiration for his personal hero never diminished, and this is perhaps a measure of the man's maturity and vision – an ability to make friends with political opponents is all too rare in Greece.

In those eight stable years of his first term, Karamanlis gave a backward, desperately poor, agrarian state, recently racked by a civil war which had killed more of the population than the world war preceding it, a firm push towards modernisation and prosperity. When he returned after the Colonels' dictatorship as the only figure in Greek political life thought to be capable of restoring normality, he continued the steady construction of a democratic European state. Early reforms included the official abolition of the dowry system, divorce by consent, the nationalisation of ecclesiastical land and the recruitment of women to the armed forces. He virtually created the tourist industry, brought Greece into the EEC and strove to eradicate the corruption and scandal which so bedevilled public life. He made great improvements to the education system – at this time three and a half million, or half the adult population, were largely illiterate. After over a century of argument between the adherents of popular or Demotic Greek and those of *Katharévousa,* the artificial version by Korais, "pure" or "lifeless", depending on your point of view, he opted for the Demotic with all its Turkish derivations. (The Colonels' regime attempted to restore *Katharévousa.*) For all these achievements, he is widely admired, especially in the conservative rural areas. Even Turkish Cypriots, when pressed, will admit to a grudging respect for Karamanlis. His successor, Mitsotakis, has yet to make his mark.

Andreas Papandreou is seen as the champion of the masses against vested interests, American manipulation and all the other enemies of the Greek people as defined by the "conspiracy" theory of politics which prevails here. In the early 1960s, he was seen as their protector against the shipping millionaires and landowners, represented in the person of Frederika, the Queen Mother. When he was persecuted by the military junta, accused of belonging to *Aspída* (the "Shield"), a left-wing society of army officers, his reputation was enhanced. As the United States is popularly believed to have first supported and prolonged the dictatorship, and then to have encouraged, or at least condoned the Turkish invasion of Cyprus, Papandreou's anti-American stance is applauded. His contacts with the PLO and other revolutionary movements in the Middle East, his independent attitude within the EEC and his hard line with Turkey all endear him to the man on the Iráklion omnibus. Greece may be a small country, but "we aren't going to be pushed around any more" is the general message.

At the time of writing, however, Papandreou and the Socialists appear about to succumb to yet another political scandal and this has all the elements – sex and corruption in high places – which so delight the debaters in the taverns and coffee shops.

CHAPTER 8

Shades of the Dew

At breakfast, Malcolm managed to jam open the tap of the orange juice dispenser. Nobody could stem the uncontrolled flow. Waiters clustered around, murmuring sugggestions and prodding ineffectually inside the glass tank with long forks. Eventually, Nikos glanced quickly round the room to see who was looking, rolled up the sleeve of his immaculate jacket and shirt cuff to the elbow and plunged his arm into the container to free the mechanism, somehow contriving to shrug his shoulders and roll his eyes simultaneously. I sometimes feel that the Greeks are engaged in a constant struggle with the various machines and mechanisms which the modern world has placed around them.

The bells were ringing for Sunday Mass as we drove through the now peaceful streets of Réthymnon. The Church of the Four Martyrs stands where four men from Perivólia were hanged by the Turks from a plane tree in 1866. The doors were now open, revealing a brilliantly decorated and illuminated interior as the congregation filed inside, dressed in their most formal clothes. From other churches in the town, the chanting was relayed to the street by loudspeakers.

The weather was deteriorating, the north wind still blowing and, as we drove across the Plain of Drámia towards Georgioúpolis, the rain began to fall. The Cretans obviously regarded these conditions as arctic and had swaddled themselves in every possible vestige of clothing. A tractor driver was dressed from head to toe in black leather, including an enormous cap with earflaps and chinstrap. As we climbed into the White Mountains above Vríses, we quickly reached cloud level and were forced to drive slowly in a thick mist which condensed on the windscreen, despite the whistling wind .

Whatever the weather, this road and these mountains seem threatening and sinister. Grim stories are told of the Allied retreat to Chóra Sfakíon in 1941. While fighting units held the Germans off to the rear, a disorganised column moved at night through the mountains over a road littered with abandoned weapons and equipment. No one knew of it at the time, but the 8th Greek Regiment distracted the enemy by continuing to fight a desperate and isolated action at Alikianós in the hills to the west. The retreating army was demoralised and in confusion: Cypriots, Palestinians and non-combatant troops all aware that priority for evacuation would be given to fighting units. There were ugly scenes and guards with fixed bayonets were deployed on the beach at Chóra Sfakíon. For three nights Admiral Cunningham sent in his destroyers, in spite of appalling losses and crews exhausted by repelling attacks from the Stuka base at Scarpanto. In the end, 5,000 men were left behind, some taking to the hills, but most surrendering. Even after the surrender, German aircraft machine-gunned the crowded beach.

Those first few months of the occupation seem to have been deceptively peaceful. Some thousand Allied soldiers were wandering about these southern mountains, sustained by patriotic villages. An escape route was devised, based around the Préveli Monastery and stragglers were taken off at night by submarine. As the Cretans began to organise, Allied agents and wireless operators were landed to gather information on enemy movements and co-ordinate the activities of the *andártes*. The Germans, for their part, were initially reluctant to enter these hostile, rocky valleys, ideal terrain for ambushes and surprise attacks. It is said that in the early days, a patrol would fire a warning volley before entering a village, to avoid an unexpected confrontation with any armed men who might be sheltering in it. Then came the dreadful famine of the 1941 winter, still remembered with horror. Many survived on little more than snails and *hórta,* or wild greens.

By the time we reached the cypress forest on the southern slopes, the wind had reached gale-force, but, just as two days before, we emerged into bright sunlight over the coast at the exit from the gorge – where in 1941 the road petered out. The black clouds were rolling over the peaks and evaporating quite suddenly in the heat. Zigzagging down the bare, tawny slope with its awesome views of distant mountains and dark blue sea, we took the left-hand turn to Komitádes and Frangokástello.

One is always conscious of the massive frowning wall of rock inland, on this occasion capped by streaming banks of dark cloud vapour. No wonder the Sfakians used to believe that evil spirits and legions of demons haunt these places. They say the shepherds, like the *shamans* of Central Asia, can determine future events from the marks on a sheep's shoulder blade, much as the ancients could by the entrails of a sacrifice. There is virtually no vegetation beyond a *phrýgana* of knee-high thornbush and spinifex, while the villages seem to crouch and cower under the threatening landscape. Komitádes, incidentally, has the fourteenth-century Church of St George, with beautiful frescoes by the painter, Ioannis Pagomenos, whose work can also be seen at Alíkampos.

We stopped to stretch our legs opposite the mouth of a ravine running inland. In spite of the high wind blowing down the gorge, the sun still felt warm. I disturbed a large black snake which slithered away into the scrub. According to folklore, all the poisonous snakes of Crete are supposed to have been expelled by St Titus but, nevertheless, I didn't intend to bother this one any further. The floor of the ravine was scattered with great boulders, washed down by some catastrophic flood many years before, and the base of the walls were honeycombed into caves which served as shelters for the goats which were grazing nearby. This landscape is typical of Crete, and particularly of Sfakiá – a name thought to mean "land of ravines". Limestone is hard and slow to erode; it splits rather than weathers. Drainage is underground through great systems of caves and the gorges are the result of the collapse of such a cave roof. They make cross-country walking particularly difficult.

After a few kilometres, the road leads down from the foothills and a side turning brought us on to a flat dusty littoral with a few flat-roofed houses and electric power lines. The hot sun picked out the bright yellow splashes of gorse against the dull green of the *phrýgana* and the ochre of the dirt road. We stopped for a few minutes to allow a large flock of sheep to cross, the dust of their passing whipping away with the wind towards the sea a few hundred yards beyond. The shepherd followed behind, controlling the beasts with well-aimed stones.

What passes through these men's minds during their long, lonely hours in these wild places, following their age-old transhumances? Do they think about their fierce ancestors, the nature of the universe, God, sex, football? They always seem pleased enough to talk to another living soul. Not so long ago, they would play a reed pipe, but perhaps not at noon time for fear of offending Pan. Recently in Cyprus, I met a young shepherd in his own electric world of rock music, between the earphones of his portable stereo set. But the nature of the work has not changed in millennia. Henry Miller wrote:

The shepherd is eternal, an earthbound spirit, a renunciator. On these hillsides for ever and ever will be the shepherd with his flock: he will survive everything, including the tradition of all that ever was.

(Henry Miller, *The Colossus of Maroussi*)

The Communist Party, KKE, gained many adherents among the shepherds and herdsmen of Greece, on the grounds that the Communist creed dignifies and applauds such simple labour, so often belittled by more sophisticated Greeks.

As we passed a small patch of cultivated land, a pair of dogs intercepted us, snarling and biting at the wheels of the car. A few minutes later, Frangokástello came into view, its sharp outline like a child's drawing of a castle on the edge of a clear blue sea. On this flat piece of land, the legends tell that the clans used to gather to dance the wild *pentozáli,* supposed to be derived from an ancient Pyrrhic war dance. Here, in the fourteenth century, the Venetians built this square fort in the hope of subduing the Sfakians, without conspicuous success. The walls of the Castle of the Franks are in surprisingly good condition, and the Venetian Lion of St Mark can still be seen over the main gate, staring out at the wilderness. It is only a shell now, however, with little to be seen inside but empty windows and doorways. Some of the stones are thought to have been taken from a more ancient site. As a building, Frangokástello is unremarkable, but seen against the backdrop of mountains and sea, crystal-sharp in the bright sunlight of this coast, it looks as extraordinary and out of place as an alien spaceship. A number of small buildings and *tavérnas* have grown around it in recent years which detract just a little from its isolated appearance.

We parked in the shadow of the walls and, after wandering through the deserted interior, climbed down the dunes, past a little café, closed till the summer, and out on to the flat windswept sand towards the sea. Little reeds had traced curious circular patterns in the white sand as they waved in the wind which whistled past our ears. Finally we reached the edge of the water, transparent and strangely still in the off-shore breeze, and looked back over the sands where the ghosts of dead heroes are said to walk. To explain this, I must gather together several disparate threads, including the story of another old Venetian fortress.

The islands of Gramboúsa, the "wild" and the "tame", are lonely places off a still lonelier cape at the extreme north-west of Crete. The Venetians built one of their key fortresses here, the others being at Soúda and Spinalónga. These off-shore citadels were so strong that Venice held them for some years after the Turks had conquered the main island of Crete. Gramboúsa was betrayed to the Turks in 1692, and subsequently its wild inlets became a notorious lair of pirates, Algerian as well as Cretan. One of their captains was apparently an ancestor of the writer, Kazantzakis. These blood-stained men preyed indiscriminately on shiploads of Muslims bound for Mecca and

Christian pilgrims on their way to the Holy Land. It appears that the Turkish administration took no action to clean out this nest of crime. During the revolt of 1821, the Turkish garrison of the fortress itself was overwhelmed by a force of Sfakians and Greeks from the islands. Pashley describes how the Sfakian chieftain, Marco Buso, fell in an early attempt to scale the towering walls.

It is not absolutely clear whether the inhabitants of the old fortress were still active in piracy by the year 1827. If they had become honest men, their black past was not so very far behind them. Some say that a thriving town was still supported by the trade. Whatever the truth of it, they were patriots, and although the revolt of 1821 had failed in Crete, they were aware that the mainland was gaining its freedom. On 27 October 1827, an allied fleet of British, French and Russian ships destroyed the Turkish fleet at Navarino (for which action the British Admiral Codrington was severely reprimanded). When the news of this victory reached Gramboúsa, a Council of Crete was convened and independence declared.

The Council of Crete selected a strange and colourful character to send on to the Cretan mainland to foment revolution. Hadzimichalis Daliannis had led a small band of Epirot volunteers all over Greece during the War of Independence – even to Beirut. Although not a Cretan, he was of true *pallikáre* material and, against all advice, garrisoned the abandoned castle of Frangokástello in the face of a large Turkish army led by Mustapha Pasha. His force, including local Cretans, came to only 385 men, and the obvious tactic would have been to retreat and carry on guerrilla warfare from the mountains nearby. Hadzimichalis Daliannis would not back down and his little band was slaughtered, Daliannis being decapitated. The songs say that the smell of death was so strong on him that his horse wept as he leaped into the saddle. Mustapha Pasha himself is said to have mourned for him, for strangely, the two men had known each other in earlier, peaceful times in the Morea.

Over the years, in the month of May, shepherds and fishermen working in the dawn mists have been terrified to see a procession of figures walking and riding in front of the castle. The curious vision has been verified by scientific observers on a number of occasions and, like the "Fata Morgana" apparition in the Straits of Messina, is not easy to explain. One theory is that a mirage is somehow projected across the sea from Libya, and that the ghostly figures are actually military manoeuvres or camel trains moving across the desert. The local people, however, believe firmly that the figures are Hadzimichalis Daliannis and his 385 *pallikária,* arisen from their graves in the sand to fill humans with dread. *Drossoulítes,* they call them, the "Shades of the Dew", or the "Insubstantial Ones".

The new Greek nation, struggling to stabilise its uncertain and precarious position while controlling the unruly brigands who were so prominent in the fight for independence, was in no position to continue hostilities with Turkey indefinitely. It was plain that the Great Powers would not accept the detachment of Crete from the Turkish Empire at this stage and Greece needed peace, a breathing space in which to establish some kind of secure base for nationhood. In the circumstances, the continued aggravation of Turkey by the rebellious island of Gramboúsa was an embarrassment.

It was John Capodistrias, the first President of Greece who quickly asked the British and French governments to suppress the Council of Crete. So it was that warships were despatched and the old fortress disarmed and dismantled, on the grounds that it was a nest of pirates. It is hard to know the truth of this episode, for indeed many of the Greek islands had turned to piracy during the war, and had to be suppressed by English, French and Greek naval forces.

A curved beach at Frangokástello leads round to a boulder-strewn promontory with a little Martello tower as a reminder of the years when coastal dwellers were constantly at risk from pirates and slavers from the Barbary Coast. Behind the tower is a small *tavérna*, and two open wooden caiques were moored to stones on the shore. The water was so clear that they appeared suspended as if by magic a couple of feet above the seabed. An old man with a deeply-lined face was attending to the mooring ropes and greeted us as we walked up. Was he a fisherman? Yes, but the catch now was very small, very poor. He looked worn down by a lifetime of toil, skin tanned to leather by the harsh sun.

The boys played in the pools between the rocks, searching for crabs, sea urchins and small fish, picking up beautifully coloured shells while we walked to the *tavérna* to see if there was any chance of lunch. The building is of plain concrete with salt-covered plate glass windows at the front. One rickety wooden table with wicker chairs was set out in the sun and wind, while inside all was bare cement: walls, floor and ceiling. A big stove stood in the corner with a pile of ready-chopped wood, together with a giant gas cylinder from which a narrow twisted copper pipe ran up to the light fitting in the ceiling. An old hammer-action shotgun leaned against the wall and a marten skin stuffed with straw was hung from a hook. A strong, friendly woman emerged from a back room; she offered a variety of dishes and then brought us a wholemeal loaf with a copious supply of strong, but exceedingly rough wine in a large brown jug.

After a while, our fisherman came in with a companion, equally ancient and as gnarled as an olive trunk, his hair long and silver, boots split to reveal bare toes. They began a long game of cards. We noticed that the pack was not the common type but more like the archaic *tarot* cards they use in Andalucia; cups instead of hearts and swords instead of spades. The propietor sat watching the game with a coffee and a glass of water, while a lean dog wandered hopefully to our table in a quest for scraps. The Sfakian dialect is supposed to be distinctive with a tendency to pronounce "ro" instead of "lamtha", but my ear isn't good enough to detect it. It is certainly true that the Greek of Crete, as a whole, is very different from that of Athens.

The faces on this southern coast would reward any portrait painter or photographer, ranging from lean, dark and Moorish, through Mediterranean to the very distinctive, so-called "Dorian" type, curly silver hair and broad, handsome features. These last men are almost always physically large and powerful, standing head and shoulder above the crowd in a Khaniá street, like eagles in a flock of chickens. As I have already mentioned, there are not many Sfakians left now in these more settled times, when men can leave the gaunt mountains to live safely on more productive land.

When our meal eventually arrived, we realised that my bad Greek had resulted in general confusion. There were man-sized plates of tiny fish fried whole, omelettes, grilled cutlets, together with mounds of fried potatoes, salad and olives. We counted fourteen plates altogether, for we had foolishly agreed to everything suggested without specifying the quantities. Nevertheless, we called the boys in from the beach and tackled the feast as best we could amid general amusement. The old fisherman may have decried the size of his catch, but the little fish were particularly delicious. As we left, we saw the hungry-looking dog wolfing down the not inconsiderable remainder outside, while a pair of cats waited their turn.

After regaining the paved road, we continued east along the coast, through the little white village of Skalotí, with its ruined Church of the Prophet Elías where Byzantine frescoes are still visible, to Argoulés, then Ano and Kato Rodákino, which must have once been famous for peach trees, if the name is any guide. All these villages are tucked close under the great slopes of bare rock above, still crowned on this day with churning grey clouds. The population of each village seemed to be smaller than the number of houses. This was an area very active in the resistance during the Second World War, the beach near Rodákino being used frequently to transfer men and materials. The villages suffered for it too, when the Germans got wind of these activities and Schubert, the "Butcher of Crete", carried out reprisals, burning many houses in Rodákino and the entire nearby villages of Kalí Sikiá and Kallikrátis. Large numbers of civilians were indiscriminately executed and some old people were burnt in their houses.

After a long, lonely, section of road, we reached the rather larger settlement of Sélia, most notable for the situation of the church on a rocky bluff above the close-packed roofs of the village. We tucked the car away in a corner of the narrow street next to a tethered donkey and went into a tiny *kafeneíon*. This establishment was presided over by a boisterously cheerful lady, who, unusually in this male-dominated society, seemed to lord it with good-natured confidence over all her customers, including the policeman, who sat meekly at her elbow. The little room was crowded with people sitting on chairs all round the walls and everyone listened with friendly attention as we were questioned on where we came from, where we were going, who was married to whom and so on. For a few drachmes we were served with a delicious orange cordial with the unlikely brand name of Bioxin, sounding more like a dangerous chemical than a drink. In Greece, they have the sensible custom of scribbling the total of even small bills on a pad to avoid confusion with foreigners; this lady was one of the many who had to ask another customer to write the figures. With the keen memory of the illiterate, she knew every customer's tally when he left.

We wandered through the streets, climbing the exposed hill to the cross-in-square church, heavy in ochre-coloured stone and surrounded by a protective graveyard wall. The wind whistled and shrieked around us and it was difficult to hear each other. But the view was worth it: range after range of blue mountains rolling away as far as the eye could see. We tried the church door, but it was locked. Isolated up in the wind, the little houses packed together below us, we seemed to be above the world.

I caught a glimpse of the *pappás*, the pope or priest, in the street below – beard, robe, stove-pipe hat, everything black. Greeks are a curious mixture of piety and anti-clericalism. It is said to be bad luck to meet a black cat, a snake or a priest, who can inadvertently bring the evil eye. A friend of mine refers to them as black crows. When one's path does cross that of a priest, one is recommended to make the sign of the cross over the genitals to ward off the spell – not that I can ever recall seeing this done overtly. But at Easter, every Greek becomes a good parishioner and Christian for one week at least – becomes, in fact, a passion player as every man, woman and child falls beneath the spell of the drama.

The really serious fasting begins in Holy Week, when a morning and evening service is held every day. After the Saturday of Lazarus is Palm Sunday, when the priest gives each worshipper a cross woven from palm and a bundle of myrtle which are taken home and hung with the family icons to bring luck. Touching a newly-married woman with the myrtle is said to bring fertility. On Monday evening, the service is known as *Nymphoí* (Bridegrooms), and an icon of Christ is carried through the church to the priest's words: "Behold, the bridegroom cometh in the middle of the night." On Tuesday, hymns are dedicated to Mary Magdalene and, in the cities, the whores go to church. Wednesday is the Day of Anointment, when the priest touches his parishioners with oil on forehead, chin, cheeks and hands. Mothers with children abroad receive a small piece of cotton wool soaked in the oil to send them. Thursday is a busy day for women. Many pastries are baked and baskets full of eggs are prepared to be dyed red. The first egg to go in the dye is known as the "Egg of the Virgin Mary", and is put on one side to protect children against the evil eye. Eggs laid on this day are also supposed to have special powers, especially those from a pullet laying for the first time, or from a black hen. Easter loaves are baked in a braided shape with a red egg in the centre. On this night, the church is draped in black, and the women mourn as if for their own flesh and blood.

On Holy Friday, the fast becomes complete. Offices are closed throughout Greece and the flags fly at half-mast. Christ has died, and his body, symbolically represented by a rich gold cloth, is taken down from the cross and laid on the *epitáphios*, a bier covered in spring flowers. The tension becomes extreme. All day the *epitáphios* lies in state while the crowds wait in line to kneel and kiss it. At night, the bier is carried by mourners through the streets in a funeral procession.

On Saturday morning, a service of exorcism is held to deter any demons or unclean spirits who might impede the resurrection which is about to occur. The priest throws laurel leaves from a basket over the congregation, who strive to catch them for lucky talismans. The paschal lambs are killed in readiness for Sunday's feast.

At eleven o'clock in the evening, the bells ring for the last time and the people converge on the church, each carrying an unlighted candle. The church is packed with people and almost dark as the priest chants, and the sense of waiting and expectation grows with each passing minute. At midnight, even the candles on the altar are extinguished. After a long pause, the priest suddenly appears with a newly lighted candle and cries dramatically, *"Christós Anésti!"* (Christ is Risen). Everyone close to him leans forward to light their candle from his, and then passes the flame to their neighbour with an embrace and *"Alithós Anésti"* (He surely is Risen). The bells begin to ring, the congregation rushes out of the church into the night to be greeted by fireworks and volleys of gunshots fired in the air, rejoicing at the recurrence of the miracle in yet another year. The streets become rivers of flickering points of light as each holds his or her candle, carefully cupped against the wind, for to bring Christ's light safely home will ensure His presence in the house for the next year. Before the door, the sign of the cross is made and the watch lamp will be lit in front of the family icons. No one goes to bed, for the parties begin at once and continue all the next day as hungry people gorge themselves on roast lamb and other good things while holding curious egg-breaking contests.

It has often been pointed out that this celebration of the resurrection is almost certainly older than the Nazarene, and that the Galileans merely adapted an ancient Greek ritual to their purpose. No one knows for certain the exact nature of the "Mysteries of Eleusis" which engaged the ancient Greeks for so long – initiates were sworn to secrecy. It has been suggested, however, that a sacred play depicted the legend of Demeter and Persephone in order to illustrate the soul's voyage into the underworld. There is some evidence that the initiate was taken on a journey of his own – perhaps a torch-lit procession through a darkened cave representing Hades, before emerging joyfully into the Elysian fields and to the temples of Demeter and Persephone. The similarity of such a drama to the miracle of Holy Week is striking.

In the next village, a highly-decorated pick-up truck was parked by the roadside, with two sly gipsy-like youths selling oranges to the village women (there are not many citrus orchards in this rocky mountainous district). They were using the old Turkish *oka* (about three English pounds) as measurement, as they still do in Cyprus, although Turkey itself was converted to the metric system long ago during Kemal Ataturk's modernisations. We bought a couple of bags, although the seller never batted an eyelid as he realised we understood the price being paid by others in the queue, and the price reduced three times during the transaction. The oranges were sweet, juicy and very large.

Reaching the coast again at Plakiás, we realised that we had truly left Sfakiá. Parking by one of the *tavérnas* which line the sandy beach, we could see little sign of the village's original fishing activity. Sunday or not, the residents were busy preparing for the coming tourist season: painting signs, refurbishing café terraces and repairing sunshades. The few boats drawn up probably spent more time taking tourists on pleasure trips than setting lines and nets. Who could blame them? The little town has a distinct air of well-being and the old men strolling during the evening *vólta* seemed relaxed and happy, perhaps in the knowledge of their children's prosperity.

Picking our way through the broken pieces of concrete and piles of gravel left by builders along the water margin, we reached the far side of the village and could look back towards the Sfakian coastline in the west, the dying sun silhouetting the harsh outlines of the capes and bluffs while laying a magical path of gold across the calm waters between us. More than ever, it seemed an empty land, populated only by the ghosts of the men who once fought over it – Dorians and Romans; captains and their *pallikária*; Venetian garrisons and Turkish soldiers; watchers crouching on the shore, straining to hear the engines of a motor torpedo boat creeping in from Egypt on a dark night.

As we returned to our car we found that the orange sellers had arrived after us and were again doing a roaring trade. Their brightly-painted Nissan was a fine example of local customising. Greeks love to hang fringes of lace from the headlining and furry toys from the driving mirror, while invocations to favoured saints are *de rigeur* for the dashboard or windscreen.

A little further along the coast to the east is the Monastery of Préveli, by the mouth of the Megalopótamos River. Many Allied soldiers left behind after the Battle of Crete have cause to be thankful to this monastery, as they were hidden here until they could be taken off by motor launch or submarine, and so to Egypt. A large number escaped in this way before the Germans became aware of these activities and sacked the monastery, expelling the monks and appropriating their livestock. The British Government made a gift of two silver candlesticks after the war, in thanks.

We, however, turned inland and through the gorge of Kourtaliótiko, where the road runs on concrete piers up a narrow passage in company with a mountain stream. At one or two points the walls nearly touch overhead, and there is a pretty little waterfall into a grotto of rocks and ferns before the cliffs open out into the normal hillside. We completed the run to Réthymnon in the dark, stopping at Kostas' little office, as Joan wished to arrange a visit to the Geráni bridge cave on the Khaniá road. This cave was discovered during the construction of the New Road, and various Neolithic remains were found, together with fine stalactites. It is usually locked, but the Tourist Office can supposedly arrange a visit.

Inside Kostas' emporium, the same lyre music, the same red rubber gloves and the same general alcoholic aroma were in evidence.

"English? My brother! My sister!" declared Kostas, putting his arms unsteadily round our shoulders. I don't think he recognised me from our previous encounter.

"Is it possible to visit the Neolithic cave at Geráni bridge, please?" Joan enquired.

Kostas stiffened slightly and then recited formally: "The cave is closed for further archaeological investigation."

"Oh, well. Thank you anyway. Another time perhaps."

"OK. Anything you want, come to me. My name is Kostas."

* * * *

Nikos' eye lit up at dinner as he poured out the *mavrodáphne*, known here as "black wine". He had seen the little plastic puppet which Malcolm had bought from a street kiosk.

"Karaghiózis!" he exclaimed, picking up the quaintly articulated and elongated figure mounted on a stick. "When I am a little boy, I never miss a show!" He showed Malcolm how to extract the sweets hidden in the handle.

Karaghiózis is a sort of shadow puppet or marionette, like a crude and simplified version of the famous Balinese shadow puppets. I am not clear whether the Karaghiózis theatre was introduced from Turkey or Syria, but for a hundred years or more, travelling show-men have toured Greece and the islands entertaining people of all ages with plays full of scandalous references and *double entendres* of the pantomime type. It is perhaps similar to the English Punch and Judy, or Italian Punchinello, in that the stories may vary slightly but the characters do not. Karaghiózis himself is everybody's favourite underdog, beset by landlords, creditors and Turkish authorities, but always surviving somehow through cunning and trickery of a kind to delight any Greek. Other characters include a Jew who speaks very bad Greek, a ruffian from the Piraeus docks, an enormous peasant in the *fustanélla* kilt of Epirus, an effeminate gentleman with a long nose, a dragon and even sometimes Alexander the Great.

Nikos felt sufficiently at home with us by now to fall about laughing at my attempts to speak his language. Did I realise that I had pronounced the word for "wine" with the stress entirely in the wrong place? "But it is good that you try to speak," he said, concerned that my feelings might be hurt. What is a stressed syllable between friends?

CHAPTER 9

The Messará Plain

I waited at the filling station while the hotel tour bus took on several hundred litres of diesel and ground off the forecourt ready for a hard day running holidaymakers to the airport and the archaeological sites. The attendant banged a defective petrol pump impatiently, but the read-out would not zero, nor the delivery commence. Everybody surrounded the pump while she sighed and encouraged us to thump it simultaneously from different angles. Smiles all round as the recalcitrant mechanism was at last persuaded to clank into life, rather as the island's saints are cajoled or threatened into answering the petitions of their supplicants.

Taking the southern route from the junction in Martyrs' Square, where the traffic always seems equally confused, whether directed by the police or not, we retraced our journey of the previous evening. This is another part of the new road system, which was planned following an American survey in order to open the island to tourism in the 1960s. This section swings round in a great loop through the plain of Messará to Ierápetra, and back to the north. In contrast to the excellent New Road along the north coast, many sections of this route are pot-holed and dilapidated, sometimes damaged by lorry traffic from the Messará. Greece, incidentally, was one of the last countries in Europe to construct railways, mostly during the twentieth century, and they never reached Crete. The "Cretan railways", as the old joke went, were no more than a train of pack mules and donkeys.

The villages around Réthymnon are charming with their luxuriant gardens, and the fig trees were now just about to sprout fresh leaves from their pale thick branches. There is a belief that the shadow of a fig tree is "heavy", and that bad dreams will result from unwisely sleeping under the shade of the branches during the midsummer heat. A Turkish Cypriot once gave us the same advice,

The harbour at Réthymnon

The gorge of Arádena

Sfakians

but for the more prosaic reason that the fig tree exudes a poisonous sap which would cause an irritating rash on hands and face.

This area was the scene of some sad events during the war, especially towards the end when Cretan resistance had goaded the occupying German forces into fury. George Psychoundakis, the "Cretan runner", describes an incident which is not untypical:

On the eighth of August, a party of our people – Levtheri Psaroudakis and the gendarmerie warrant-officer, Stratidakis, and Mr Tom (Dunbabin), led by Antoni Zoidakis from the village of Ay-Yanni in the Amari – was heading for Priné. Mr Tom was on his way to meet the leaders of EOK and EAM to discuss the differences which separated the two organisations and come to an agreement about co-operation with each other, because things had reached a dangerous pitch between them. Mr Tom and his companions were about to cross over from the foothills of Vrysina where a path cuts across the main Retimo-Armenoi motor road. This stretch of the journey was dangerous because of the Germans, for they had guard posts, trenches and machine gun nests all over the place. There are some vineyards close to the foothills, and somewhere near the road there, two Germans were sitting. Both parties feigned indifference on both sides, and our people continued on their way in single file at wide intervals. Antoni Zoidakis came last. The Germans must have got wind of something, for as the last of these strangers passed they fired at him with their pistols. He stopped one of the bullets but did not go unavenged, for with the first report, Mr Tom, who was last but one among those bushes, turned round and emptied his pistol at the Germans. One was killed there and then, and the other seriously wounded. The ones in front doubled back on their traces, as there was danger ahead. Poor Antoni was left there wounded: perhaps his wound was not a mortal one, and perhaps he might have been saved.

Some more Germans soon arrived. They tied Antoni to the back of their car and dragged him behind them all along the road to Armenoi. There they threw his unknown corpse, unrecognisable now, on the side of the road, forbidding anybody to bury him. When a couple of days had passed, they threw him into a hole and filled it up.

(George Psychoundakis, *The Cretan Runner*)

The sun was bright in the sky, despite the early hour, and the olive trees rang with birdsong as we stopped to stretch our legs by a little brook, bordered by lush green grass and yellow bog-iris. It might have been June in an English water meadow. The land began to rise steadily until we reached the mountain village of Spilí in the eparchy of St Basil. There was an alpine freshness in the morning air, and the aromatic blue smoke of the wood stoves hung over the rooftops in long skeins. The little square, shaded by numerous trees and the mountainside close above, was still cluttered with drifts of last year's dead leaves and filled with the sound of gushing water from the famous fountain. A great trough runs under the hillside on the edge of the square, and nineteen stone lion heads constantly pour clean spring water into the channel. This cool, damp corner, the white-painted walls stained by moss and lichen, must be a delightful oasis in the heat of midsummer.

The village looks prosperous and the square was filled with pick-ups, tractors and brightly coloured motorcycles. Most of the houses are two-storeyed with balconies and little gardens of lemon trees and almonds with white blossom. Above the steep terraced paths leading between ivy-clustered walls to the top of the village, the foothills of Oros Kédros loom in steep cliffs above the russet-tiled roofs. We walked up the street to look into the shops: country shops stocked with the goods country people require, their shelves storing rather than displaying tinned food, flour in sacks, beer, wine, *raki* and oil, paraffin lamps and candles, plates and saucepans, salt, sugar and soap, crates of soft drinks, sheep bells and rat traps. By contrast, at the modern pharmacy, we bought a tube of toothpaste from an elegant woman who would have looked at home in a smart Athenian restaurant.

The road begins to descend again through the olive groves and skirts a military base, the reddish soil churned up by tank tracks and steel-helmeted sentries gazing stonily out across the lines of barbed wire. It is hard to contemplate the Greek Army now without thoughts coming to mind of those grim years of the Colonels' dictatorship, the ESA military police and all those television documentaries about torture. Western Europeans sometimes find it equally hard to understand why the Greek people, who profess to love freedom so much, could have permitted such a thing to happen. The reasons are many and complex, but it should be remembered that the Greeks had not really experienced a great deal of genuine democracy in their short history anyway. They were desperate for stability, terrified of another civil war and easily scared by talk of a planned Communist take-over. The scandals and conflicts of 1965-67 between the Government, the King and the Military had exasperated their patience. With the Greek readiness to believe in corruptness and conspiracy, the various perks available to politicians – no income tax, free telephone and postage, free travel on Olympic Airways – were a further irritation.

Some Cretans suffered as much as any in Greece during those sad years of loyalty undertakings and muzzled speech, until the Junta finally blundered its way out of power. Sardonic little jokes and stories were, for most Greeks, the only possible protest:

Tourist to Athenian taxi driver: "Are you free?"
Taxi driver: "No, I'm Greek."

There was a little Greek dog who swam across the Adriatic to Brindisi. Italian dogs gathered round and smelt him, and said, "So, you're a Greek dog. Have you come to Italy to get some bones?" The little Greek dog said, "No, plenty of bones in Athens. I just wanted to have a bark."

After the wide bed of the River Platís, where the water trickled through bleached stones, we reached an area carpeted with so many yellow flowers that the meadows seemed to be covered in gold. Far away to the north, we could now see the Oros Idi, with the highest summit of Psilorítis floating in pure white above the morning mists. As we progressed along the road, this mountain began to dominate the view, majestic and unattainable, the highest peak of Crete at 2,456 metres, and invariably snow-covered in winter. The ancient Greeks believed that high mountains were the homes of the Gods, and from this angle the view of Ida certainly has an ethereal and sacred quality. Ida is an old Doric word for a timber tree, but Cretans usually call it Psilorítis, simply meaning the "High Mountain".

In fact, a fit walker can climb Psilorítis in about six or seven hours in summer, either starting from Kamáres to the south, or Anóyia to the north, from where a road leads up to the Nídha plateau at about 1,300 metres and the Ida cave. The summit is a desolation of rocks and stones, but there is a shelter and the Chapel of Tímios Stavrós, or the Holy Cross, to which some Cretans make a pilgrimage in September.

This is an area associated with legends of Digenis Akritas, a half-mythical figure like Robin Hood, who defended the frontiers of Byzantium against the barbarians. His exploits were told in an epic poem of the Middle Ages and are woven throughout the folklore of all the Greek world. The *akrites* were the soldiers of the border provinces of the eastern Roman Empire, while *digenis* means "born of two races", for the hero may have been the son of a Saracen Emir from Syria and a Greek woman of the Doukas family whose fortress he captured near the Euphrates. In modern times, Digenis Akritas is better known as the *nomme de guerre* adopted by Grivas during the EOKA campaign in Cyprus.

We were now entering the Messará plain, the largest flat area of the island, and the most intensely cultivated. The soil of this twenty mile strip is the richest in Crete and supports 50,000 inhabitants. It has been famous for its wheat since Roman times. In 1855, Messará wheat was awarded an honourable mention at the World Exhibition in Paris, although since that time Crete has become a net grain importer. Modern methods of agriculture and fertilisers are now being intensively applied, but the Messará, like the rest of Crete, is suffering from the gradually decreasing supply of water. The western river, Geropótamos, is barely adequate to supply the complicated irrigation system of ditches and plastic pipelines running through the fields, while in the east, the well-named Anopodáris (upside-down) River only flows intermittently. Apart from the traditional staple wheat crop, there is tremendous expansion in the growing of tomatoes, cucumbers, cut flowers and various other market garden crops for export to Athens and the rest of Europe.

The formation of co-operatives is to some extent alleviating the problems caused by the constant sub-division of parcels of land as dowries or inheritances to be split between a number of children. The Greek dowry system, which was officially abolished by Karamanlis, has been described as the ruination of agriculture. The marriage of each daughter required a division of land until a typical farmer might own a dozen or so *perivólia*, or small gardens, spread over a wide area. The conventional view has always been that this is extremely inefficient, but there is a recent tendency to revise this opinion, for various reasons.

Incidentally, on Corfu they used to operate what strikes me as an infinitely superior system. When a daughter was born, the father would plant thirty cypress trees. When the girl married, the trees would be cut down and the wood sold to provide the dowry. In Cyprus, by contrast, the parents of a bride are still expected to provide a house for the young couple. Pity the poor man with four or five daughters, for he will have to work hard all his life to fulfil his obligations.

There is a story that when Greece adopted the Gregorian calendar in 1923, a small village somewhere in the Messará refused to comply and doggedly stuck to the old system devised by Julius Caesar. For many years afterwards, they were some two weeks out of step with their neighbours and celebrated a lonely Christmas and New Year's Day on what they considered to be the correct dates. Not such an incredible story when one considers that the monks of the Holy Mountain of Athos keep the Julian calendar to this day. There, each twenty-four hour period begins at sunset, and so the clocks have to be reset daily.

For a few kilometres we drove in the white dust of constant lorry traffic, past acres of polythene sheeting stretched over the tomato plants: a heavily-populated landscape of men working on pipelines and windmills ready to pump water up to the surface during the coming summer drought. Then we entered Timbáki, a noisy, bustling town, full of diesel fumes from the lorries collecting produce. The bus terminal was crowded with people straggling over the road; the cafés and bars were full of youths, their motorcycles lined up outside. Almost every building seemed new, concrete and dusty, while it was plain that the ultimate status symbol here is a new four-wheel drive Japanese pick-up truck, so many were parked along the street. The Messará breeds wealth, and there is a world of difference between these thriving, entrepreneurial farmers, covered now by the OGA social insurance scheme, and with an opportunity to reach quite a reasonable standard of living, and their peasant grand-fathers, or those still scratching a living off poorer land up in the hills.

A little further across the flatlands, the ancient site of Phaestós is signposted to the right, across the Geropótamos. We pulled into a virtually empty car park on a rocky outcrop above the plain, and on leaving the car took off our jackets in the hot southern sun. An old man was making his way down the path, dressed in baggy breeches, boots and with an embroidered *sakoúli* on his back. The tapping of his stick on the ground was the only sound.

No sign now of the famous caretaker, Alexandros, who guided Henry Miller round this site in 1939, and seems to have been obtaining plenty of mileage out of the fact years later. He was forbidden to accept gratuities he used to tell tourists, but he did collect coins as a hobby. He must have retired years ago, but his meeting with Miller is one of the more enjoyable parts of the latter's famous book, *The Colossus of Maroussi*. The colossus, incidentally, George Kitsimbalis, endeared himself to me at least, by once remark-ing to a writer: "An awful lot of bad books have been written about Greece and I'm sure you're going to add to them." Quite.

A few serious-looking students were carefully studying odd cor-ners of masonry, while the guides sat back in their chairs by the tourist pavilion and enjoyed the sun without bothering to offer their services – somewhat to my relief. I always prefer to wander around archaeological sites in my own time and drink in the atmosphere, without worrying too much about whether each little room was actually a grain store, a lustral basin or a lavatory.

The ancients seem to have taken more care than we over the background to their cities, apart from considerations of defence, water and commerce – take Carthage or Pompeii, for instance. Phaestós is built in a superb situation on a hill above the Messará, with the snows of Psilorítis to the north. To the south lie the Asteroúsia mountains towards the sea, and at the far end of the plain can be seen Mount Díkti and the Lassíthi range. It seems strange that buildings on such a high, exposed site could become buried in soil and debris, but it was not until the Italian archaeologist, Federico Halbherr, began to excavate in 1900 (almost simultaneously with Evans' work at Knossós) that the importance of this ancient palace was realised. Work has continued almost ever since under Italian direction, more recently by Doro Levi.

The Messará has been occupied since the Neolithic period. It is believed that the first men to reach Crete came from Asia Minor or North Africa in about 6500 BC. From pottery remains, it has been deduced that they worshipped a fertility goddess and gradually evolved from hunting and cave dwelling to a simple form of agriculture, living in crude clay-brick houses. In about 2600 BC, further settlers arrived, whether from Asia or North Africa cannot be stated with certainty. The races mingled and formed what Evans termed a "Minoan" culture, mining copper on Crete and importing tin to make bronze. Obsidian was brought from Anatolia to make knives and, as the trade routes were opened up, a distinct craftsmanship in the working of metal and precious stones, as well as pottery, evolved.

Phaestós itself was built in about 1900 BC, roughly at the same time as the other great Minoan palaces of Knossós, Mália and Káto Zákros. It has been argued that the same masons built Phaestós and Knossós, following careful examination of marks on the component stone blocks. At any rate, the two palaces appear likely to have had close relations and the old legends suggest that Phaestós was ruled by Minos' brother, Rhadamanthys. Phaestós is strategically situated for trade with Asia, Africa and the other islands of the Aegean – and, of course, surrounded by the rich agricultural land of the Messará. The reorganisation of Minoan society around the palaces of rulers, or priest-kings, proved rapidly successful and Cretan ships, built from the native forests of cypress and cedar, began to trade widely over the seas. Colonies were even founded on other islands and the Minoan thalassocracy expanded to become the dominant power in the eastern Mediterranean. An earthquake in 1700 BC seems to have had little effect on the development of these interdependent states, despite damaging the palaces, which were rebuilt on the same sites more magnificently than before.

Scholars are still arguing about the famous script known as "Linear A", which developed at about this time. Apparently devolved from a Cretan pictorial script, it was used to record commercial transactions, but the nature of the spoken language is unclear. This Neo-Palatial period, the Minoan Golden Age, saw the flowering of the art and culture which caused such excitement as Evans gradually revealed the treasures of Knossós. By this time, such goods as amber from the far-away Baltic were reaching the island, and some believe that these sturdy little men (they averaged not much over five feet) sailed through the Straits of Gibraltar and north as far as Scandinavia. Minoan ships carried about thirty rowers and a square sail – they certainly could not have sailed close to the wind. By about 1500 BC, the script had changed to what is called "Linear B", and Evans always believed this to have been a natural development of "Linear A". Evans also believed that the various Cretan-style artefacts which Schliemann found on the mainland at Mycenae fitted in with his theory that Mycenae and Pylos were provincial outposts of Minoan Crete.

In 1939, excavations were carried out at Mycenaean Pylos, the Palace of Nestor, and (on the very day that Italy invaded Albania and south-eastern Europe began to slide into the chaos of the war) "Linear B" tablets were discovered, correlating to those of Crete. For nearly a decade, the tablets remained safely in an Athens bank vault during the Second World War and the Greek Civil War. Then in 1953, Michael Ventris, a young architect who had been given access to the tablets, together with the Cambridge scholar, John Chadwick, claimed to have deciphered "Linear B". Ventris and Chadwick argued that "Linear B" bore no direct relationship to "Linear A", but was something quite different – an early form of Greek. I understand that the first word to be recognised was "ti-ri-po", tripod.

Ventris died tragically in a car crash in 1955, but his work had created a considerable stir in the world of archaeology. If an Achaean Greek language was in use in Crete by 1500 BC, the obvious inference is that the Mycenaeans were dominant at that time, possibly having conquered the Minoans. Certainly it did not seem so likely that Mycenae was merely a colony of Crete. In spite of the differences between the languages, it is believed that some of the old Minoan words found their way into Greek – for instance, *thálassa*, the sea, and *kiparíssos*, cypress tree. The English words "hyacinth" and "terebinth" (turpentine tree) may be derived from the ancient Minoan language.

In about 1600 BC, the great palaces were again damaged by another earthquake and quickly restored. However, the exact nature of the catastrophe which overwhelmed the palaces in 1450 BC is today the subject of the most intense controversy among archaeologists. The most dramatic theory is that a huge eruption of the strange volcanic island of Santoríni, or Théra, to the north, caused earthquakes and tidal waves which destroyed the palaces within a few hours. Santoríni is a sinister place, known as the "Devil's Island" or "Island of the Apocalypse", although Pátmos is where St John is reputed to have experienced his "revelations". The last major eruption was in 1956, but there is evidence that at the time in question there was a huge explosion with three times the force of Krakatoa, which would have produced great quantities of volcanic ash lying up to 130 feet deep. One thinks of the version of the Argonauts legend in which the heroes encounter a mysterious and terrifying darkness lying on the face of the waters, the biblical story of the Parting of the Red Sea, and Deucalion and the Flood. Less spectacular, but possibly more plausible, is the idea that the palaces were simply sacked and burned by pirates. Whatever happened, only Knossós recovered to any approximation of its former glory, until a further catastrophe destroyed it too in 1370 BC.

During the Post-Palatial dark ages, it is unclear whether Phaestós was a deserted ruin, or whether a few Minoans (or Achaean/Minoans?) held on, remembering better times. There is a theory that Minoan refugees fled by sea from these disasters to settle in Italy, Sicily, the Cyclades, Attica, Rhodes, Cyprus and the Levant. It has been speculated that the legendary land of Atlantis did not lie beyond the Pillars of Hercules after all, but was, in fact, Minoan Crete. In classical times, a tribe in Tunisia were known as the "Atlantes". Another theory is that the powerful Canaanite tribe known in the Bible as "Philistines", and with whom the Israelites came into such constant conflict when they reached Palestine, had originated in Minoan Crete. Although they are conventionally believed to have come from western Anatolia in about 1200 BC, there are a number of details which might accord with Cretan ancestry. The Philistines were of Mediterranean rather than Semitic stock, skilled in seafaring, and are thought to have introduced vines and olives to Palestine.

All of these speculations serve only to make the Minoans seem a more mysterious people than ever. Professor Hans Wunderlich has introduced yet another angle: the question of Egyptian influence in Crete. There are Egyptian tomb paintings of the fifteenth century BC which clearly show Cretans carrying offerings. Wunderlich argues that the palaces were nothing of the kind, but actually mausoleums sacred to the dead in the Egyptian fashion. In support of this theory, he states that many of the surfaces constructed in gypsum would never have stood up to the wear and tear of regular human occupation.

Common sense would seem to suggest that the sites of the destroyed palaces were reoccupied to some extent, and the city of Phaestós is claimed to have been strong enough to send a contingent to the Trojan War under the Cretan King, Idomeneus. Homer mentions Phaestós and nearby Górtyna in his description of the wrecking of Menelaus' ships on their return from the siege. As the Dorians, armed with iron swords, invaded Crete at the end of their long sweep through Greece from Yugoslavia and Bulgaria, the remaining Minoans must have been reduced to serfdom, with the exception perhaps of a few who preserved their culture by withdrawing to the hills and remote parts of eastern Crete. The general area of Phaestós was certainly occupied and it may have been an independent city with its own coinage. In classical times, the people of Phaestós had a reputation for wit. Crete was now far from the centre of world affairs, but Cretan mercenaries were apparently highly valued. Alexander the Great pitted Cretan archers against elephants and chariots, while the historian, Polybius, recommends their use in night patrols, ambushes, raids and the taking of prisoners. All this is very much in accordance with the modern Cretans' reputation as guerrilla fighters. Phaestós would now certainly have been over-shadowed by the new and powerful city of Górtyna, and in 180 BC the latter took over the sea port of Kommós and destroyed what remained of the old city and palace. For two thousand years this great shelf above the plain must have seemed a mysterious and haunted place to the peasants below, as the broken pillars and walls gradually became buried and disguised.

We loitered in the hot sun on the stone flags of the courtyard, where the sinister mandrakes have insinuated their roots, and watched a raven stalking along the meadow below. The wind had dropped to a flat calm for once. Phaestós is a place of flowers in the spring: anemones, pink and white ranunculus, and later orange orchids in the long grass below the boundary fence.

Unlike Sir Arthur Evans at Knossós, the excavators have not attempted to reconstruct this palace to any major extent, and the main impression is of spacious courts, each at a slightly different height, linked by broad staircases. The proportions are restful and pleasing to the eye against the magnificent backdrop of scenery. With the aid of the guide book, you can discover a fine theatre, magazines filled with the great storage jars, or *píthoi* (which are made to this day in Crete and Sicily for oil and grain), shrines and royal apartments, guard rooms and corridors, porticos placed to give views of the mountains, and the court where the Minoans may have played their famous bull-leaping game, if indeed it was a game. Here and there, the situation is slightly confused by the presence of Archaic Greek, Roman and Christian remains, built above the ruined palace. The great treasures of Phaestós are now safely in the Archaeological Museum in Iráklion, notably the exquisite Kamáres-style pottery, later jugs and bowls painted with delicate reeds and flowers, a carved dolphin and the mysterious Phaestós Disc. This circular piece of terracotta, seven inches in diameter, was unearthed in 1908 and has 45 symbols, stamped with metal punches in a spiral pattern, which show axes, fishes, running men, helmeted heads, divided into groups of three, four and five. No one knows what it means.

Between Phaestós and the Libyan Sea lies a villa, or minor palace, built in about 1550 BC and excavated by Luigi Pernier at the turn of the century. Its ancient name is unknown, and so the site has been named after the nearby fourteenth-century Church of Ayía Triáda (Holy Trinity). Connected to Phaestós by a paved road, it may have been a satellite community, or perhaps a summer house for the rulers of Phaestós. It is a secluded and shady place, but, nevertheless, has wonderful views over the plain. The area along the river below, famous for its fruit trees, is locally known as "The Paradise". The primitive painter, Markakis, was once a warden here.

The villa of Ayía Triáda was built with features specifically designed to withstand earthquakes, yet it was destroyed by fire in 1450 BC. Among the contents recovered were nineteen talents of copper, imported from Cyprus and together weighing more than half a ton, each ingot being shaped so that two men could carry it. There were wall paintings of such charming subjects as a wild cat hunting a bird and a lady sitting in a garden, the beautiful "Harvester's Vase" and "Chieftain's Cup", a wonderful conical libation vessel of black steatite, with boxers carved in relief, and, in a tomb a hundred metres from the palace, a limestone sarcophagus painted with scenes of rites for the dead. This is one of the most thought-provoking of all the finds, and shows calves and a model boat being offered to the dead, the pouring of libations and the sacrifice of a bull. In the background stand the double-headed axes which were of such symbolic and sacred significance.

Nearby is the Church of Ayios Yeóryios Galatás, a simple stone chapel with some frescoes from the Venetian period. Local people tell a story that milk was mixed with the mortar when the church was built (the word *galatás* meaning milky).

Beyond the town of Míres, the road was torn up for repair. The inside of the car was soon filled with a choking white dust, fine as talcum powder, which had dulled the dark green leaves of the orange trees beside the road. The Messará shimmered in the midday heat and the distant snows of the mountains seemed unreal. Some of the earliest archaeological finds were made near here: the "Tombs of the Messará", excavated by Cretans with Italian assistance in the nineteenth century, and which can now be seen from the village of Plátanos. These circular stone burial chambers were built on the plain before the emergence of the Minoan civilisation, by a people organised in small family groups or clans. Their artefacts, including weapons, idols and jewellery, indicate that even this ancient race indulged in foreign trade, for the obsidian stone from which they made their knives could only have come from the Dodecanese or Anatolia. There were other links with the cultures of Egypt, Babylon and Mesapotomia.

We came quite suddenly on the sign for Górtyna and stopped by a group of road builders eating their lunch sitting on an upturned lamp standard and handing a flagon of wine from one to the other. Passing with almost a conscious wrench to what seemed to be modern surroundings, we found ourselves wandering among the tumbled blocks and pillars of the Basilica of Ayios Títos. This Christian church, now surrounded by olives and carobs, was built in the sixth century AD during Crete's first Byzantine period. The part left standing, with its great Roman barrel vault, still looks massive and imposing, imbued with the confidence of an empire which had ruled most of the civilised world for so long. The monogram of the Emperor Justinian was found on the capitals and Christianity was obviously prospering in Crete by this time. The original frescoes are not, of course, to be seen, it being one of the tragedies of Byzantium that when iconoclasm became official in AD 717, under the Emperor Leo the Isaurian, most earlier decorations were destroyed. Nevertheless, it comes as rather a surprise among these ruins, to find a brightly painted side-chapel, freshly swept and obviously in regular use. Titus, the saint for which the church was named, was a disciple of St Paul, who became the first Bishop of Crete, later to be martyred and buried in this place.

Paul gave one of his aides the unenviable task of bringing Christianity to the island, for he himself did not seem unduly impressed by the Cretans: "One of themselves, even a prophet of their own, said, 'The Cretians are always liars, evil beasts, slow bellies.' This witness is true. Wherefore rebuke them sharply, that they may be sound in the faith . . ." A little later in his epistle to Titus, Paul advises: "Put them in mind to be subject to principalities and powers, to obey magistrates, to be ready to every good work, to speak evil of no man, to be no brawlers, but gentle, showing all meekness unto all men." Did Paul have the *pallikária* of Sfakiá in mind? Vain hope!

St Paul's own landfall in Crete had been made not far away at Kalí Liménes (the Fair Havens) as he sailed to Rome, a prisoner in the nominal charge of the unfortunate centurion, Julius. Paul must have liked Kalí Liménes at least, as he wanted to stay for the winter, and, never one to take a back seat when decisions were being made, argued with the centurion and the ship's master who wished to winter at Phenice (Phoenix near Loutró in Sfakiá). The centurion, struggling to retain his authority, had his way in the end and they set off along the coast, only to be caught by a wind known as *Euroclydon*. This blew them past the island of Clauda (Gávdos), eventually all the way to Malta. To this day, the fishermen call the violent north-easterly storms which suddenly blow up on this southern coast *Euroclydon*, or "St Paul's Wind". The moment when Paul stood up in the storm-tossed boat saying: "Sirs, ye should have hearkened unto me, and not have loosed from Crete and to have gained this harm and loss," must have been hard to bear for Julius. One can imagine him muttering darkly to himself as the insufferable saint, now in his element, took command of the situation. I have often wondered if the viper which bit Paul on the seashore in Malta found its way into the firewood entirely by accident. Of course, the saint was wholly unaffected.

There is a conflicting legend in Crete that Paul did, in fact, land at Loutró and so antagonised the population that they scourged him, doubtless being unaware that this had already been tried without effect. At the small fishing village of Kalí Liménes today, you can see a chapel marking the spot where the saint is said to have landed and preached, while a little island offshore is named after him. Incidentally, Sir Arthur Evans once went camping on the beach at Kalí Liménes, and was all but swept away with his tent in rather ludicrous circumstances.

We wandered through the scattered columns of Ayios Títos, the air full of the strident humming of insects by the brook which runs nearby. Steven and Malcolm quickly tired of history, and took to trying to catch frogs in the reeds at the water's edge. This is the stream of Lethaios, where Zeus consummated his union with the beautiful Phoenician princess, Europa, having brought her across the sea on his back, while in the form of a bull. Rather prone to human passions, Zeus was always ready to adopt the form of an animal, or perhaps a shower of gold, at the drop of a hat, if it would make him more attractive to the object of his desires. Europa, of course, set us all on the road to the EEC, and the result of her love-making with Zeus under a plane tree was Minos, of whom more later. The philosopher, Theophrastus, the "Father of Botany", claimed that the famous plane tree was still standing by the stream in the third century BC. This little stream was later to reveal a dramatic secret.

The Turkish authorities in the nineteenth century were generally unhelpful and obstructive to archaeologists, while the lack of roads, incidence of disease and brigandage made Crete a dangerous place to travel. Nevertheless, Robert Pashley explored and identified a large number of ancient sites which he described in *Travels in Crete*, published in 1837. Later, Captain Spratt was commissioned to survey the coastal waters for the British Admiralty and made a series of journeys into the island, during which he took the opportunity of investigating many sites. His experiences, *Travels and Researches in Crete*, were published in 1865. These two works are generally regarded as the pioneering surveys of the island, but no real archaeology was involved, only the observation of what could be seen above ground level as pointed out by the local population. Incidentally, both Englishmen engaged the services of Captain Manias, a reformed Sfakian pirate with a good knowledge of all the secret inlets and anchorages. Manias had spilled much blood in 1821, and in 1824 his caique had captured and successfully ransomed 64 Muslims from the Sitía district. In their different ways, both Pashley and Spratt became very fond of the old rascal, who was, it seems, one of nature's gentlemen, once retired from his old profession. He died of fever in Ierápetra while in Spratt's service, and they buried him in his long boots.

During the later nineteenth century the Turks became more reasonable, and in 1878 the Pasha gave permission for a number of educated Cretans to found a society for the preservation of ancient monuments. This was associated with a museum in Candia in which to exhibit the various objects, which, over the years, had been found by peasants and retained as curiosities. Prominent among the members of this society was the aptly named amateur archaeologist, Minos Kalakairinos (Minos Fairweather), who stumbled on the site of Knossós when digging south of the city. (Evans came later.) Another interested Cretan, Joseph Hadzidakis, explored ancient sites all over the island in the company of the Italian archaeologist, Federico Halbherr. Halbherr was an exotic figure, riding a black

Arab mare, doubtless relying heavily on his companion's local knowledge as they passed through this wild landscape in the dying days of the Ottoman Empire. Their experiences must have been extraordinary, and surely they must have been filled with the heady sense of the discoveries lying ahead of them as they made one find after another. The cave at Psychró on the Lassíthi plateau, the identification of the palace of Phaestós, the Kamáres cave on Mount Ida, the initial identification of Káto Zákros in eastern Crete and the Amnisós cave were all scored in quick succession.

The site of Górtyna was far from unknown. The most recent of Crete's ruined cities, its position is accurately cross-referenced by classical literature and most of the buildings must have been above ground when the Church of Ayios Títos was built. The Italian, Buondelmonti, who passed through in the fifteenth century, spoke of counting "two thousand columns and statues upturned by time". Although much looting had occurred since that time, it was an obvious place for Halbherr to investigate.

To return to the stream of Lethaios: further upstream is a mill which dates from Venetian times and ground the village's corn until it was abandoned about twenty years ago. The last miller was well known for playing the Cretan bagpipes, an instrument which has almost disappeared now. Halbherr happened to be there in 1884 when the water was let out from the mill leat, exposing great blocks of stone embedded in the mud. On the stones, in an archaic Dorian dialect, was inscribed an almost complete code of the civil laws and customs which governed the city of Górtyna, covering property, inheritance, marriage and divorce, adoption, mortgages and citizenship. Of course, this description makes the recovery of the "Code" sound more simple than it was. The peasant who owned the land stubbornly refused to sell it off, or allow the stream to be diverted, for a considerable period. It should also be mentioned that Halbherr had received a cryptic clue, in that some years before an inscribed block had been noticed, incorporated into the mill itself.

We walked up the stream from St Titus until we reached a place where it becomes enclosed by artificial walls and diverted around the first century AD Odeon of Górtyna, which is built on the site of an earlier Hellenistic theatre. Enough of the brick and stone roof columns remain to give a clear impression of this building with the roof in place, although now the wild carobs and grasses wave in the breeze behind the outer rows of seats. A little arched brick shelter has been rather tastefully incorporated into the pillars to shield the reconstructed "Code" from the weather. The characters are clearly cut in the long row of ochre-coloured stones and run in "ox plough" fashion, left to right, then right to left, one line after another. There are elements of Minoan and earlier tribal customs incorporated in the "Code of Górtyna", and, conversely, many of the laws here were incorporated into Roman law, and thus, eventually, our own. It is surprising how familiar this insight into a society of the early fifth century BC seems today. Divorce law and the subsequent division of property (divorce apparently being as common then as in modern Western societies) is defined in such a way as to give virtually equal rights to both parties. A husband had no control over his wife's dowry and any money or property she might inherit in her own name. Most offences were punishable by fines; there is no mention of the death sentence or any savage or barbaric penalties. The most noticeable feature is the strict division of their society into freemen, serfs and slaves, and the different value placed upon each class of man. Thus, the evidence of a serf would carry greater weight in court than that of a slave, and the penalty for a crime committed against a freeman would be greater than for the same crime committed against a serf. Presumably, in the early days of the city, only the Dorian conquerors would have been eligible for citizenship, the unfortunate Minoans who had not fled to remote districts finding themselves among the serfs and slaves.

Crete must have been a dark, forgotten place after the fall of the Minoan palaces, but as the Dorians gradually established themselves, they began to form trading associations of their own, particularly with the Near East. As the Bronze Age yielded to the Iron Age, Górtyna rose to become the foremost centre of power and civilisation on the island. Their society appears to have been similar to that of mainland Sparta: young male children of the aristocracy being taken from their parents at an early age and rigorously trained as warriors. Nevertheless, during the Classical and Hellenistic periods, Crete, by virtue of its geographical position, was something of a backwater, overshadowed by Athens and the great city-states of the mainland. There is a theory that the Cretans, who played no part in the Persian or Peloponnesian wars, were, of all Greeks, the least affected by foreign influences. The Greeks themselves regard Crete as the most "Greek" of all the islands in racial and cultural purity. Presumably, at this far-flung outpost of the Balkan peninsula, one can assume that the ancient Greek blood has intermingled the least with that of the various races who invaded from the north at different times. In the third century BC, Górtyna, as the dominant city of Crete, joined the "Confederation of Oreioi", together with Cyrenaica in Libya. At one time, there was an alliance with Rhodes, and the Cretans sent help when that city was under attack by Demetrios Poliorcetes, the "besieger of cities", during the carve-up of Alexander's empire after his death. In a time of general lawlessness and civil war, Crete gained a particular reputation as the home of mercenaries and pirates. This piracy eventually proved an irritation to the Roman Empire, whose trade was threatened. The Cretans also unwisely contracted an alliance with Mithridates, King of Pontus on the Black Sea, with whom Rome was at war.

The first Roman attack on Crete was made in 72 BC by the Praetor Marcus Antonius, who was defeated at sea by Cretan ships under the command of Panares and Lasthenes. Two years later, the Proconsul Quintus Caecilius Metellus invaded Crete with three legions, capturing first the city of Kydonía, and then besieging in turn the cities of Knossós, Lýttos, Eléftherna and Lappa. It was a bitter, hard-fought campaign, involving desperate resistance, for Metellus' reputation for cruelty in victory was such that many garrisons fought to the last man, or committed suicide rather than surrender. In 67 BC, Ierápetra was taken and the island surrendered. It is said that Górtyna betrayed Crete to the conquerors by agreeing to assist Metellus, and thus avoided the destruction meted out to the other cities. Górtyna eventually rose to new eminence as the capital of the combined Roman province of Crete and Cyrenaica, while the Romans themselves, who claimed only to have invaded to restore peace and order to warring factions in the island, eventually stayed for 450 years.

The Romans had great plans for this new addition to their Empire. Górtyna was to be rebuilt as a magnificent city, presiding over a Messará which would become a granary for Rome. A large amount of building took place, coupled with irrigation projects for the wheat-lands. It is thought that, as a prosperous Roman province, Crete probably had a larger population than today. The geographer Strabo describes the walls of Górtyna as measuring 50 stadia (about 9.5 kilometres). When the modern motor road was being constructed across the Messará, long stretches of the original Roman pavement were uncovered. Individual Cretans did not rise to any great prominence within the Empire, although it is interesting to note that the Emperor Nero apparently employed a Cretan named Andromaches as a personal physician, surely a hazardous position in the extreme.

When Diocletian split the Empire, Crete fell to the East, and when Constantine built his capital of East Rome on the site of the Ancient Greek city of Byzantium, he founded a dynasty which has deeply marked the culture of all modern Greeks. The traditional story of the conversion of Constantine is that when marching to battle with his army, a great cross was seen shining in the sky with *In hoc signo vinces* written across it. The Emperor's mother, Helena, promptly became perhaps the first archaeologist, discovering the location of Calvary and unearthing what are claimed to be the True Cross, the Sponge, the Lance and the Crown of Thorns. The religious relics industry has thrived ever since.

In fact, Constantine's Christianity was more politic than anything else. Many of the armies opposing him during the ruthless wars he prosecuted against his fellow Emperors during the struggle for supreme power contained a large element of Christian troops, known for their superstition and easily impressed by such relics as Helena managed to produce. Constantine himself was only baptised on his deathbed and was believed to have tended towards Mithraism, if anything.

Byzantium was a strange and inward-looking society, Greek in language and literature, but Roman in law and administration. While the barbarians massed on the frontiers, the rulers and bishops occupied themselves in endless and bitter quarrelling about fine points of religious doctrine. It was a society which allowed little personal freedom, for travel was forbidden and sons were obliged to follow in the professions of their fathers. Their's was a static world, a fixed pyramidal hierarchy ruled by the Emperor and the bishops, each figure decked in rich robes and jewels as in the extraordinary paintings of the time, where all realism is sacrificed to symbolism. Yet how magnificent a world it was, with its beautiful books and frescoes, an immutable, totally confident world, awaiting the year 1000 when the Resurrection would come and Christ would rule again on earth. (Byzantine dates, however, were normally calculated not from the birth of Christ but from 5505 BC, the biblical date of the Creation.)

While Christianity may have prospered, Crete found itself in a vulnerable situation, as the protecting power of Constantinople was far away. In 623 AD, the island was raided by Slavs, the Byzantine fleet no longer being able to dominate the Aegean. The coast was frequently subject to attack by Gothic pirates, and later the rising power of the Arabs became a greater and greater threat. Finally, in 824 AD, Abou Hafs Omar, an Arab corsair leader, destroyed the city of Górtyna and conquered the island. The Metropolitan Cyril of Górtyna was martyred and the Church of Titus destroyed, while nineteen cities were burned. A dark age settled on Crete for a hundred years, as the island became a slave market and pirate's haven. Only in remote parts of Sfakiá did Christianity survive.

Across the stream from the Odeon are the remains of the *acrópolis* and a Hellenistic theatre. A ruined aqueduct can still be made out, which carried water from the brook upstream of the mill, around the contours of the hillside and down to the lower part of the city across the modern road. Here the Praetorium looks splendid with great pillars lying like felled trees around the cracked flagstones. A temple to Pythian Apollo, the Sanctuary of Isis and Serapis, another theatre and two Nymphae have also been uncovered. A little further south, near the footpath between the villages of Mitrópolis and Ayii Déka, the "Ten Martyrs", there is an amphitheatre and a stadium. The ruins are fenced off from the surrounding olive trees, but otherwise hardly seem to have been excavated or disturbed. No one else was about to interrupt the hum of insects in the drowsy heat of noon. I would never have believed that a March sun could be so hot in Europe.

All this history had given us dry throats and we felt distinctly in need of refreshment as we drove back through the Messará. A simple little village *tavérna* with an outside table by a south-facing wall was what we desired, and we set off hopefully into the hills to the north of the main road, only to find ourselves heading into lonely country towards the Ida range. Turning downhill once more, we passed through an area with a very Italian appearance, large villas being surrounded by high walls and poplar trees. We found plenty of noisy, grubby bars in the towns of Míres and Timbáki, but none promised the peaceful meal we had hoped for. We passed an old couple seated at a little café table under a verandah festooned with vines, drinking soup from the same bowl. But the dust from the wheels of the trucks roaring past a few feet away swirled around them and we didn't stop.

At the western end of the plain, we took a side turning to the sea at Kókkinos Pírgos, "Red Tower", a strange little port which once lived by trade with Africa, although now the warehouse and customs office is locked up and abandoned. The Cretans use this village as a summer resort and there is a row of *tavérnas* along the single street which look on to the beach. On this day they were all closed, and the little hotel, smart and newly painted as it was, didn't serve meals at this time of the year, nor did the large open-air bar at the end of the street where the workers from the tomato fields were playing cards and backgammon in their lunch hour.

The sea barely lapped the deserted and rubbish-strewn beach in oily ripples, so bright with reflected sunlight it was painful to look at. Out to sea are the twin islands of Paximádia, or "Dry Bread". Once, they say, a giant fish swam inshore from the deep sea to devour the people of the coast. Zeus dropped a great loaf of bread into the sea as an alternative food source for the fish, which could only swallow half, and spat out the remaining pieces to float for ever as islands in the Gulf of the Messará, occupied only by rabbits and foxes.

We were disinclined to go back to Timbáki, and we turned north towards Apodoúlou and the Amári valley. As the road climbed into the mountains, the air grew cooler and fresher, and we began to feel the wind again. The dust and the lorries of the plain were left behind with the lush sub-tropical vegetation and we were surrounded by green grass and oak trees. The road twisted and ascended, and we began to catch glimpses of the snow-covered Psilorítis to the north, miles away, and partially veiled by a long horizontal streak of cloud clinging to the shoulder.

CHAPTER 10

The Amári Valley

The mountaineers have a tradition of contempt for the plainsmen which is reflected in a number of folk songs:

> Fie on the young men down in the plains,
> Who taste the good things of the world,
> the choicest foods,
> And are base to look at like the creeping lizard.
> Joy to the young men up in the hills,
> Who eat the snow and the dew fresh air,
> And are fine to look at like the orange tree.
>
> (Trs. Michael Llewellyn Smith *The Great Island*)

Or the complaint of a daughter from the mountains, married to a husband from the lowlands:

> Mother, you've made a poor match for me in giving me to
> the plains.
> I don't hold with plains, I don't drink hot water.
> My lips will wither, will turn to yellow leaves
> from the warm water, the great heat of it.
> Here the nightingale sings not and the cuckoo does not
> speak.
> The plains nourish horses and the mountains heroes,
> And the girls waste away and become husks.
>
> (Michael Llewellyn Smith *The Great Island*)

Once again, the shepherds we met along the road were men with tough weather-beaten faces and tall leather boots, made as they say to "stamp on the earth that's going to eat us".

I walked into the *kafeneíon* in Apodoúlou to ask if we could have lunch; conversation stopped in the crowded little room with the door closed against the chill mountain air and the stove sending wood-smoke into the room as the wind blew back down the chimney. Unfriendly faces stared inhospitably.

"No, no food here. Try the next village," they said. In Níthavris, a village which played a famous part in the resistance, and near which the captured German General Kreipe was hidden for a time, the atmosphere was equally stony and restrained. A family group sitting against a wall in the single street of Kouroútes did not want to speak to us at all, but then a young girl asked: "Deutsches?"

"Ochi, eímaste Angloi."

Everybody relaxed and became more friendly. "Go on to Fourfourás," they said, "you will get food there."

We had resigned ourselves to going hungry for the rest of the day anyway, and the sight of the mountain snows closer and closer above us was compensation enough. Once, according to myth, these "roots" of Ida were populated by great giants, the *sarantapéchi*, or "forty-cubitt ones". When the earth was covered by the Great Flood, they took refuge at the summit of Psilorítis. Although the waters rose up to their necks, they would have survived, were it not for the worms which wriggled up through the mud under their feet to infuriate them. When they bent down to catch the worms in their fingers they toppled off the mountain and were drowned.

When we finally turned the last corner into Fourfourás, there was an apparently empty concrete *kafeneíon* by a bend in the road. Across the street, a man stood outside his workshop mending an old Briggs and Stratton agricultural engine, using the top of a wall as a bench. An elderly, bespectacled lady sat on a wooden chair just inside the door, reading a local newspaper. She looked rather careworn and tired, but smiled when she saw the children.

"Deutsches?" came the inevitable question after we greeted her.

"No, English. Can we eat here please?"

She smiled again, and indicated her little counter where there was a small pile of sausages on a plate. Would we like some salad? She pointed to a patch of lettuces outside near where I had parked the car. This seemed just fine in our present state of hunger, and we sat down with anticipation at a table in the cold room. Apart from the tiny bar in the corner, the tables and the chairs, the building was no more than a bare concrete shell with a glass front. There was no stove.

She brought a jug of sharp wine and something fizzy for the boys. The salad couldn't have been fresher and tastier, and the sausages, when they arrived in their own gravy with a little bread, contained a delicious gamey meat, almost like venison, though we couldn't find out what it was. Unfortunately, her frying pan was small and she had to cook them up in relays to satisfy our appetites. Smiling and shy, she sat down again at her paper with her spectacles on her nose, but looked up and patted Malcolm on the head when he went up with his phrase book to say, "Thank you, it was very good."

High above Fourfourás is the cave where the British agent, Tom Dunbabin, made his headquarters during the German occupation. From here, he could look out over the valley which he so loved, and the villages of the Amári which he always said were the most beautiful in Crete. And from here, he watched helplessly as the same villages burned for a week.

Through more picturesque valleys and the little village of Vizári, we drove until we reached the Venetian Monastery of Asómatos. Like Arkádi, not so far away across the mountains, this was a centre of resistance to the Turks. In addition, the whole Amári valley was particularly active in resisting the German occupation, and many British agents operated here with the local *andárte* bands. The men of the Amári have something of the reputation of the Sfakians in the White Mountains of the west and, although I may have poked a little fun at these captains, in truth, they proved their courage often enough at that time. The shepherds of the Ida mountains and the Amári were staunch friends to the Allies. Two powerful groups of *andártes* operated from the slopes of Psilorítis: that of Michael Xilouris to the north, and that of the legendary Petrakoyeorgis to the south.

We doubled back to Monastiráki, where the Germans found a Minoan site during the occupation (presumably it wasn't all bitter raids and reprisals), and passed the Agricultural College with its kumquat tree, founded by the monastery. After the pretty town of Amári, the road narrows to a little rough track which climbs steeply out of the valley towards the flank of Mount Kédros, where the oaks and pines grow thickly, as in the high sierras of Spain. When we paused at the head of the road to look back, Psilorítis floated on a tablecloth of cloud above the chasm, while the bulge of Mount Samítos filled the right foreground. We had to stand and stare for five minutes before moving on.

This valley is a very mysterious place. Hidden in its woods are tiny Byzantine churches, with extraordinarily rich and ornate frescoes. The people don't pay them much attention, content to worship in the larger, modern churches in the villages. In a month you wouldn't be able to search out all the little chapels lost in these hills. They say the people of the valley emigrated to Africa, and there is a whole colony of them in Lourenco Marques. One of the villages, Génna, was once Turkish, but was repopulated by refugees from Smyrna.

There are two caves under Psilorítis. The Kamáres cave, four hours' climb above the village of the same name, was discovered by shepherds in 1890, who alerted the Italian archaeologists working in the area. Here was first found the beautiful style of Minoan pottery known as Kamáres ware, which form some of the finest exhibits of the museum in Iráklion. The Minoans seem to have brought offerings to the cave in vases and dishes in the hope that the gods would send them good harvests. Higher up, on the north side of the mountain, is the great Ida cave, discovered in the 1880s, and containing a large number of bronze weapons, shields and vessels, dating from the eighth and ninth centuries BC. The cave is reached from the large village of Anóyia and the high plateau of Nídha, where the snow lies for six months of the year, although it is a good summer pasture.

The Ida cave has long been one of the claimants for the honour of being the birthplace of Zeus; the other is the cave at Psychró under Mount Diktí. The Cretan Tourist Organisation has attempted to resolve the situation to the satisfaction of both factions, and has declared that Zeus was born in the Diktean cave, but brought up on goats' milk and honey in the Ida cave under the care of the Curétes. The Curétes, it will be remembered, were the warriors who clashed their shields to hide the baby's cries from his father, Cronus, who sought to devour him. Another associated myth is that King Minos, the son of Zeus, returned every nine years to his father's birthplace, whichever cave that may be, and received instruction in law to pass on to mortals, rather in the manner of Moses and the Commandments. Many eminent students of Greek mythology, including Robert Graves, have argued over these caves, but it seems clear enough that the ancient Greeks worshipped Zeus in the Ida cave, as one of the bronze shields found there clearly shows Zeus with the Curétes.

The mysterious philosopher, Epimenides, who came from Phaestós in the sixth century BC, was supposed to have slept in the Ida cave for fifty-seven years. Epimenides was called to Athens as a great exponent of Cretan law, whether before or after his long sleep, I am not clear. His remark that: "All Cretans are liars; Epimenides is a Cretan; is Epimenides a liar?" is one that the islanders have never been allowed to forget. (I would answer that all Cretans tell lies to some degree, but they vary in the extent to which they bend the truth.)

On the wilder parts of Kédros, I am told that a rare pink can be found, unique to this mountain. On the highest peaks there is an alpine crocus known as the "Glory of the Snows". But the strangest story about Kédros is that the mountain has one hundred and one springs. One hundred springs are known to the shepherds of Kédros, but the one hundred and first spring contains the Water of Immortality, and whoever drinks from it will live through all eternity, if only he can find the right place in this tangle of rocks and trees. The story of Alexander the Great and the Water of Immortality is told all over Greece with variations, for Alexander has become a legendary folk hero, only loosely based on historical fact.

When King Alexander had conquered the world, he was still a young man, and he became restless and concerned that he might die and thus be cheated of all the power and possessions for which he had striven. He called his wise counsellors and asked them the secret of a long life. They replied that such things were in the hands of the Fates, but the only sure way of surviving to enjoy his empire was to be in possession of the Water of Immortality, for the man who possessed this water need no longer fear death. However, the water could not be easily won, for first he must pass between two clashing mountains which crushed every traveller who attempted to ride between them. Then he must fight the dragon which guarded the water, a dragon who never slept.

Alexander felt that these tasks would not be insuperable to a man who had, after all, conquered the world and so he mounted his horse, Bucephalus, rode like the wind through the clashing mountains and slew the wakeful dragon, bearing home the magic water in a glass. But, foolishly, he did not drink the water at once, for he lay down to sleep first. As Alexander slept, his sister came, fussing and tidying, and, not knowing what the water was, she threw it away. The water fell on to a wild squill plant and that, they say, is why a cut squill never withers or goes dry.

When Alexander found what had happened, he was consumed with fury and when he regained his powers of speech, he cursed his sister:

"May you grow into a mermaid, fish from the waist down, and suffer torments in the sea until the End of Time."

It seems that the gods heard Alexander's curse and took it to heart, for sailors and fishermen say that ever since that time, the crew of ships in lonely parts of the sea have sometimes come across the poor mermaid crying and lamenting. She still loves her brother, for she invariably asks the ship's master for news of him:

"Does Alexander live?"

Now a foolish captain might answer truthfully and tell her that Alexander is long dead, in which case she will so churn up the sea in her paroxysm of grief that the ship will be lost and all the sailors drowned. But a wise man will answer:

"Yes, he lives and reigns," and the mermaid will be reassured and send the ship on its way with sweet songs.

As an interesting contrast, a similar story about Alexander is told in Persia, where Freya Stark heard it from a Mirza, or nobleman:

> . . . they spoke in the King's hall of the wells of life in the Lands of Darkness, and the King asked where they lay; and none could tell him until Elias, a stripling at the court, stood up and spoke of the waters, white as milk and sweet as honey, that rise through six hundred and sixty springs out of the darkness of the west. Whoever washes there and drinks will never die.
>
> Alexander, who wished to live for ever because his kingdom was so great, prepared for the journey. He asked what he should ride and Khizr Elias bade him mount a virgin mare, for their eyes are made of light . . . and each took in his hand a salted fish, to test the waters when they reached them.
>
> Now when they came to the western darkness, Elias wore a jewel, and by its glitter saw on every side white wells of water, and threw his salt fish, and it swam away; and Elias washed and drank and lives for ever. But Alexander of the Two Horns missed the path and wandered, until he came out by another road, and died in his day like other mortal men. Unto God we return.

(Trs. Freya Stark, *Alexander's Path*)

In the concrete village of Kardáki, where the cobbler used to provide a haven for escaping Allied soldiers, we met a man leading a mare, a rare sight in Crete now, though I presume they must exist in order to breed the ubiquitous mules. There sometimes seem to be more donkeys and mules than people in this land. Next came a cow, very Swiss in appearance, with curved horns and a large bell, led on a halter by an old woman who waved cheerily to us. These are even rarer, except occasionally in high mountain villages. In the woods near the village is the isolated Byzantine Chapel of Ayios Ioánnis, and also a monument to villagers executed by the Germans.

Gerakári is the highest of the Amári villages; Mount Kédros, not so far above, is nearly 1,800 metres. The surrounding country, with leafless deciduous trees, bracken, brambles and rough brown grass, looks wintry and northern, while snow is common here well into the spring. No Mediterranean oranges and lemons are grown, but potatoes, apples and cherries. The Morello cherries are famous, and they are made into a summer drink called *visinádha*. Above the village is the plateau of Yious with many springs. An ugly place now, Gerakári, and when you look closely you see that everything is new and everything is in grey concrete, hastily built, and so unlike the whitewashed villages of Crete. In Gerakári, it was Alexander Kokonas OBE, the schoolmaster, who hid Allied soldiers, but the village was generally patriotic and helped the resistance whenever they could.

The day of reckoning for the Kédros villages came in August 1944, when Gerakári, Kardáki, Vríses, Drigiés, Gourgoúthi, Smilés and Ano-Méros were burned, together with the more distant villages of Anóyia, Kamáres, Kría Vríssi and Saktoúria. The last year of the occupation proved to be the worst. The Germans gave out that the villages were burned as a reprisal for the abduction of their General Kreipe, but some doubt this, for that operation had taken place three months before. In October, the Germans withdrew to an enclosure around Khaniá for the remainder of the war, so perhaps the reign of terror had been instigated to cover their withdrawal. When they burned a village, they would shoot all the men they could lay their hands on. The women would be locked up in Réthymnon for about a fortnight and then released to manage as best they could. "The English forget us," they said to Dilys Powell in Vríses, where 39 died, "don't they know the sacrifices we made?"

George Psychoundakis, author of *The Cretan Runner*, probably the most interesting book on the resistance movement, watched these once beautiful villages burning from Tom Dunbabin's cave on the far side of the valley. Later, he wrote a poem on their lost beauties, very much in the heroic Cretan style:

> . . . You were the secret shelter for each Greek and
>   English rival
> Of tyranny, who grasped a gun for liberty's survival!
> But when the Dark Hour came at last the storm clouds
>   broke asunder
> Barbarian tempests flung their fire, high mountains
>   crashed with thunder.
> And now you lie there, cold and dead, ruined and
>   black with burning.
> Empty and silent in the hills and dark with fire and
>   mourning.
> Where are your *pallikária* now, your chosen
>   warriors sleeping,
> Who fell that evil day and filled Amári's vales with
>   weeping?

Where are your idle afternoons, your mornings bright
    with sunlight?
Your founts, your belfries in the dusk, your churches
    pale with moonlight?
Where are your dove-white houses now, your soft winds
    and your waters,
Your happy throngs in summertime, your golden sons
    and daughters? . . .

(George Psychoundakis, *The Cretan Runner*)

By the time we reached Apóstoli in the late afternoon, the sun was hidden by clouds and the chilly wind had a touch of the distant snows about it. A good road reaches this point at the northern entrance to the Amári, and we thankfully stopped at a large modern *kafeneíon* for a warming coffee and a glass of *tsikoudiá*. An old man in mountaineer's dress was sitting by a roaring stove and politely brought up chairs for us to share its warmth, while he piled on more oak logs from the stack on the floor. It seemed a prosperous place, with a large glass and chromium counter displaying a selection of hams and sausages, a television and an enormous twin speaker portable radio. The old man's pride and joy was obviously his little grandson, just learning to walk, who wobbled unsteadily over the few feet between his grandfather and his mother, a smart, sophisticated woman, whose clothes must have come from Iráklion's better shops, if not Athens.

A rugged looking Mercedes truck with an enormous ground clearance pulled up outside, and the little boy's mother left him for a moment to serve the bearded driver with coffee and a white goats' milk cheese, which he cut up and began to eat without bread. Swelling with pride, the family handed the little chap to Joan to hold for a moment, while an older girl, rather eclipsed by the attention paid to the younger, male child, peeped shyly around the counter. As we left, we gave the children some bars of chocolate: a gift to children being the only present the Cretans will allow you to get away with. Greeks are generally indulgent towards children, and they have certainly always been very kind to ours. Incidentally, Greek children do not have an individual birthday in the sense that ours do, but a "name day", this being the day of the saint of the same name. These celebrations are continued enthusiastically into adulthood, and so on St George's Day, for instance, all the men named George of a village will entertain each other with food and drink in a sort of peripatetic party which will continue long into the night. All Saints Day is used to take care of those who do not possess a saint's name.

I have jumbled memories of the villages beyond Apóstoli. White villages and brown villages: they say limewash has an antiseptic quality and the dictator, Metaxas, wanted to force all the villages in Greece to use it. In practice, it is done more according to tradition. A row of poles leaning against a wall, each carrying a complete new sheepskin, stiff with dried blood, waiting to be cured. Carved double doors partly open, revealing the great storage jars which are built little by little from the bottom, until several large men could hide in one. Clay brick ovens for outdoor baking. A ruined water mill, inhabited only by goats now, the interior floor supported by a single great arch above the water which trickles through the machinery and spreads out over the silt which covers the floor. Cats creep about the crumbling walls and their eyes stare from the dark recesses. It is reckoned to be unlucky to kill a cat here, and so kittens starve.

Thrónos was so named as the throne of a bishop in the first Byzantine period. In the Church of the Panayía is a mosaic floor, which is all that remains of an early Christian basilica. Above the village is the ancient site of Sýbritos, a name still used by the shepherds for their summer pasture.

There was no sunset to cheer us under the lowering clouds, and the wind was cold as we made our way down the dark valley to Réthymnon. Even the cicadas under our window were silent that night.

CHAPTER 11

The Plain of Omalós

The next day was cloudy; the wind was still blowing, but it was a little warmer as we took our now familiar drive along the New Road to Soúda Bay. The port is busy now and looks modern, but in 1940, amazingly, there was not one crane, symbolic of the difficulty in turning this island into a fortress at the southern perimeter of Europe.

On 28 October 1940, Mussolini's army confidently crossed the frontier into Greece from Albania. Instead of sweeping rapidly across this weak, under-developed country with a population of only seven million, they were astonished to find themselves fiercely opposed and then pushed back across the border. At this time, the Cretan Division, like much of the Greek army, was poorly equipped. Nevertheless, the men were so insistent that they be sent to the Albanian front that they threatened a hunger strike. They had their way, and as bitter fighting continued in Albania throughout the winter, the Greeks gradually gained ground. Soon, a humiliated Mussolini was complaining that only the Greeks would be so barbarous as to use such weapons as the sword and bayonet in modern warfare, or to make use of such savages as these men from Crete.

Greece wished to send every available man into Albania, and asked Britain to undertake the defence of Crete. Churchill was more than willing to commit Allied troops to aid Greece in every way, for he saw it as essential to deny the Axis Powers the south-eastern corner of Europe and access to the Middle East. Crete, meanwhile, was to be made impregnable. The British navy, based in Egypt, would protect the island from invasion by sea, while the garrison would deal with air attack. General Wavell, the Commander-in-Chief, Middle East, who had been less than enthusiastic about Allied assistance to Greece at all, was charged with undertaking this, in addition to his responsibilities in the Western Desert, Abyssinia, Iraq and Syria. In practice, little in the way of modern, heavy fire-power was moved on to the island. The lack of ports on the southern coast was an immense handicap in this respect, although British naval superiority in the eastern Mediterranean was virtually undisputed at this time.

By contrast, the air defence situation was appalling. The three fighter squadrons requested never materialised, for these machines simply were too precious in the Middle East to be risked. The handful of serviceable machines on Crete in the spring of 1941 found themselves contesting the skies with forces of German aircraft forty or fifty times greater in numbers. The survivors were withdrawn completely to Egypt just before the invasion, and throughout the subsequent Battle of Crete the Germans enjoyed total air superiority, an advantage which they exploited masterfully.

During these preparations, Crete found itself under seven different commanders in a four-month period. Eventually, on 30 April, Wavell appointed General Bernard Freyberg VC, the Commander of the New Zealand Division and an old friend of Churchill. Freyberg, incidentally, had been one of the party who buried Rupert Brooke on Skíros during the First World War.

Little serious attention seems to have been paid to exploiting the fighting qualities of the Cretans themselves. By the spring of 1941, most of the Cretan Division were dead or captured in Albania. Following their support for the Venizelist revolt in 1935, the dictator, Metaxas, had disarmed the island as far as possible, and now there was a shortage of rifles. At the approach of war, British intelligence had employed the archaeologist, John Pendlebury, ostensibly as a British vice-consul, but in fact to make contact with potential guerrilla leaders among the people. A rather quixotic figure with a glass eye and a long cloak, he was much loved by the Cretans as he roamed over the mountains from village to village. Yet, when he and Freyberg asked Wavell for ten thousand rifles for Cretan irregulars, their request was never fulfilled.

In April 1941, Hitler's patience ran out and he finally came to Mussolini's aid. A large-scale armoured invasion through Macedonia rapidly overran Greece, and the Allied expeditionary force was evacuated to Crete in some disarray. They were under constant air attack on the way to Soúda Bay, which itself was threatened throughout the daylight hours. Two oil tankers had been hit, and one lay burning for five days in the water. Conditions ashore were confused, with no tents or blankets and a shortage of hot food. Some armed men took to wandering about the surrounding hills, scavenging for themselves, and the Military Police had problems in restoring order. A few stragglers from the Cretan Division eventually reached the island too, wounded and starving, having made their way across the seas in requisitioned caiques. Almost their first act was to assassinate the Commander of the Division, who had escaped from Epirus and returned to Khaniá without his men. This was generally approved by the local population, who regarded him as a traitor.

General Karl Student, Commander of XI Air Corps and later to command the German forces at Arnhem, had conceived a plan for the airborne invasion of Crete. Goering, when he heard it, was filled with enthusiasm, for here was a project for the Luftwaffe which might restore some of the prestige lost during the Battle of Britain. Hitler, strangely negative about the whole Eastern Mediterranean area, took more convincing that it was even necessary. He was at this time more concerned with "Operation Barbarossa", the impending invasion of Russia, and wanted all his forces intact and ready for this great advance. Mussolini's failure in the attack on mainland Greece and the subsequent necessity to bail him out with German troops had already caused Hitler intense irritation. Moreover, he had a particular affection for the parachutists, whom he later described as "the toughest fighters in the German Army, tougher even than the Waffen SS." Yet, illogically, he so cherished these troops that he was unwilling to risk them against serious opposition.

Hitler eventually agreed on the grounds that he could not afford to leave the island in Allied hands, and that it would make a valuable advanced air base to attack the British in the Eastern Mediterranean. The operation was then delayed by transport problems within Greece, the two and a half million gallons of aviation spirit required eventually having to be brought from Trieste in small vessels along the Adriatic coast.

German intelligence was extremely poor: estimates of the numbers of defenders varying from only three battalions to 100,000 men. Most amazingly of all, they believed that the population would take a neutral stand, if not actually welcoming the invasion. I cannot imagine what grounds they had for this belief, but paratroopers were told to expect a friendly reception from the Cretans. As we have already seen, the German assault met with a truly hostile and terrifying reception and, especially among the parachutists, heavy casualties. Hitler, thereafter, could never be persuaded to use his airborne forces intact. Most were frittered away piecemeal in Russia, Italy and Normandy.

* * * *

On the northern outskirts of the city of Khaniá are wide groves of orange and lemon trees, bordered today by a rash of yellow flowers in the thick green grass. So fertile are these lands that a nearby village is named Perivólia, "the Gardens". A dirt road leads to the rich orange groves around Mesklá, fortunate in its abundant water supply, and sometimes known as the "Garden of Eden". The fourteenth-century Church of the Transfiguration is famous for its frescoes, and on the floor of a smaller chapel the mosaic floor of a temple to Venus is still visible.

There is a rather grim legend attached to this village of Mesklá, which may be no more than the invention of a Venetian official, the monk Antonias Trivian, who was still in Crete when the Turks captured Candia in 1669. All that is really certain is that there was a major rebellion against the Venetians in western Crete in about 1527. The Cretans of the districts of Sélinos, Sfakiá and Kydonía, objecting to forced labour in Venetian galleys and on defence works, revolted and established their own independent state. They refused to pay taxes or acknowledge Venetian authority. As "Rector of Western Crete", they elected Yeoryios Gadhanole, known as Kandanoleon, from the remote village of Koustoyérako in the mountains of the Sfakiá–Sélinos border. He set up his headquarters in the shadow of the White Mountains at Mesklá, with the support of a number of families who claimed noble Byzantine ancestry – the *árchontes*. This situation continued for some time, although it seemed obvious that sooner or later the Venetians would marshal their forces to take countermeasures.

Kandanoleon had the extraordinary idea of contracting a formal alliance with Venice. He arrived at the house of the Venetian aristocrat, Francisco Molino, at Alikianós and suggested a marriage between his son, Petros, and the baron's daughter, in order to mend the rift between the Venetian and Cretan nobility. Following the marriage, Kandanoleon would pass the governorship of Western Crete to his son. After he recovered from his initial astonishment, Molino thought quickly, then agreed to the match and the betrothal took place immediately. The wedding date was set for a few days ahead, and it was agreed that Kandanoleon could bring up to five hundred of his relatives and friends, while Molino would supply a great banquet and invite about fifty Venetian guests from Khaniá.

The wedding appears to have been a great success, a hundred sheep and oxen being roasted, and no shortage of wine. It was, in fact, a typical Cretan wedding party, and, by the end of the day, the whole Kandanoleon contingent had collapsed and were snoring stertorously. Their Venetian counterparts, however, had not drunk as deeply

The Minoan palace at Phaestós

Frangokástello

Kritsá

as had appeared, and opened the gates during the night to allow in the troops of the Rector of Khaniá, who had been tipped off by Molino. The drunken Cretans were trussed like chickens as they slept.

Kandanoleon and two of his sons, including the bridegroom, together with 33 of the guests were hanged in the morning from a nearby tree. Others were hanged at the gate of Khaniá, another group at Kandanoleon's village of Koustoyérako, some at Apokorónas Castle on the Candia road and at the village of Mesklá. The remainder were sent to the galleys. This was only the beginning of the Venetians' revenge, for the *Proveditore General*, Marino de Cavalli, went with his soldiers to a village called Photeiniaco, near Mourniés, which had taken a prominent part in the rebellion. Cavalli hanged twelve leading villagers on the spot and, in order to spread terror throughout the district, had the bellies of four pregnant women slit open with the sword and the embryos extracted. The village was burned to the ground and never rebuilt; it appears on no map today.

After more savage reprisals in the district of Kydonía, Cavalli sent word to the leaders of Frangokástello, Sélinos, Apokorónas, Kíssamos and Sfakiá, that they should attend him in person and swear their allegiance to Venice. Not surprisingly, the Cretans were not too happy about that idea, and felt safer sitting tight in their mountain strongholds. Cavalli's next move was to outlaw them, and to declare their land and property forfeit, while offering the rebels one terrifying opportunity to reinstate themselves with the authorities. Any outlaw who brought Cavalli the severed head of an outlawed male relative, be it father, brother, nephew or cousin, would receive the state's pardon. This dreadful order was actually complied with by a priest of the Pateros-Zappa family, who, with his two brothers and two sons, paraded before Cavalli in Khaniá, each carrying the head of a close relative. This was a scene of such horror that even the Venetians were moved to pity, and following the mediation of Catholic and Orthodox priests who travelled to Sfakiá as temporary hostages, the Cretans swore loyalty to Venice and a lasting peace ensued.

This story is generally believed in the island, although the dates, the historical evidence and numerous details do not tally. Even the existence of Kandanoleon is open to doubt.

The villagers of Koustoyérako, Kandanoleon's birthplace, were during the Second World War staunch supporters of the resistance. They were associated with the British SOE agent, Xan Fielding, and the legendary New Zealander, Sergeant "Kiwi" Perkins or "Kapetán

Vasili". When the Germans surrounded the village, the men were all away in the hills. Nevertheless, the Germans intended to carry out reprisals on the basis of ten Cretans to be executed for the death of every German soldier in that district. The women and children were lined up in the square in front of a machine gun and the officer prepared to give the order to open fire.

However, a small group of Koustoyerakiots, led by Kostis Pater-akis, whose family was particularly prominent in the resistance movement, were hidden on the mountainside fully 400 yards away. With commendable marksmanship they killed the officer with the first volley and, moments later, several more Germans before they could take cover. The survivors fled to the lowlands, taking further casualties as the Cretans followed them through the narrow valleys.

When a large German force returned to obliterate the village, they found it deserted, for the women and children had joined the men in the mountains. They remained there in safety for the rest of the war, living in sheepfolds and shepherds' huts. The Germans destroyed the village with dynamite, but dared not move higher into the hills where they knew a hundred rifles were watching and waiting for them.

Halting on the mountainside below the alpine village of Lákki, we looked across the valley at the great blue-domed church high above us. The green fir trees and terraced vineyards were alive with almost deafening birdsong, for even the nightingales seem to sing in the daytime here. For a moment, the arcadian scene was lit by the sun's rays finding their way through the clouds. Higher up, above the village, the scenery changed to barren rocks and tree heather again, while the mist began to collect on the windscreen and wisps of cloud drifted below us in the valleys.

We passed two shepherds talking beside the road and leaning on their crooks. They grinned as their dogs, supercharged with aggression, chased our car down the road while biting at the tyres. There used to be a belief that the soul of a heathen Turk would be housed in the body of a dog after death; perhaps that is why the dogs here are treated so harshly. There is a custom of calling one's dog by an enemy's name in order to have the pleasure of speaking sharply to it. During the Second World War, they say, Crete was full of dogs answering to the name of Hitler, Mussolini and Goebbels. During the Civil War, Stalin and Molotov came into favour. Whereas Cretans are not usually actively and sadistically cruel to animals – which, after all, usually have a value to any countryman – they are relat-ively indifferent to any incidental suffering which may occur. It is assumed, for instance, that hunting dogs have to be kept half-starved in order to be of any use. The Anglo-Saxon obsession with kindness to domestic pets is as incomprehensible to them as it is to most of the world.

This was the Sfakians' route out of their mountain lair to the vulnerable plains below, either for purposes of brigandage, or, as so often in the last century, in a holy crusade for the freedom of Crete and extermination of the hated Turks. The captains met on the high plateau of Omalós to begin the "66", the "Great Revolt", but the same pattern of events recurred almost every decade. The old muzzle-loaders which their fathers had used in the "21" would be dug out from their hiding places. Beacons were lit on the mountain peaks to raise the countryside, crossroads and strategic points were occupied, while Turkish villages were blockaded. Women and children would be sheltered in remote monasteries among the foothills as columns of smoke began to rise from the burning villages of the plains.

At other times, it was not the Turks, but their fellow Cretans who had cause to fear the presence of the Sfakians in the mountains above, who combined an enthusiasm for brigandage with their patriotism. Lowland Cretans tell a story against the Sfakians, a special adaptation of the Creation. When God made Crete, they say, he carefully ensured that each district had a crop to sustain its inhabitants. Thus, the men of Khaniá grew oranges, the fields of the Messará were covered with wheat, in Kíssamos they tended their vines, and in Sélinos the olive groves. God came last to Sfakiá and found he had no gift left but dry stones. As might be expected, these mountaineers became truculent and demanded to know how they were expected to survive among such barren rocks.

But the Creator pointed out that he had been more generous to the Sfakians than to any other Cretans: "You've got eyes haven't you? Just look down at the plains where all those farmers are working hard to grow such fine produce – just for your benefit!"

But my favourite "Sfakian" story is the one about two little fisherboys who were playing on the beach somewhere between Réthymnon and Khaniá. They looked up from their game to see a Sfakian *pallikáre* down from the mountains, gazing sternly out to sea. He was dressed in the normal manner of a Sfakian on a journey: silver pistols and dagger thrust in his sash, long rifle on his shoulder, crossed bandoliers and curved sword. The lowland fisherboys began to giggle behind their hands as small boys will.

The Sfakian's dignity was affronted and he called them over, twisting his ferocious moustaches with annoyance.

"How dare you laugh at me?" he demanded. "Don't you realise that I am a man of Sfakiá, a man who fears nothing? There is nothing I cannot do."

"Really?" said one of the boys, "I'll bet you can't swim as well as we can."

The doughty warrior, without more ado, marched into deep water, where he promptly sank out of sight, weighed down by all the hardware. The two boys dived in, grabbed an arm each, and assisted the captain to dry land. He was not one whit chastened by his experience, however, and his first words when he had regained his breath were:

"There you are. The sea can support whole fleets of ships, yet it has not the strength to bear one man from Sfakiá!"

As we crossed the rim of the Omalós plateau, over 1,200 metres above sea level, and descended to a corner of the flat alluvial plain, we noticed the gaping black mouth of a cave to the right. This was uncovered in 1961 and forms a sort of drain hole, what is called a *katavóthras*, to allow the water to escape from the enclosed plateau. There is a little notice close by to commemorate an exploration by Birmingham University in 1967, when the swallow hole was found to plunge down for over 1,000 metres and to be 20 kilometres in length, including a large subterranean lake. Our expedition made do with a torch from the glove pocket as we clambered down the little hollow, grown with arum and saxifrage, into the dripping, boulder-strewn chamber inside the entrance. The way slopes steeply downhill in the manner of most of Crete's limestone caves, the floor consisting of a frozen avalanche of great rocks beginning outside the cave's mouth and disappearing into the bowels of the White Mountains. We didn't venture out of sight of the daylight showing through the entrance.

The Omalós is a desolate and eerie place, deserted at this time of the year, although the winter snows had melted, leaving patches of marshy ground. In a hard winter, the snow will remain on the plain until April, after which life slowly returns to the earth, the Cretan tulips appearing in May, and then hyacinths, white peonies and cyclamen emerging in summer on the slopes above, with the orchid of Provence showing in shaded crevices. These strange upland plateaux, or *poljas*, fertile with alluvial soil and looking for all the world like dried up lakes among the barren mountains, are in fact quite common throughout the limestone Dinaric Alps, almost invariably drained by underground cave systems. It is this subterranean drainage which causes such problems for agriculture in Crete, for the rocks are so porous that it is impracticable to build storage dams. In summer, the men of Lákki, and Ayía Iríni on the Sélinos side of the White Mountains, make their way up here to live for a while in the little dry stone huts at the edge of the plain and grow a crop of barley, and the potatoes for which the Omalós is renowned. Now the cold mists drifted over brown sere grasses with no sign of new spring growth. A raven gave a sepulchral croak and flapped raggedly away just under the cloud cover a few feet overhead. Rare birds of prey are sometimes seen here – the lammergeyer, booted eagle and griffon vulture – but there was no sign of anything so exotic on this dismal day.

A small hummock rises from the plain with a little group of buildings: a chapel and the house of the Kydonian leader, Hadzimichalis Iannaris, hero of the "66", whose name indicates that he had made the pilgrimage to Palestine to visit Jerusalem during Holy Week, and bathed in the River Jordan. Hadzimichalis first fell foul of the Turks in a café brawl. Following the Russian defeat at Sebastopol in 1855, a group of Turks in Khaniá were drinking and celebrating and began to insult the Orthodox Greek church which they linked with the Russian. Hadzimichalis, stung by their remarks, proposed the health of the Tsar and in the ensuing fight he wounded several Turks. He was imprisoned by Mustapha Pasha, and only released on contributing to the hospital bills of his victims. Later, when imprisoned again, he prayed to St Pantaleimon and promised that if he escaped, he would build a chapel in the saint's honour. When eventually he broke free with the help of friends from Lákki, he forgot his promise and built a house for himself. It fell down at once and, taking the hint, he built the chapel first before rebuilding the house on the original site, where it stands solidly to this day.

There is a little bus stop here and a *kafeneíon* which probably does a roaring trade in summer as the coachloads of tourists pass through on their way up to the Samariá Gorge. Today, all was deserted and locked up. As we approached the end of the road, we could hear the wind whistle around us and the mists began to accelerate, like the smoke tracer in a wind tunnel, towards the lip of the precipice.

Wrapped in sweaters and jackets we walked to the edge, unable to see anything much for cloud, but from the deep reverberating note of the wind we sensed that an immense open space lay in front and below us. Suddenly, the veils of mist cleared for a few seconds to reveal the massive bulk of Mount Gíngilos in front of us: a great grey bastion, millions of tons of rock reaching from the bottom of the gorge 750 metres below our feet to the ice and snow-covered peak 2,100 metres above sea level, and even 900 metres above our viewing platform, so that we had to strain our necks back to see it. Tantalisingly, the cloud closed in again, and then every few minutes, more frequently as the sun grew higher and the vapours evaporated, the scene was momentarily revealed. The "rotten cliffs" of Gíngilos are pockmarked with gulleys and crevices where the snow never melts.

The head of the gorge is to the right, a long scree with occasional firs finding a precarious foothold. The lower walls of the canyon are covered in rich green cypresses and occasional maples, although the actual valley floor cannot be seen. To the left, the chasm winds below Gíngilos and its twin Mount Volakiás, and then towards the sea to the south and so out of sight around the corner. From this gulf issued the deep booming roar of wind which sometimes seemed to include the sound of rushing torrents. Beyond is the high Madará, the central range of the White Mountains, bare rock and snow leading up to Páchnes, the greatest of them all. There are no roads between here and Askýfou, truly a formidable tract of wilderness. Below our feet, we could look down through the feathery branches of the cypresses at the *xylóscala*, or wooden steps, a zigzagging path cut into the cliff all the way to the bottom.

This is the deepest gorge in Europe; there may be finer mountains in Switzerland, but this particular scene makes an awesome and dramatic impact on the spirit. All the tourist brochures extol the magnificence of Samariá at some length, so I will say no more, though we leaned over the balcony of the deserted tourist pavilion for more than an hour as the sun gradually cleared the mists. Water from the melting snows makes the walk down to the coast at Ayía Roúmeli impracticable in the spring. Now that the gorge is a National Park, it is officially closed during the winter months, certainly until April, and possibly even later if the rains have been heavy. A warden's notice at the head of the steps threatens a severe fine for anyone who ventures into the canyon during the closed season.

A few families, members of the Viglis clan, used to live in this sinister place at the little village of Samariá. They claimed to be of Byzantine stock, descended from the *Archontópouli*. Even by the standards of the White Mountains their life must have been desperately lonely and isolated. The name Samariá is a corruption from their Venetian Church of Ossía Mariá, dating from the fourteenth century and with beautiful frescoes. The Viglis family had a reputation for good looks and fair hair, and were notorious, even amongst other Sfakians, for sheep stealing and blood feuds. In 1948, there was a full-scale vendetta between the Samarians and the men of Lákki, with the Omalós forming a kind of no-man's land. Moreover, in those days, the gorge was a haven for outlaws, and a few hunted Communists used it as a refuge after the Civil War. George Psychoundakis describes a chilling encounter with what he calls "wind boys", a group of outlaws living in the gorge during the Second World War. At that time, the Germans maintained a guard post on the Omalós plateau and, in order to avoid this, it was necessary to descend into the gorge and climb the far side by a precipitous ibex path, and so across to the Sélinos mountains. The route was pointed out by a shepherd, Roussos Viglis, who warned Psychoundakis that if he and his companion encountered the "wind boys", they should use the Viglis name as a safe conduct. In the bottom of the gorge they met the outlaws, who behaved in a suspicious and sinister manner, seemingly undetermined whether or not to kill the two resistance men, who only had a pistol between them. Later the "wind boys" opened fire from a distance and, although the pair eventually escaped, the hand of Psychoundakis' companion was smashed by a rifle bullet and the fingers permanently paralysed. Roussos Viglis later told Psychoundakis that the leader of the "wind boys" was his own nephew, though he disowned him and wished that Psychoundakis had killed him.

When the area was made into a National Park and game reserve for the ibex, the Viglis family was offered compensation to move away, and their village of stone houses has been deserted now for twenty years.

The gorge is reputedly the birthplace of the nymph, Britomartis, daughter of Leto and companion of Artemis, the huntress. On Aegina, Britomartis is known as Aphaea, and the Dorians built a temple to her. Perhaps she remains in Samariá to protect the ibex, as she once did the deer.

Through the narrowest part of the cleft, the *Sídheroportes*, or Iron Gates, lies the tiny village of old Ayía Roúmeli, now almost empty. Beyond the ruins of a Turkish fort is the sea, with the new village on a little plain, site of the ancient Hellenistic city of Tarrha. The people of Ayía Roúmeli, once hunters and shepherds, now make their living from the summer tourists walking through. Of course, no roads lead here or are ever likely to. In order to return to civilisation, you must take a boat to Chóra Sfakíon (about one and a half hours) or to Paleochóra in the west. If the sea is rough, you may have to stay here or walk back up the gorge.

During the Battle of Crete, King George of Greece and Tsoudheros, the Prime Minister, were evacuated from Khaniá with an escort of New Zealand soldiers. They made their way up into the White Mountains, fired on by groups of German parachutists and nervous Cretans alike. After a freezing night under the mountain snows, they walked through the gorge to Ayía Roúmeli to be evacuated by a British submarine. It was firmly believed by the Allies that the survival of the monarch and the formation of a government in exile was essential for the morale of the Greek people. In the event, as anti-monarchist elements in the resistance gained the ascendancy on the mainland, this proved to be less than true and the seeds of civil war were already sown.

We took the road back to Omalós and on to Lákki, where we walked to the church, whose blue dome had shone so spectacularly across the valley in the morning. The inside of the cupola, which symbolises heaven to the Orthodox, shows the Pantocrator, Christ in Majesty, painted on a huge scale and glaring down, condemnatory and terrifying. This is no gentle Jesus, meek and mild, but a frowning Ayatollah, staring in anger at the sins of mankind, left hand on the Gospel, and right, according to tradition, with thumb and third finger touching to form a circle.

The Orthodox tradition of religious painting, from Byzantine frescoes to the more modern icons, often strikes Western eyes as formal and stylised, in spite of the richness of the colour and the variety of themes. The choice and positioning of subjects was, in fact, subject to rigid rules. Below Christ in the dome come the apostles and prophets, then the saints, with the Holy Virgin in the apse. Often, there is a gruesome and explicit Last Judgement, just to remind you to behave well, as you leave. More appealing are the martial saints, particularly the popular St George, who appears everywhere on the island (George must be the commonest male name here), usually slaying a rather small and harmless-looking dragon. Cretans have a firm trust in St George, who they always believed would turn up one day and send the Turks packing.

Incidentally, many of the frescoes of saints in the older churches have been damaged by the digging out of the eyes from the plaster with the point of a knife. This desecration is usually attributed to philistine Turks, but I did hear that there used to be a belief that the plaster of a saint's eye, sprinkled on the food or in the wine of one desired, would act as a love potion.

Other favourite subjects are the *Mystic Feast* (the Last Supper), various scenes from the Pentateuch and the *Assumption of the Blessed Virgin*. Often an angel and a devil strive for the Virgin's soul, while she lies with her hands crossed. The angel's sword is drawn and has cut off both the devil's hands, which fall through the air spurting blood from the wrists. There is a rather charming scene known as the *Well of Life*, in which the Virgin and Child sit together in a sort of giant bath tub, from which streams of water pour to refresh the world.

Another favourite saint who appears regularly is Pantaleimon, the "All-Compassionate". Born in Nicomedia on the Sea of Marmara, in the third century, St Pantaleimon was brought up by his mother as a Galilean, although his father was pagan. After training as a doctor, he rose to high position, being appointed as a personal physician to Galerius, who had been made Caesar of the East by the Emperor Diocletian in 293 AD. Under the influence of Galerius' court, he neglected his Christianity and tended towards paganism once more, until he encountered St Hermolaus, who brought him back to the Faith. When Diocletian began the last and severest persecution of the Christian sect in 303 AD, Pantaleimon insisted on treating Christian patients without charge, and dispersed his money and property among the Christian poor. Galerius Caesar was a reasonable man, who counted Pantaleimon as a friend and valued his medical skills. However, when Pantaleimon was denounced to him, he found his position difficult and tried to persuade him to publicly reject Christianity. But Pantaleimon refused to apostatize and carried out a miraculous cure of a paralytic. Arrested and tortured, he remained obdurate and was sentenced to death. The saint's stubborness continued, for he refused to die, his body magically resisting burning at the stake, attack by ravenous wild beasts, drowning, liquid lead and the wheel. Eventually, the exasperated Romans tied him to an olive tree and beheaded him with a sword, whereupon he consented finally to expire, although his veins bled milk instead of blood, and the olive tree burst immediately into fruit. They say that the phials of his blood (which are now kept in Madrid, Ravello and Constantinople), miraculously liquefy on his feast day, similarly to that of the famous St Januarius at Naples, who protects the city from Vesuvius.

When the great fresco painters abandoned Crete for the monasteries of Mount Athos and the Metéora, their place was taken by the painters of icons, an art form which continues to this day. The iconostasis on which these boards hang, gilded and bright with colour, or darkened with age and the smoke of countless candles, is a rood screen of ornately carved wood dividing the nave from the chancel. There are three doors in the iconostasis, and some say there is a connection with the three thresholds in the proscenium of ancient Greek tragedy.

In Lákki, the *tavérna* was obviously used to catering for the summer tourist traffic, although the only other customers on this day were two old men playing backgammon by the stove. The owner grilled us some lamb cutlets and served some reasonable wine, while we sat and watched the traffic of the village: laden mules plodding up and down the road, driven by women with their black shawls wrapped around the lower part of the face.

Further down the road to Khaniá is a memorial naming two resistance fighters who died in February 1944, one of them being the

New Zealander, Sergeant Perkins. Gunner Perkins, as he then was, had escaped from the prison camp at Galatás after the Battle of Crete, and with a companion had wandered for months over these western mountains, sustained by hospitable Cretans for whom they understandably developed a great affection. On a number of occasions they were chased and nearly caught by German patrols as they attempted to buy or steal a boat to sail to the North African coast. Eventually, in the spring of 1942, Perkins encountered a group of commandos landed from a Greek submarine and obtained a passage to Egypt.

It was obvious that Perkins had a natural affinity for the island and its people, and he was given special training in irregular fighting and sabotage before returning to Crete in July 1943 (on the same boat as George Psychoundakis who was returning from leave in Cairo). Perkins was to assist Major Xan Fielding, the British agent responsible for the west of Crete, and quickly familiarised himself with the resistance network. After the Germans burnt Koustoyérako on 2 October, Perkins, now known as "Kapetán Vasili" to the Cretans, together with the Paterakis family, organised the men of the village into an aggressive and effective band of *andártes*. Arms were dropped to them from Allied aircraft, and they constantly attacked German positions at night, often recovering sheep which the occupying forces had confiscated.

On one occasion, a patrol of twenty German soldiers were ambushed in a cheesemaking hut, high in the mountains. Perkins personally killed ten of them by throwing in a grenade, the rest being taken prisoner and then shot, such being the harsh conditions of guerrilla warfare at this time. Perkins was hit by a bullet which travelled through his shoulder and parallel with his spine for some distance. His companions were uncertain as how to deal with the wound, and Perkins encouraged them with the words, "Haven't any of you killed a sheep before?" It was said to have been a butcher who eventually located the bullet with the point of his knife and extracted it.

On the way to Así Gonía to rendezvous with another British agent, Perkins and four companions were surprised by fifty Germans, Perkins and one other being killed instantly, the other three escaping, although wounded. The Germans recovered his body and buried it by their barracks at Lákki.

"Kiwi" Perkins was the kind of *pallikáre* that Cretans admire most, and his grave is said to have been covered with flowers. I once heard a story about a young Cretan couple who wanted to emigrate to New Zealand a few years ago. The quotas were full and the immigration authorities turned them down. Then the girl's father wrote in their support, saying that he didn't know whether it had any relevance, but during the war he had sheltered Sergeant "____", a New Zealander on the run from the Germans. Permission was granted for the young people to enter New Zealand.

Down in the rich orange-growing country under the mountains near Fournés, a little church stands beside the road, surrounded by white marble graves decorated with arum lilies and pot plants. The fields around the churchyard were covered with the *ranunculus asiaticus* anemones which even appear in Minoan painting. The bell rope was loosely tied to the outside wall in the usual Greek fashion. The bells of Crete's churches and monasteries were such potent symbols of the island's freedom that the Turks, early in their occupation, ordered the Christians to give them up into the keeping of the authorities. Many cast a substitute to hand in, and hid or buried the original bell, keeping the location a secret for many generations down the centuries. Even today, great bells must still be buried in the ground in remote places, or forgotten in obscure caves and clefts in the mountains. In other ways, Christianity operated with minimal restrictions under Turkish rule, at least in times of peace, although permission was needed from the Sublime Porte to build a new church or carry out repairs.

In the town itself, we took a stroll around the larger church, fronted by bulbous palm trees. The church was locked, but the spiral iron staircases to each of the twin campaniles were unobstructed. The nineteenth-century wrought iron was spindly, and at twenty or thirty feet above the ground began to sway and creak alarmingly. We all decided that the view was quite adequate from halfway up and descended quickly.

Across the street is an old Turkish *konak*, a house with wooden balconies, and carved doors and shutters against soft honey-coloured stone. Perhaps once an *aga* ran his estates from here, while his wife and family stayed safely in their town house within the walls of Khaniá. The playground of the school was crowded with small children, who came openly and happily to the railings to talk to us, while a group of old women, swathed in black, stopped their knitting to smile.

We parked near the port in the city of Khaniá and wandered inland towards the newer part of the city, and along Hadzimichalis Iannaris Street. The wall has been knocked down here, where once the main or Réthymnon Gate stood by the Bastion of Piatatora. In its place, a cross-shaped, covered market was built in 1911, a copy of the great Marseilles market, all cast iron and glass, like a Victorian railway station, and a meeting place for all of western Crete. In Turkish days, there was an open bazaar here and along Apokorónas Street, which divided the Greek and Turkish quarters.

Most of the day's business was over, and the tradesmen were packing up as we made our way along litter-strewn aisles between the stalls in the greenish light filtering through the glass roof, as if at the bottom of an aquarium. Cretan butchers love to display the more dramatic aspect of their wares. Often one comes across the severed and bloody head of a cow nailed to a shop doorway in a village street, the expression indescribably mournful, as well it might be. If the shop has pork, the pig's head will be on the doorway as a useful indication of the delicacies available within. Here, the butchers' tables were greasy and bloody, dismembered carcasses and odd remnants lying on the concrete. Almost nothing is wasted, for Cretans enjoy eating all sorts of offal and odd delicacies: sheep's eyes, testicles, heads of pigs and goats, lambs' intestines are all prized. Most of the meat was lamb, beef and goat-kid, but chickens and rabbits were also hung up, together with partridges and mountain hares. Blood puddings, salt pork in barrels and pigs' trotters were laid out under smoked and york hams (for like most mountain people, Cretans understand about curing hams), great ropes of sausages and salami. The rich, savoury smell of the preserved and smoked meats merged into the pungent odour of the cheeses for which Crete is famous: goats' milk *féta*, *graviéra*, *myzíthra* and many other varieties. The cheese-sellers also displayed large tubs of thick-crusted, creamy yoghurt, some being squeezed in muslin to remove surplus liquid until it is as thick as cottage cheese.

The fish merchants, not to be outdone by the butchers, had nailed the leathery tails of giant tuna over their stalls, and were now clearing away boxes of unsold fish and hosing down the floors. Striped moray eels, looking flaccid and flabby like clumsily abandoned football scarves, lay beside trays of octopus and squid, and the delicious red mullet or *barboúnia*, Crete's favourite fish when baked with thyme. Salt cod was packed in barrels. Sometimes there are swordfish, but this is a rare treat, for these seas are, on the whole, barren fishing grounds which have been further depleted by the illegal use of dynamite – some of the older fishermen have fingers missing from both hands to show for it.

The vegetable sellers still had large quantities of big tomatoes, cucumbers, courgettes, aubergines, chillies, red and green peppers, and fierce purple onions, together with all the varied green salad leaves, artichoke, dandelion and horseradish, which are known collectively as *hórta*. All the familiar northern European vegetables are available here, long before their season, with great pumpkins and squashes to come later. The clear, sharp smell of fresh coriander tied in luxuriant green bunches overlay the confusion of less powerful scents. Enormous bundles of fennel lay next to boxes of asparagus and large black mushrooms. We made our way past bags of herbs and spices, black peppercorns, cloves, nutmegs, mace, shelled almonds, cinnamon, bay leaves, marjoram and rosemary.

The fruit stalls were mainly occupied with the winter's crop of oranges and lemons, and a few of the bananas which are now grown here. Later there would be an exotic collection of strawberries, melons, peaches, green and black figs, grapes, medlars and, of course, the quince (*kydonis*), which originated here in Khaniá. Large amounts of space were given over to bags of dried pulses, chick peas, beans, lentils and the sunflower seeds, or *passatémpo*, which people nibble here constantly, together with various nuts, especially chestnuts from Kíssamos. The various types and shapes of Greek bread were stacked next to *kouloúria*, rolls with sesame seeds, barrels of biscuits and cakes. There were trays of *baklavás*, layered pastries sticky with nuts and honey, *bougátsa*, a light pastry filled with cheese, and the famous *halvá*, made from honey and sesame seeds. These fattening but delightful snacks are sold from street barrows all over the Middle East. Like most southern Europeans, Greeks tend to have a sweet tooth and, apart from the famous honey, there were endless varieties of jams and preserves in odd combinations, such as melon and lemon.

I spent a pleasant ten minutes looking through a wineseller's stock, surrounded by unfamiliar labels. Apart from the unnamed local wines, there are many registered bottlers in Crete, most of whom, sadly, do not export. Joan was still fascinated by the herbs. Cretans may have a simple cuisine, but they love to cook lamb and chicken in a smoky fragrance from the thyme, rosemary and mint in which it has been rolled. You crush these pungent herbs underfoot with each step in the mountains, and the islanders will tell you that the fine flavour of the lambs is due to their aromatic diet. The honey made during the flowering of the wild thyme is similarly famous. The olives in Crete are somewhat small and dry, nothing like the large, sweet, black olives of Kalamata on the mainland. A man was selling a range of fresh ground coffees: all the very fine grains used for making Greek coffee (never call it Turkish), with a great deal of sugar and very little water, in little long-handled pots over the fire. Finally, there were the sweet sellers with sticks of liquorice and many different types of *loukoúmi* (again, not to be called Turkish delight here any more than it is in Turkey).

133

* * * *

Driving along the shore of Soúda Bay on the way back to Réthymnon, we were reminded of an episode in Kazantzakis' truly great novel, *Zorba the Greek* (which must be the perfect book to take on your travels in Crete). One of the characters is an old, broken-down French tart, Madame Hortense, who constantly reminisces about the days of the Great Powers' occupation, when the fleets of four admirals, English, French, Russian and the Italian Canevaro, rode at anchor in the bay. Hortense, young and beautiful then, and apparently in the process of making a courtesan's grand tour of the Levant, from Alexandria to Anatolia via Beirut, was the toast of the fleet, rowed from flagship to flagship in an admiral's barge until she could hardly stand from exhaustion. In the dark, she could only tell the admirals apart by their perfume: eau-de-cologne for England, violets for France, musk for Russia and patchouli for her favourite Italy. In spite of their impressive gold braid and plumed hats, she would pull their beards and then beg them not to shell the Cretan rebels on shore (as already mentioned, this was done on at least one occasion in an attempt to keep order):

"How many times the woman you see here has saved the Cretans from death! How many times the guns were ready loaded and I seized the admiral's beard and wouldn't let him 'boom-boom!' But what thanks have I ever had for that? Look what I get in the way of decorations . . ."

(Nikos Kazantzakis, *Zorba the Greek*)

Prevelakis tells that the character of Hortense was not pure fiction. She arrived at Soúda from Provence, via the brothels of Marseilles, in order to service the fleets off Crete. She was taken on board first by the Russian admiral, Andreyev, who then politely passed her around his colleagues. When the fleets left she spent twelve hard years in a Khaniá brothel and then turned to a more respectable living in the Turkish baths at Réthymnon, adopting the name of Fatima. When the Turks were expelled in 1923, she revealed her true nationality to the French Consul and was allowed to stay.

We stopped off to look at Georgioúpolis again, approaching the village from the Cape Drépanon side. One of the villages on this Sickle Cape was used by Michael Cacoyannis for his film of *Zorba*. This received a bad reception among some Cretans, who felt that they had been shown as barbarians. Nevertheless, there is no event portrayed in the film which would not be quite credible in the Crete of sixty years ago, or is greatly at variance with the Cretan Kazantzakis' own writings.

We were lost for a while on the cape, wandering in labyrinthine lanes, until a shepherd directed us and we emerged under the eucalyptus trees of the village. Joan and Michael stayed by the tables of the fishermen's *kafeneíon*, while I followed the boys over the tumbled rocks of the causeway to the little chapel in the sea – this time at risk of being soaked by the big waves pushing in past the cape from the Aegean and intermittently breaking over the stones. The north wind still whistled, the sea was dark blue, flecked with white, and the luxuriant trees bent and showed the silver undersides of their leaves around the little cluster of houses beneath the grey backdrop of the mountains.

There were strange scenes in Georgioúpolis in the early months of 1945. The German forces had by then withdrawn to the area around Khaniá, and, as the war in Europe slowly came to an end, a sort of uneasy truce was observed for the most part between the beleaguered German garrison, regular Allied forces and the various bands of guerrillas. The German territory began at Georgioúpolis, and of course in those days the old road to Khaniá ran through the middle of the village. A wooden barrier across the square marked the boundary, and here messages were passed and the Bishop of Khaniá arranged an exchange of prisoners: a German officer, non-commissioned officer and private, for each partisan. George Psychoundakis describes Pericles Vandoulakis of Vaphé being released in this way. Vandoulakis had a long and distinguished career in the resistance, once escaping German custody, until he became such a thorn in their side that they would have paid a great deal for his head. On this occasion, his captors were unaware of his identity, having swallowed a false story he had fed them. Psychoundakis remembers him sitting in the back of a British lorry, a few feet on the safe side of the barrier, taking great delight in explaining to the chief of the Khaniá Gestapo just who had slipped through his fingers, before being driven away. (The exact nature of this "accommodation", if such it was, between the Allies and the German enclave around Khaniá, is unclear. Other German garrisons marooned elsewhere in Europe surrendered. Supporters of the Left contend that its sole purpose was to prevent EAM/ELAS gaining power – there were too few Allied soldiers on Crete at that time to enforce order throughout the island – and ensure that the administration was eventually delivered into the hands of the Right.)

Georgioúpolis is earmarked for tourist development next; it was featured on British television soon after we arrived home. There are a few little guest houses and rooms to let in summer, and it is becoming popular among those who like a quiet holiday, staying in a Greek village. It would make an ideal base for visiting most of western Crete and the place has great charm. If the developers build two or three large hotels, the men won't need to fish any more of course, but I wonder what the village square will seem like then? On this evening the *vólta* was in full swing, elderly gentlemen ambled along, chatting and fingering their loops of worry beads, teenagers idled by the central *kafeneíon* and housewives gossiped around their doorsteps.

CHAPTER 12

The Road to Iráklion

In a car uncomfortably jammed with suitcases, bottles of wine and oranges, we set off the following morning along the Old Road in the direction of Iráklion, through flat land where sunflowers and peanuts are grown. An occasional mule-powered pump stood idle, chains of buckets growing rusty until the water table sank again in the summer drought. Hedges of mutilated prickly pear divided the fields: a vicious plant which no one willingly brushes their hand against twice. In the old days, the flesh of the prickly pear was used as insulation, to line the walls of ice houses. The sun was shining again as we left Mount Vrísinos behind Réthymnon to the right, and passed the turning to the potters' village of Margarítes, birthplace of the Abbot Gabriel Marinakis of Arkádi. The countryside was gentle and green, the olive groves busy with workers, and every now and then we passed a donkey or mule ambling along the road, whose side-saddle rider would salute us. We stopped at a village garage for fuel and fell into conversation with a delightful old chap on a little two-stroke motorcycle.

"Deutsches?" he asked as usual, and then his brown, lined face split into a broad grin when he heard that we were English. As we shook hands, he managed, in a couple of sentences, to convey his resistance credentials, disapproval of everything German, and the continuance of a special relationship between Cretans and the English (really very kind, considering how much English prevarication cost them in the nineteenth century. Cyprus, it seems, is forgotten, or forgiven at least.) He insisted on riding ahead to show us the road to Pérama.

After asking in the village, we turned left for Pánormos, "Everyman's Harbour", a little coastal settlement close to the site of a Hellenistic-Byzantine port, with the ruins of a fifth-century church. Soon we came to a picturesque, narrow bridge over the Mylopótamos, the "Mill River". As far as I know, there are no water mills still grinding corn in Crete, although windmills certainly do. One often comes across the derelict remnants of a mill, wherever there is a slight head of water which can be counted on with any regularity: simple constructions with the wheel set horizontally so that the jet of water strikes it on the side and the minimum of internal gearing is required.

We waited for the *pappás* in his flowing black robes and stovepipe hat to cross the river before we drove over, and turned immediately right for the village of Melidóni. Here, a little girl playing on a corner pointed out the road up to the cave, and we climbed a steep slope up the western flank of the Kouloúkonas Mountains. No doubt the villagers earn some money in summer guiding visitors to their famous cave, but now the hillside was deserted, except for scattered goats with their tinkling bells. We moved a wire fence from across the road, taking care to replace it securely behind us, and soon reached the head of the track, by a small white chapel with a fine view over the valley. Behind is a sort of hollow, or sunken grotto, where the mountainside has collapsed inwards: an area where pine trees grow among tumbled white and honey-coloured boulders. The hollow must hold the damp, because the ground was green with succulent iris leaves and scattered with the tall white-flowered stems of spring asphodel.

The chapel was newly swept, with fresh flowers and olive oil lamps burning before the iconostasis. The most remote shrines in Crete – and there must be thousands, some perched on the most inaccessible crags – always seem to be regularly tended and cared for by someone. A power line runs into the hollow to the cave mouth from the chapel, but the uninsulated electrical connections looked so dangerous that we didn't risk switching on, and made do with our torch and a few candles. The entrance slopes steeply down, as in all these water-worn limestone caverns, and then opens out into a large first chamber with more to be seen beyond. The stalactites picked out by our flickering candle light were really quite fine, like the pillars of a Gothic cathedral.

This is the cave of Talos, the legendary giant of brass constructed by Hephaestus to guard Crete for Minos. His veins contained ichor, the blood of the gods, sealed by a plug in his heel. Three times a day, he lay in a furnace until his metal body reached red heat, and then he stalked the cliffs looking for strangers. Any he found were burned to death in his fiery embrace. Talos appears in some versions of the story of Jason and the Argonauts, and it was said to have been the witch, Medea, who destroyed him in his sleep by removing the plug in his heel. In Hellenistic times, a cult worshipping Hermes seems to have used the cave. The cracked stone altar in the first chamber, around which human bones and skulls are piled, is of more recent significance to modern Cretans, however.

During the general Greek revolution of 1821, the Turks of both Crete and Cyprus were filled with dread and, in order to instil a greater fear into their potentially rebellious subjects, attacked the symbols and representatives of the Christian Church. In Crete, the control of the authorities over the Janissaries and Cretan Turks was weak, and armed mobs rushed through the city streets, killing every Christian they could find. The hanging of the Bishop of Kíssamos in Khaniá, the murder of the Metropolitan of Iráklion together with his bishops, and the barbarous use of the *soúvla* (the old Turkish practice of impaling live prisoners on a stake), far from intimidating the Christians, aroused them to a fury. The revolutionaries were seized by a combination of blood lust and religious fervour, with overtones of sexual repression. Many "Soldiers of the Cross" vowed not to sleep with their wives during the war. No male prisoners were taken by the Christians, and captured Muslim women were similarly killed, apparently to prevent the physical and moral contamination of the *pallikária* by sexual contact with infidels. Many Sfakians enrolled in the "Brotherhood of the Church", a mysterious early Christian ceremony which dates back to the time of the Emperor Justinian, and was strictly forbidden by the Orthodox Church and the state. These ties of brotherhood were regarded as being as strong as those of blood, so that it was not later permitted to marry a close female relative of such a "Brother in Christ". No quarter was asked or given by either side and atrocities comparable to those at Trípolitsa on the mainland occurred.

For three years, the Turks lost effective control of Crete, the Sultan being hard-pressed in attempting to suppress the mainland revolt and unable to spare valuable troops to assist his Cretan garrisons. In 1824, having made little headway in his endeavours to control these rebellious Greeks, he made a deal with his powerful vassal, Mehmet Ali of Egypt. For his aid in defeating the insurgents, both in Crete and on the mainland, Mehmet would receive the Pashaliks of Crete and the Peloponnese.

Mehmet Ali was an Albanian leader who had assisted the British to drive Napoleon out of Egypt in 1801. He had been made Governor by the Sultan in 1805. In July, Mehmet Ali's son, Ibrahim Pasha, a competent and feared general, sailed from Alexandria with a powerful squadron of ships and began systematically by capturing and brutally sacking the seafaring island of Kássos (Kassiots still argue over how the island was betrayed), before attempting to reach Crete.

He was twice foiled by the Greek admiral, Andreas Miaoulis, before a mutiny of Hydriot sailors (their pay was in arrears) forced the Greek fleet back to Nauplia. It had been assumed that the Egyptians would not attempt naval operations in winter, but Ibrahim Pasha arrived at Soúda Bay during December, before continuing to the Peloponnese two months later. After landing at Modón, he captured Navaríno and eventually Messalónghi. For three bloody years he waged a bitter war against the rebels, a war which he very nearly won, but that is another story.

Many of Ibrahim Pasha's troops were Albanian mercenaries, and these were among the large army left in Crete under Khussein Bey in order to pacify the new Egyptian possession. Khussein Bey proceeded about his task with a cruelty at least equal to that shown by the Cretan fighters in their earlier attacks on the Turks. The population of Melidóni abandoned their village in the face of the advancing Egyptians and hid with their goods and animals within this cave, having supplies for six months. Their hiding place became known, but an intermediary sent by Khussein Bey to order the villagers to come out was shot down in the cave mouth, as was a Greek woman sent to offer safe conduct. Twenty-four Egyptian soldiers were killed in an attempt to rush the defenders. When they tried to block up the opening with rocks, the Cretans cleared them away overnight. Finally, Khussein had a great brushwood fire lit in the entrance, in order to fill the cave with smoke. The Egyptians cautiously waited eighteen days before sending in a Greek prisoner, who reported that all 300 had been suffocated. The English explorer, Pashley, was probably the next to enter the cave, in 1834. He wrote that: "The bones and skulls of the poor Christians are so thickly scattered, it is almost impossible to avoid crushing them as we pick our way along." The bones were high in every cranny where the victims had attempted to escape from the choking smoke.

It is a terrible story, and seems the more so in the dripping inner chambers of the cavern, out of sight of the entrance in the fitful candlelight. In spite of these horrors, the '21–'24 revolt did advance the cause of Cretan freedom. As the war on the mainland continued, the interest of Western politicians became engaged, quite apart from that of philhellene volunteers such as Lord Byron, Church and Cochrane. Ibrahim Pasha's campaign finally lost its impetus, Russia diverted Turkish attention by invading her territory and, most important of all, Admiral Codrington, commanding English and French warships, annihilated the Turkish and Egyptian fleets at Navaríno. Crete's minor insurrection of 1828 collapsed with the defeat of Hadzimichalis Daliannis at Frangokástello. The island secretly sent representatives to attend the Fourth National Assembly of Greece, held at Argos in the following year, but the motherland was in no position to protect her outlying populations still under the domination of the Ottoman Empire. In 1832, the tiny modern state of Greece was founded, with Prince Otto of Bavaria as its first king, but Crete was left for the moment, as the Sultan had promised, under the Pashalik of the Egyptian, Mehmet Ali.

At first, the change of ruler seemed to be to the Christians' advantage. It should be remembered, of course, that by this time the majority of Cretans had renounced their religion and turned Muslim. A few years before, the religious proportions were said to have been 200,000 Muslims to 60,000 Christians, and these renegades were, if anything, more resented by the Christians than the Turks themselves. Mehmet Ali installed the Albanian, Mustapha Pasha, to govern the island. A relatively humane and intelligent man, he realised that the Turkish settlers and renegade Cretans, who had been accustomed to lord it over the Christians during Turkish times, would be unlikely to accept Egyptian rule willingly. He therefore bolstered the Christian minority's power as much as possible. He announced that he intended "to establish the tranquillity and cause the prosperity of Crete, and to deliver the Christians from the vexations to which they were formerly exposed." Councils of representatives were established at Khaniá and Candia, the Christians being allotted more than their fair share of seats. Many exiles were now freely allowed to return.

The island over which Mustapha Pasha ruled was in a state of extreme devastation, the population having been halved by the two revolts. Pashley, the main source of information on this period, describes the once crowded Messará as "full of ruins from the '21". In many villages, the number of surviving males could be counted on one hand, and the people camped under the walls of the fire-blackened, roofless houses. He saw one village consisting entirely of widows and children. As already described, only 2 males out of 64 survived from the Kurmulidhes family, once so rich and powerful.

The honeymoon was short. The Albanian troops who remained in the countryside, like the Janissaries of earlier years, were barely under the control of their masters and their depredations caused great resentment. In spite of their promises, the Egyptians could no more than the Turks resist the temptation to squeeze the Cretans with heavy taxes. Mehmet Ali was already entitled to one-seventh of Crete's entire revenue, but, in addition, he imposed a tax on all wine produced, whether sold or drunk by the vintner, and increased the taxation on olive oil exports, together with many other commodities.

The new councils quickly became mere puppets in the hands of their president, a man of mixed Turkish-Egyptian race. In 1833, a strange law was proposed, which insisted that all land must be fully cultivated by the owners; mountaineers accustomed to live mainly by their flocks and by hunting, felt this to be an intolerable restriction on their freedom. The real purpose of this regulation was to increase Mehmet Ali's personal holdings – all uncultivated land fell to him by default. In villages where most of the adult male population had died during the revolt, full cultivation of the land was impossible.

In this year, Mehmet Ali made a personal visit to his possession, accompanied by Colonel Campbell, the British Consul General. In a temporarily magnanimous mood, he suggested that the Cretans should submit a petition, setting out the details of their grievances and, in due course, the document was given to Mustapha Pasha for onward transmission to Mehmet Ali. The list, it appears, was a long one, complaining of the many taxes, the quartering of ill-disciplined troops in the villages, and excessive use of the *bastinado*, a punishment involving the beating of the soles of the feet. Mustapha Pasha lost his nerve; he decided that it would be more than his life was worth to present such a document to his master. He therefore paid some fifty Greeks to draw up an alternative memorandum, which complained of nothing at all, but expressed only the "happiness and affection" of the Cretans under Egyptian rule. Mehmet Ali presumably smiled on reading this and continued imperiously back to Egypt. Colonel Campbell was totally taken in.

The aggrieved Cretans, after their recent and bitter experience of armed revolution, tried a peaceful approach for once. At the village of Mourniés, a few miles from Khaniá, they formed an Assembly to petition the authorities. At the same time, aware of the Great Powers' new interest in Greek matters, they sent deputations to the consuls of Great Britain, France and Russia. These officials, in some embarrassment, recommended that they return home quietly, but the Assembly, unarmed and composed of Muslims as well as Christians, remained at Mourniés. Mustapha Pasha sensibly took no precipitate action and gave them some vague assurances. As time went by, many Cretans returned to their villages and fields. A hard core remained, however, and finally Mehmet Ali, the man who had defeated the Mamelukes and ruled Egypt with a rod of iron, lost his patience. In spite of the intercession of Mustapha and the other pashas, he had ten of the Assembly hanged on 3 December and further executions took place elsewhere on the island *pour encourager les autres*.

For all Mehmet Ali's power, he depended largely on British goodwill. At the Convention of London, 15 July 1840, he agreed to cede Crete, Syria and Arabia back to the Sultan of Turkey, in return for which he and his descendants were formally confirmed in the hereditary title of Khedive of Egypt. When the Turks took over again, they retained the services of Mustapha Pasha, who was faced almost at once with a rebellion in Sfakiá, where a provisional government was formed and union with Greece declared. The rebellion was quickly crushed and King Otto of Greece was widely criticised for sending no assistance. All parties now realised that change was in the air and the Cretans constantly petitioned for new roads (it has been estimated that by the mid-nineteenth century the roads of Crete were in a worse condition than in the Minoan period), new schools and proper maintenance of port facilities. At the same time, they complained of high taxes, discrimination against Christians in the law courts and countless other matters. The creaking and monolithic Ottoman administration did little more than make promises. These petitions were sent not only to the pashas, but to the Russian Tsar, Queen Victoria and Napoleon III, for it was intended that the "Cretan Issue" should not be forgotten by the Powers.

The plan to unite Crete with Greece had many supporters at this time, including Lord Palmerston in England. The "Central Committee of Cretans" on the mainland advanced the cause of union with the Greek government. Unfortunately, the Great Powers were concerned with larger matters. In 1853, Tsar Nicholas I proposed that Russia be given a protectorate over all Orthodox Christian subjects of the Ottoman Empire. In return for Britain's acquiescence in this, he suggested that she annex Egypt and Crete into her own Empire. Turkey was now too weak to resist such pressure. Britain, however, saw this supposedly altruistic motive as a disguise for Russian expansionism, a first step in their plan to gain Constantinople and a foothold on the Mediterranean. The British rejection of the proposal resulted in the Crimean War of 1854-56. The Treaty of Paris, with which the war was concluded in 1856, stipulated that there should be no external interference in the affairs of the Ottoman Empire, and thus the Cretans found themselves once more isolated from the forces of liberty in the west.

In spite of all these reverses, the revolutionary movement in Crete had acquired a momentum of its own. It is remarkable that during Venetian rule the Cretans rebelled only under extreme provocation, but in the later Turkish period uprisings occurred constantly every few years. There was a scent of liberty in the air of the nineteenth century, and even in their remote mountains the Cretans could smell it. One feels that however benign and enlightened the Turkish administration, they would have constantly been forced to suppress a restless population. Cretans talked of nothing now but *énosis*, and it seemed that in spite of all they had suffered, the desire for freedom could not be stifled until finally it erupted again in the Great Revolt of 1866 and the holocaust at Arkádi.

Michael freely admits to feeling uneasy underground, and we were all relieved to regain the fresh air and brush down our muddy shoes. We sat on the side of the mountain for a while, eating oranges in the sunshine, while the distant sounds of the village below floated up to us through the clear air, mingled with the tinkling of goat bells. "A goat is indestructible," say the Cretans. "How can you harm the devil himself?" Nevertheless, when the time comes, they enjoy goat meat as much as any other.

An ancient blind woman was tapping her way across the bridge, seemingly oblivious to the motorcycle which roared by a few inches away from her. We waited for her to pass, and then drove on towards Iráklion through countryside which becomes increasingly more wooded. The normal sparse *phrýgana* of the open hillside is replaced by a maquis of bracken and Spanish broom, tree heather, myrtle, laurel and lentisk, chaste tree, Judas tree and Christ's thorn. The little hills are covered with thick groves of twisted holm oaks, where occasionally a thin curl of blue smoke indicates the presence of a charcoal burner engaged in his solitary vigil. Most village houses now possess a couple of burners operating on bottled gas, but charcoal is still used for the clay ovens and for grilling *souvlákia*, or occasionally in an iron brazier on the floor during cold weather. The narrow winding valleys with their little patches of field and vineyard have an air of secrecy, and seem in the spring to be as lush and green as parts of Devon. The scenery is on a small scale and friendly, the people are welcoming and altogether I like the look of these little villages surrounded by their fertile gardens as much as any on Crete.

We were approaching the great wine-producing areas of the island and vines were to be seen everywhere, some pruned back to barely knee-height, others supported on trellises nearly as tall as a man. In spite of the gentle domesticated appearance of the countryside, we came upon a great eagle circling low over a spinney, round and round, without even a wing-beat to increase its momentum. When we came too close, it simply banked and floated away over a ridge, leaving a fleeting impression of matt brown feathers untidily arranged in a massive span. The eagles follow the flocks, especially at lambing time, taking advantage of a death, an unprotected lamb or an afterbirth.

The name of the village of Drosiá indicates refreshment, and the *tavérnas* are famous for roast sucking pig, but it was still early and had some miles to cover. We were now close to the Psilorítis, although the surrounding foothills do not allow many views of the snowy giant. Emerging from the valley of the Mylopótamos, we had passed from the *nomós*, or prefecture, of Réthymnon to that of Iráklion. Up a rough track to the left lies the abandoned Monastery of Ayios Pantaleímon, where the painter, El Greco, may once have studied, and beyond is the village of Fódhele, which claims to be his birthplace. Further along the road is a right-hand turn which leads to the Minoan site at Tílissos, a series of villas excavated by Hadzidakis early in the century. A little further and we had crossed the New Road and were approaching the suburbs of Iráklion, still surrounded by vineyards bright with yellow March flowers, although the land looked dry and dusty.

CHAPTER 13

The Great Fortress

The Minotaur still grumbles and occasionally roars in its subterranean chambers below Iráklion, for the city is built on a fault and is notorious for earthquakes. Minor tremors are quite common and every generation or two comes a severe shock, such as those of 1926 and 1931. In addition, nearly a third of the city was destroyed during the Second World War, so that some of the population were forced to live in caves in the surrounding countryside for years afterwards. Even the streets remained unpaved until 1935. It is therefore unsurprising that much of the outer part of the city is new, concrete and rather unattractive. The "Street of the 62 Martyrs" is full of workshops and modern businesses: sheet-metal workers, garages, agricultural equipment retailers and the like. We entered the massive Venetian walls, fully forty-five yards thick in places, at the Khaniá Gate and drove straight through the city centre with its white-gloved traffic policemen, still known by the old Arabic name, the *mejdan*, and on to the Platía Elefthérias, Freedom Square, managing to find a parking place on the road down to the new port. From high above, the regular ferry in from Piraeus was dwarfed against the pier, and the sea glittered and sparkled in the bright sunlight.

The City of Heracles has changed its name in the most confusing way over the years, and I hope I will be forgiven for referring to it elsewhere as Candia or Megalokástro. No Minoan remains have been found, but the Palace of Knossós a few miles inland would almost certainly have maintained a port here. In the first century AD, Strabo describes the port of Knossós, using the name Herakleium, after the seventh labour of Heracles, the capture of the Cretan bull. This bull had been sent to Minos by Poseidon, God of the Sea, in order that the king might sacrifice it to him. But according to the legend, Minos so admired the magnificent white animal that he kept it unharmed and the enraged Poseidon drove the bull mad, so that it did great damage around Crete until Heracles came to restrain it. Yet another Cretan bull legend, quite apart from the Minotaur, and Zeus and Europa!

In the early Byzantine period, this place was called "Kastro", so we can assume that there was a fortress or castle here. The known history of the city really begins when the Arab Emir, Abu Hafs Omar, arrived with forty ships to conquer Crete in 824, having been driven out of Cordoba. This Saracen pirate (the Greeks are believed to have given the Arabs the name of Saracen, from the Arabic word *sharc*, or east) landed in Crete and promptly burned his ships, a dramatic gesture to remind his men that they must fight or die for such a rich prize. He built a fort with a ditch here and named it "Rabdh al Khandak", the "Castle of the Moat". There is a story that the exact site on which to build the fortress was indicated to the Emir by a hermit living on this coast. The occupation by Spanish Saracens lasted until 961, but there was little building or colonisation as they only required Crete as a base for their piratical forays. They must eventually have rebuilt their fleet, for in 901 they sailed north to sack the city of Salonika. During the period of Arab occupation, Constantinople made five attempts to recover Crete, two of them at the instigation of the Emperor, Michael the Stammerer (one feels instant sympathy), but without success.

In 961, the Byzantine general, Nicephorus Phokas, commanding a new and powerful fleet, beseiged the city of Al Khandak. The fortress was strong, and it was plain that the siege would be a long drawn-out affair. Phokas received intelligence that a relief force of Arabs from Asia and Africa was secretly on its way to attack his army in the rear. When he heard that they had landed, Phokas sent a number of Armenians to ambush them at night, which they did with great success and much slaughter. Nicephorus Phokas then achieved a grim reputation for himself by having the severed heads of these defeated Arabs catapulted over the walls of the citadel.

Other strange things occurred during the ten months of the siege. On one occasion, an Arab woman of remarkable ugliness climbed up into one of the towers and began to treat the Byzantine army below to a tirade of insults and curses, before exposing herself to them in a series of obscene positions. The simple, superstitious soldiers believed that this must be a witch casting the evil eye on them, and terror spread through the army before an archer had the presence of mind to shoot her down from her perch. Later, in a moment of boredom, the besiegers amused themselves by catapulting a living donkey into the city. When the Arabs finally surrendered through starvation on 7 March the following year, the Greeks sacked the city, but Nicephorus Phokas treated the Arab ruler and his family with courtesy and had them taken to Constantinople.

Crete was once more in the fold of Byzantium, but in a state of devastation. The ancient capital at Górtyna had been in ruins for more than a century. The old episcopal cities of Kydonía, Sýbritos, Láppa, Kíssamos, Khersónnisos, Ierápetra and Knossós were destroyed. Phokas began to rebuild the administration of the island, appointing an Archbishop of Crete, seated now in Al Khandak, where a new cathedral dedicated to St Titus was to be built. Under the Archbishop, metropolitans were assigned to new territories and there are villages named Episkopí to this day to mark the sites of their palaces. The castle of Teménos was built on the important route to the Messará, and Phokas introduced a feudal system with a Duke of Crete at its summit, supported by a Byzantine aristocracy, and in which the defeated Arabs found themselves the serfs of Cretan masters. Two years after Nicephorus Phokas left Crete, he became Emperor, and the Byzantine fleet became once more the dominant force in the eastern Mediterranean, eventually recapturing Cyprus also.

Little is known of life on Crete in the second Byzantine period. It seems likely that Constantinople despatched groups of colonists to strengthen trade and commerce. It is known that the Emperor Alexius Comnenus I also sent a mysterious group of privileged Byzantine noble families to provide Crete with an aristocratic ruling class of known pedigree. Far from being resented for their extensive grants of land, these *archontópouli* in later centuries achieved a charismatic hold over the minds of Cretans, although it is unlikely that all the claimants were genuinely descended from the original twelve families. These were the clans who led the rebellions against the Venetians, and it is intriguing to consider that some at least of these families must be directly descended through Byzantium from the patricians of the Roman Empire. By this time, the name of the Arab citadel had been corrupted to "Khandax", or something similar.

Crete was again in the Empire, but far from secure, as the Empire itself was under constant threat from the growing power of the Muslim races to the east. In spite of occasional periods of vigour, Byzantium was steadily weakening, seemingly unaware of the steady barbarian encroachment around their island of ancient, crystallised civilisation. Perhaps the cruellest blow of all was struck by fellow Christians during the disastrous Fourth Crusade to the Holy Land, led by Prince Boniface of Montferrat. He had intended to begin by conquering Egypt, but his allies, the Venetians, who had by now established themsleves as the main naval power in the Levant, enjoyed favourable trading relationships with Egypt and the Muslims of the Holy Land. They had ideas of their own, more connected with profit than religious fervour, and they persuaded the Crusade to turn on Constantinople, the city which they had ostensibly come to protect being taken and sacked in 1204. Count Baldwin of Flanders was made Emperor in place of Alexius III, and the Empire was carved up. Much of the Orthodox Christian hate for Roman Catholicism must stem not from the schism, but from the time of this treacherous action.

Prince Boniface himself received Crete, which does not appear to have been to his taste, for on 12 August 1204 he signed the *Refutatio Cretae*, which gave the Venetians title to the island in exchange for 1,000 silver marks and the mainland territory of Salonika. The Venetians were delighted, for Crete was one of the key positions in their plan to control the sea routes to the east and give them access to the caravans which came overland with the fabulous riches of Asia.

Unfortunately for them, while all this horse-trading was taking place, the Genoese Enrico Pescatore, Count of Malta, had quietly landed on Crete and was now firmly in the saddle. The Genoese had much the same trading ambitions as the Venetians and the Cretans seemed to favour them. It was not until 1212 that Venice was able to defeat the interloper and take over the new acquisition, and even after this Genoa continued to harass them for a considerable time. In 1293 they captured Khaniá with the aid of Cretan rebels and managed to hold the city for some years.

The first Venetian Rector (or Governor), Jacopo Tiepolo, renamed "Khandax" as "Candia", which became gradually extended to the whole island. This is the name by which Crete and its capital was known to Franks, or West Europeans, until recent times (Shakespeare called it Candy). The Venetians were in many ways admirable and energetic colonists, determined to make the most of the island's resources. They were also capable of extreme and calculated cruelty towards subject peoples who would not co-operate. They imposed heavy taxation on agricultural produce, whatever the actual yield of the harvest in any given year, and forced Cretans into service in the galleys of their navy and the building of their great fortresses. Some noble Cretan families collaborated and grew wealthy in the general expansion of commerce. Others, less fortunate, lost their lands and property to Venetian colonists and took to the mountains of Sfakiá, Ida and Lassíthi, to nurse their bitterness while living as brigands, ambushing the conquerors' mule trains on their way through the passes to the south.

There were a bewildering series of rebellions in the early period of Venetian rule. Almost immediately after taking office as Rector, Tiepolo had to call for reinforcements to quash an uprising. The centralised administration from Venice, together with high taxes, alienated some of her own colonists, who rose in 1268, in an attempt to achieve independence. In the last twenty years of the thirteenth century, the Cretan *árchonte*, Alexios Kallergis, rebelled and caused havoc until the Rector was obliged to come to terms, making him a Knight of Venice. The divided Kallergis family were involved on both sides in the revolution of 1333, and in 1341 Leon Kallergis attempted to enlist the aid of the Turks against Venice. When the Venetians captured him, he was sewn in a sack and thrown in the sea.

In spite of all these problems, the Venetians were steadily re-building and fortifying. The Governor-Duke Dandolo's taxation demands to raise money for the repair of Candia harbour in 1362 led to an uprising of Venetian knights, who destroyed St Mark's banner in Candia and publicly renounced Catholicism for the Orthodox Church. This brought the Cretan *árchontes* in on their side, including the Kallergis family again, and an independent "Republic of St Titus" was proclaimed. Such a serious revolution, based on the remote plateau of Lassíthi, was only put down with difficulty, using reinforcements from Italy and other Venetian possessions in Greece.

All this time, the power of the Ottoman Turkish Empire was growing. At one time, the Greeks, under the Byzantine Emperor Justin II, had contracted an alliance with a war-like tribe from Central Asia in order to help protect Byzantium from the Huns and the trade route to China from the Persians. Later they were to regret their friendship with this wild group of Seljuk, Turkmen and Krim Tartar herdsmen who had wandered into Asia Minor and become converted to Islam. Under their leader, Orkhan, son of Othman, they pressed forward to the west and overran the Asiatic part of the Byzantine Empire. Orkhan founded the tribute of fifth sons, the "New Soldiers", or Janissaries, who were to be in the vanguard of each new conquest. The Greeks, or "Citizens of Rome", as they called themselves, seemed to have believed, in the face of all the evidence, that Byzantium and the Orthodox Church were everlasting and immutable. This, in spite of the fact that the Empire now consisted only of the City, Salonika and the Peloponnese. In 1453, their world and the Roman Empire of the East finally came to an end.

The fall of Constantinople on 29 May 1453 to the Turks is to this day neither forgiven, nor forgotten, in the minds of the Greek people, particularly as the Turks proceeded to make it the capital of their Empire. The City fell on a Tuesday, a day which has been declared unlucky and ill-starred ever since. The legend is that Constantine built the City, and a Constantine will return to take it back, for no one saw Constantine XI die while the hordes of Asiatic soldiers with the green flag of the Prophet at their head rushed into the great cathedral of Ayía Sofia. Surely they were silenced for a moment in these awesome surroundings as they realised the magnitude of their achievement. They had turned the world upside down. Mehmet II, "The Conqueror", is said to have murmured these lines from Saadi as he walked through the remains of the Emperor's palace: "The spider spins his web in the Palace of the Caesars, And the owl sings her watchsong on the Towers of Afrasiab."

Nikos Kazantzakis described sailing past Constantinople on a Greek ship bound for the Black Sea during the dangerous time of the population exchanges:

We left the Greek coast behind us; one morning Constantinople came palely into view on the shadowy horizon.

A gentle rain was falling; the white minarets and black cypresses pierced the fog like masts from a sunken city. Saint Sophia, the palaces, and the half-crumbled imperial walls were lost in the silent, despairing rain. Crowding all together at the ship's bow, we struggled to make our gaze bore through the thick mist in order to see.

One of my companions cursed. "Damn her, the whore! Sleeping with Turks!" His eyes filled with tears.

"Over the years, in time, she'll be ours once more," murmured another.

(Nikos Kazantzakis, *Report to Greco*)

Byzantium, Constantinople, Miklagard, the Polis, Istanbul: through the centuries the peoples of the East have dreamed of possessing her. The Roman imperial eagle gained a second head in 330 when Constantine founded the Eastern Empire, and this symbol lived on after the fall until 1917, as the emblem of Russia, for Tsar Ivan III had married a Paleologue princess. Once the Russians also longed to own the city they planned to name Tsarograd.

Sultan Mehmet, from the first, showed great political astuteness. Far from attacking the Orthodox Church, he installed with his own hands a new Patriarch with magnificent ritual and even greater powers than before. Thus he neatly emphasised that all power in the Empire flowed from him, and that he would rule the Greek people through the hierarchy of their own church.

Cretans fought in the defence of the City and their ships brought the dreadful news back to Candia. A flood of refugees began to reach Crete, some carrying priceless manuscripts salvaged from the City's libraries, although much, including plays by Euripides, had been burned and lost for ever. Crete became an important centre for copying these manuscripts which eventually reached the West via Venice and, in this way, saved much of Hellenistic culture from being lost to us. Cretans, such as Markos Mousouros, edited the works of Plato, Sophocles, Aristophanes and Euripides for the Aldine Press in Venice. Crete, once regarded as a remote and primitive outpost, suddenly found itself the artistic and literary centre of the Greek world. As Ancient Greek and Venetian influences mingled, that strange phenomenon known as the Cretan Renaissance came about. The fall of the City brought the last great chance for the healing of the schism between Orthodoxy and Roman Catholicism, in the vision of the Siennese scholar, Aeneas Silvius Piccolomini. As Pope Pius II, he worked to persuade the Catholic princes of Western Europe to launch a last great crusade, with the aim of recovering the City and the Empire for Christianity, and simultaneously uniting the divided church. The great project died with him.

Venice kept a fearful eye on the rising Ottoman tide; they were well aware that Crete was equally important to the Turks. In 1522 the Sultan, Suleiman the Magnificent, turned the Knights Hospitallers out of Rhodes, and they passed through Crete on their way to Malta. Turkish pirates had been a major hazard to coastal towns and villages for many years, carrying off the people as slaves. This was not an occasional, but a regular hazard of life in those days. Pashley claimed that during the entire Venetian occupation, the population decreased from 500,000 to 200,000, due to the depredations of the pirates, loss of life and exile during the various revolts, and a series of plagues which swept the island.

In 1538 Khaireddin Barbarossa arrived in Cretan waters: no ordinary pirate, but in command of two hundred ships borrowed from Suleiman the Magnificent, with conquest in mind as well as the taking of livestock and slaves to feed the markets of Algiers. In two cruises through the Aegean, he had already captured a number of smaller islands, including Santoríni nearby. Barbarossa sailed along the north coast of Crete, leaving a trail of plundered and burning villages, and sacking the town of Réthymnon. The walls of Candia, then in the process of being strengthened by the military engineer Sanmicheli from Verona, were enough to deter him, however, as he preferred hit-and-run tactics to a prolonged siege. In 1571, coincident with a rebellion in Sfakiá, the Turks returned to western

Crete and burned unfortunate Réthymnon again. In the same year, under Selim the Sot, they captured Cyprus from Venice. By 1585, the Venetian Bailiff at Constantinople was reporting that large numbers of Greek refugees were reaching the City from Crete, in order to escape famine and tyranny. Many were skilled craftsmen who took jobs in the shipyards. These men talked to the Turks of the unprepared condition of the Venetian fortifications, the shortage of food and the dissatisfaction of the Greek population with Venetian rule. The Turks listened with interest.

Venice was badly frightened, and reacted by sending out one of their most forceful and competent administrators to take command of the island and organise its defence. Giacomo Foscarini, Proveditore-General and Dictator of the Island of Candia by decree of the Serene Republic, arrived in 1574 and immediately set about reforming the administration and feudal systems which had become largely corrupt. Military service was now a matter to be taken seriously, and fortresses were built as rapidly as possible at Gramboúsa, Soúda Bay and Spinalónga. Sanmicheli's enlarged walls at Candia were now considered to be the strongest in the world. A major setback must have been the return of the plague in 1592. Over half the population of the city died, with obvious weakening of the defences.

In the event, the attack did not come until 1645 when, as already described, the Turks landed in the west and took Khaniá. In that year, the Maltese Knights of St John had plundered Turkish ships of gold and, it is said, women bound for the harem of the Sultan. They sheltered in a Cretan port, before returning home, and this was considered by the Sultan to be sufficient justification for the attack on Crete. Three years later, having swallowed up Réthymnon on the way, the Turks began to besiege Candia. Venice attached an importance to this last city almost beyond reason. They knew that if Candia was lost, there would never be any hope of regaining control of the eastern trade on which their wealth had been founded, and so the Republic went to extraordinary lengths to raise money for the cost of defence. The Venetians still had access to the harbour to supply the garrison, and their ships continued to harass and distract the Turkish convoys elsewhere in the Mediterranean. At other times, the Venetian fleet lay close to the deserted island of Nísos Día, now a reserve for the Cretan ibex, which can be seen from the walls of the city. The defenders were not only Venetians, but also the Knights of Malta, together with mercenaries from the Greek mainland, France, Savoy and various Italian and German states, to the number of ten thousand under the command of Francesco Morosini. The Cretans in the countryside for the most part seemed to favour the Turks.

After eighteen years and immense expenditure on powder and shot by both sides, the situation was very little altered. The walls remained intact, although the dwelling places within the town had been reduced to a shambles by the bombardment. In exasperation, the Grand Vizier, Ahmed Kuprili, took personal command of the besieging forces and began to press the defenders so hard that in 1669, at the Pope's request, King Louis XIV of France sent ships and seven thousand troops to aid the garrison. When these reinforcements arrived, red flags were flown from the towers and all the bells of the city were rung for what seemed to be deliverance from their long ordeal. In fact, it was the beginning of the end.

The new force was jointly led by the Dukes of Beaufort and Navailles, the former losing his life in a sortie soon after their arrival. There was talk of Venetian cowardice on this occasion, and the Duke of Navailles refused to initiate any further sorties unless 4,000 Venetians would lead the way through the surrounding Turkish fortifications. Morosini, the garrison commander, demurred on the grounds that his soldiers were weakened and exhausted – after two decades of siege some must have grown quite old within the walls. The French eventually went home, and other volunteers of different nationalities gradually melted away until Morosini was at last left with only his 4,000 Venetians. Realising the hopelessness of the situation and wishing to avoid further slaughter, Morosini surrendered Candia on 5 September 1669, after twenty-two years, three months and twenty-seven days, the longest siege Europe has ever known.

The terms were honourable: the garrison to leave unhindered within twelve days and Venice to keep her island fortresses at Gramboúsa, Soúda Bay and Spinalónga. During the twelve days, it was said that an extraordinary and unaccustomed silence reigned over the city while Venetian and Turkish soldiers met peaceably under the ramparts to salute each other with respect and discuss their past struggles. In no case was the truce disturbed. At the peace conference, the Englishman, Colonel Thomas Anand, was one of Morosini's representatives, while the Greek, Paniogotes Nikouses, advised the Grand Vizier. This man later rose to the post of Grand Dragoman of the Sublime Porte, the first of many Greeks to reach high positions within the Ottoman Empire. The statistics of the siege are stupendous, and read more like those of a battle in the Great War than one of the seventeenth century. The Turks lost 119,000 killed and wounded, the Venetians 31,000. The Venetian batteries fired more than a quarter of a million cannon-balls, using 50,000 tons of powder, 18 million pounds of lead and 13 million pounds of wick. The

Turks claimed to have fired 100,000 cannon-balls and stated that seven Pashas had died, eighty Principal Officers and over 10,000 of their elite Janissaries, besides the other militia.

After twelve days, the city now being virtually empty of civilians, except for a tiny colony of Jews, a citizen formally handed over the keys of Candia to the Vizier, and received in turn the courteous gift of a robe and gold coin. The Vizier wished to extend a similar gift to Morosini, who declined politely. While the Turks marched in through the breached walls at the San Andrea bastion, the tattered defenders went down the hill to their ships. Most educated Cretans left too: poets, writers and painters, carrying the manuscripts and remnants of Hellenic and Byzantine culture to the relative safety of the Ionian islands. The preserved head of St Titus, the most famous relic of the island, was embarked for Venice, and Crete was left to Islam and the *pallikária*.

Under the treaty of 1669, the forts at Soúda, Gramboúsa and Spinalónga remained in the Venetians' hands. Yet the Turks took pains to isolate these islands from any contact with the Greek population. Any Cretans found to have had dealings with the Venetians were either impaled on the *soúvla*, or dropped on a frame covered with iron butchers' hooks known as a *gaunche*, and left to die in agony. In 1691 the fortress at Gramboúsa was lost to the Turks, but the following year, Domenigo Mocenigo, the Venetian Captain-General, persuaded 2,000 Cretans to rebel and attack Khaniá from the land, while Venetian ships supported them from the sea. The rebellion was a failure, but Mocenigo embarked the defeated Cretans and gave them land in the Venetian Peloponnese, where whole Cretan villages were founded, in the Máni and elsewhere, and where the Cretan 'akis' surname suffix is still common.

While Franks continued to refer to the city as Candia during Turkish rule and well into this century, Cretans called it *Megálo Kástro*, the Great Fort. Old people still sometimes call it *Kástro*, and the inhabitants are known as *Kastrini*, renowned for shrewdness in money-making. The archaic name of Iráklion was officially re-adopted in 1922.

Perhaps the best way to see the city today is to take a walk around Sanmicheli's famous walls, still largely intact, in spite of the efforts of the Turks and the more drastic changes of the twentieth century. The walls have now been cleared of the clutter of later buildings and undergrowth which used to obscure them, and one can follow them for three kilometres, completely encircling the landward side of the old city and passing seven great bastions. Until this century, the original four Venetian gates remained in use; now only the Khaniá, or Pantocrator Gate, on the west and the Kainoúria Pórta, or New Gate, to the south can be seen. The Harbour Gate was destroyed by the English Admiral Noel, when bombarding Turkish rioters in 1898, while the nearby Ayios Yeoryios Gate was demolished in 1913 during the building of Eleftherías Square.

While Pandelis Prevelakis has provided us with a guide to old Réthymnon, his friend, Nikos Kazantzakis, has done the same in his own way, for his birthplace. In the monumental novel, *Freedom and Death*, set in the Megalokástro of the late nineteenth century, Kazantzakis freely drew on the experiences of his own family and childhood. This, more than any other work, captures the extraordinary and unreal atmosphere of the *pallikária*'s fanatical struggle against the Turks, an atmosphere so charged and dramatic that the novel has been described as surreal. Yet it has the ring of truth, for many events were taken from life. The young Kazantzakis experienced the terror of a Turkish massacre of Christians, standing beside his father who kept a loaded gun aimed at the street door. After the riot, his father forced this little boy to kiss the cold feet of the three Christians the Turks had hanged from the branches of the infamous plane tree, which must have stood on the site of Eleftherías Square. The ferocious Captain Michales was very largely based on the author's father, the product of a society where scholarship was scorned and physical courage admired above all things, where the ancient books and parchments from monastery libraries were cut up to make cartridge cases, and lead stripped from the church roofs to make bullets.

The Megalokástro of *Freedom and Death*, barely a hundred years ago, seems almost a mediaeval city behind its great walls, manned by a Turkish garrison: "At nightfall, the trumpets were sounded, the guards picked up the keys and double-locked the city gates. Till sunrise, no one could leave or enter." (Nikos Kazantzakis, *Freedom and Death*)

As one looks harder, traces of this older city can be seen beneath the modern veneer. The Ayios Yeoryios Gate was also known as the Lazaretto Gate, for here the lion-faced lepers would cluster to beg for alms from travellers before returning at night to their village of Meskínia outside the walls. They were still there when Arthur Evans came to Knossós. Kazantzakis also calls this place the Three Vaults, for there were three bores or tunnels in the wall, choked early in the morning by the cursing drivers of mules, loaded with fresh produce for the city's market. Today, Dimokratías Street leads to an open gap in the wall, but the map provides a clue, for the road above is still known as Treís Kamáres, the "Three Arches".

About halfway round the wall, the Martinengo Bastion projects to the south, and here Nikos Kazantzakis was buried, following his death in Germany in 1957. The author is much admired in Crete, but perhaps less so by his Greek literary contemporaries. The name of the man claimed to have been one of the greatest writers of the twentieth century by such as Mann and Schweitzer was forwarded several times to the Nobel Committee, but he never received the prize. His champions say that the Greek Government brought political pressure to bear, on the grounds that if not a communist, he was a fellow traveller. At one time perhaps he was, but it is a ludicrous over-simplification of such a complex character to categorise him so neatly. In his autobiography, *Report to Greco*, he described the four successive influences on his thinking as Christ, Buddha, Lenin and Odysseus. He grappled with many philosophies, but he never lost his love for his birthplace and was always a patriot. During the dangerous and disturbed time of the population exchanges, he worked for his fellow Greeks in Thrace, Macedonia and the Caucasus, where they found themselves under attack from Bolsheviks and Kurds alike.

The Orthodox Church, more accustomed to unquestioning faith and obedience than to Kazantzakis' independent, sometimes arrogant, approach to spiritual matters, refused to grant him a religious burial. Whatever his views on the existence of a supreme deity, he was nothing if not anti-clerical in some of his writing, and once the very mention of his name to a priest would be certain to result in a change of subject. The Church initially made trouble about the famous inscription – "I hope for nothing, I fear nothing, I am free" – as smacking of atheism, and in 1963 someone damaged his tombstone with a charge of dynamite. This was a harsh judgement on a man who claimed that he "wrestled with God" all his life and once seriously considered becoming a monk. "Water sleeps, but souls do not", he wrote of his anguished uncertainty, and on the nature of faith itself:

Three kinds of souls, three prayers:
1. I am a bow in your hands, Lord. Draw me lest I rot.
2. Do not overdraw me, Lord. I shall break.
3. Overdraw me, Lord, and who cares if I break!

(Nikos Kazantzakis, *Report to Greco*)

The Church has now relented so far as to set up a plain wooden cross at the grave.

There are fine views from the city wall. The island of Nísos Día to the north is sometimes known as Dragon Island from its shape. The stock of ibex is now said to be diluted by inter-breeding with wild goats which also roam the island. Curiously, the place is overrun with rabbits, which are unknown on Crete itself, where there are only hares in the mountains. Inland, one can see Mount Strombóúlas, with the Chapel of the Crucified at its peak, and the strange, isolated Mount Ioúchtas, supposedly shaped like the profile of the reclining Zeus. In the south-west, further in the distance, are the snows of the Ida range.

I don't suppose that many travellers will come to Crete and fail to visit the Archaeological Museum at Iráklion, probably combined with a trip to Knossós a few miles to the south. One could spend several days studying the detailed displays, but if pressed for time, or one of those whose expression becomes slightly glazed during the discussion of Minoan culture, you can see the best features in a couple of hours. The museum stands by the city wall, close to Eleftherías Square by a little garden with a monument to the Duc de Beaufort, and rather a fine view down to the harbour. The lobby is a noisy, bustling place, as are most of the rooms. Greeks don't feel it necessary to whisper in museums and chat away at full volume over the heads of the seated attendants, who on this particular day were all hunched over electric fires – it must have been all of twenty degrees outside in the sunshine! Perhaps this susceptibility to cold weather is the result of living in a city where forty-six degrees centigrade has at times been recorded in the shade during a hot summer day.

We emerged from the museum in time for a very late lunch in the square. Iráklion is at its most modern here, where the brightly striped awnings of the cafés and restaurants run far out to the street in Parisian style, so that you can watch the world, or at least the traffic, go by. The restaurant took a pride in its appearance; the tablecloths were spotless and a waiter in an immaculate white jacket brought us Amstel beer and fruit juice while we rested our weary feet. Did lepers really beg at the gate over there, just a few years ago? A Mercedes taxi stopped, and an elderly man in mountaineer's dress got out; his high boots shone like glass, while his tweed jacket and smartly-cut riding breeches would have looked in place at an English fox hunt. Other customers, businessmen perhaps, or office workers on the late Greek lunch hour, fingered their worrybeads, read their papers or chatted over coffee and ouzo, as if the afternoon had no ending. 'Khaniá for arms; Réthymnon for book learning; Iráklion for drinking . . .'

We walked down Dikeosinis Street, past the old Turkish barracks which now house the Prefecture and the office of the Tourist Police. The shops in this part of Iráklion are glossy enough to indicate that plenty of money is spent here, and it cannot all come from tourism. Furriers, jewellers and luxury furnishings are represented in abundance, and we particularly noticed ornate wedding dresses with delicate lace trimmings. The nearby statue of Daskaloyiannis looked grim and out of place amidst all this modern frivolity.

Venizélos Square is sometimes still called Fountain Square, after the fine Venetian fountain by Francesco Morosini (the uncle of the commander during the siege). It was built in 1647, but the four lions incorporated in it are much older. Across the square, with its book-shops, is the thirteenth-century century Basilica of St Mark, used as a mosque during Turkish times, but now restored. Inside is a collection of reproductions of some of the best early Byzantine frescoes from the churches of Crete, many of them having been painted or plastered over in later centuries. This is a rewarding visit, for you will have to drive many miles to see all the originals, scattered as they are in the remotest corners of the island. The old Venetian Armoury, a little further on, is now the City Hall, with a seventeenth-century loggia, which has been restored after earthquake damage. A few yards away is the Church of Ayios Títos, the island's patron saint. Founded in Byzantine times, the church was added to by the Venetians, and then turned into a mosque by the Turks when they took Candia. It reverted to the Orthodox Church in 1923 as the last Muslims left, and in 1966 Venice finally returned the skull of St Titus which it had held since 1669. However, the Venetians are still keeping the church's other great relic, the icon of the Virgin Messopanditissa, which remains in Santa Maria della Salute in that city.

Across 25th August Street is a modern park, named after El Greco, that mysterious figure who managed to combine his Byzantine style of painting with the Renaissance, and thus to bridge the gap between the mediaeval and the modern world. Domenico Theotokopoulos was born in 1541, and was always known to have come from the island of Candia, often signing himself "The Cretan", not just "The Greek". His birthplace at Fódhele to the west of the city was only established (or virtually established), during this century by the discovery of references to a family of this name in contemporary documents. The supposed family home is now no more than a ruin, and little is known of Theotokopoulos until he arrived in Rome at the age of 29. He may have spent some years in Venice as a student of Titian. After studying Michelangelo and Mannerism, he moved on to Toledo in 1577, where he lived until his death in 1614, painting actively all over Spain.

El Greco was undoubtedly a genius, quite unconcerned with realism or nature, a visionary whose paintings, like those of William Blake, came from his innermost thoughts rather than the world around him. His figures, while possessing all the richness of Italian colour, have an ethereal, mystical quality, distorted and elongated. Some say that his eyesight was actually physically defective and he suffered from astigmatism. Heavens populated by angels, and crowds of sinners floating unsupported in the air show the Byzantine influence. His work, invariably spiritual and heroic, was not always well received – it is recorded that Philip II of Spain, patron of Titian and collector of Bosch, neither understood, nor admired the *Martyrdom of St Maurice* which he commissioned from El Greco. Even the wonderful painting *Espolio* was at first refused by Toledo Cathedral, although it seems that his adopted city eventually realised his worth. *The Burial of Count Orgaz* still hangs in the Church of San Tomé, an enormous and disturbing canvas, full of movement and hallucination.

25th August Street, which takes its name from the day of the massacre in 1898, runs past a street named for Epimenides, and down by the old Jewish and Armenian quarters to the Venetian inner harbour. The largely undamaged fortress on the mole, still known by the Turkish name of *Koúles*, was once a hated prison where Cretan rebels were left to rot. As at Khaniá, the Venetians constructed vaulted chambers, or *arsenali*, at the harbour for ship-building and some parts remain. Another curiosity is the old salt warehouse, for this commodity was once a highly-prized government monopoly. Slightly inland from the west of the harbour is the Historical Museum, which takes over from the Archaeological Museum, beginning in the early Christian period. There are various objects found at the Basilica of Ayios Títos at Górtyna, together with Byzantine frescoes, icons, Venetian sculpture and Turkish remains. Also on display are reconstructions of a peasant dwelling from the turn of the century, Kazantzakis' study at Antibes and the study of the Réthymniot, Emanuel Tsouderos, Prime Minister of Greece during the Battle of Crete and the later stages of the war.

Nearer the centre of the city, in a square of the same name, stands Ayía Ekateríni, the Church of St Katherine. This building was a centre of learning during the sixteenth and seventeenth centuries: the "Mount Sinai Monastery School" of the Cretan Renaissance, where theology and art were taught. The church is now a museum of religious art and contains work from all over Crete. It has been claimed that El Greco studied here, but it is certainly known that his contemporary, Michael Damaskinos, did so, and six of his finest paintings are displayed: *The Burning Bush, The Adoration of the Magi, The Last Supper, Noli Me Tangere, The Divine Liturgy* and *The Ecumenical Council.* Damaskinos, like El Greco, travelled west to Venice, and the early paintings are very Italian in style. The theologians, Meletios Pigas and Kyrillos Loukaris, who became Patriarchs of Alexandria and Constantinople respectively, were also once students of the school. The Patriarch Kyrillos, together with the Cretan Pope Alexander V, worked for the reunion of the Orthodox, Catholic and Protestant churches. Another learned Cretan of this period, Nathaniel Canopus, was at Balliol College, Oxford, for ten years, and is said to have brought the habit of coffee drinking into England.

Across the square is the Church of St Menas, the protector of the city, and both the building and the mystical figure of the saint feature prominently in *Freedom and Death.* Cutting across to 1866 Street, which serves as the city's market, one can walk down to Kornaros Square, with its beautiful Turkish fountain and the earlier Bembo Fountain, which incorporates a headless Roman statue from Ierápetra. Vincenzo Kornaros from near Sitía, the greatest writer of the Cretan Renaissance, is famous above all for the epic romantic poem *Erotokritos*, written shortly before Candia fell. A poem of courtly love, in fifteen syllable couplets, obviously influenced by the Italians, the *Erotokritos* strikes some as stilted and repetitive – it is certainly long. Kornaros seems to have appreciated the vulnerability of the society he lived in and the threat of the dark age coming:

> Whoever seeks the great things of this world,
> And does not know how here he is a traveller on the road,
> But takes pride in his nobility, boasts of his wealth,
> I hold him a cipher, he is to be accounted mad,
> These things are blossoms and flowers, they pass by,
>   they are gone,
> And the times change them, often they destroy them.
> Like glass they shatter, like smoke they are gone,
> They never stand unshaken, but they run away, they go . . .

> (Trs. Michael Llewellyn Smith, *The Great Island*)

Whether you enjoy the epic or not, it cannot be denied that to modern Greek literature, as well as to folk consciousness, it has assumed an importance comparable with the works of Homer. There has always been a love of poetry and song among the peasants and fishermen of Greece, which would be quite unfamiliar to English working people. Perhaps it has been a comfort during the centuries of enslavement and sustained hope during prolonged sufferings. The *Erotokritos*, a sort of *Midsummer Night's Dream* more than ten thousand lines in length, came to assume an extraordinary significance to the Greeks before they became a nation, a unifying force which they could identify with their national aspirations. It entered the folklore of Crete, recited by professional ballad singers, and many of the couplets have separately found their way into the island's *mantinádes*. The poem was handed down through word of mouth by illiterate country people and it was not uncommon, until recently, to hear all the ten thousand lines recited from memory. In 1669, it was carried away to Venice with the exodus from Candia, and here it was actually published for the first time in 1713, in acknowledgement of its popularity among the Greek island people. The modern Greek poet and Nobel Prize winner, George Seferis, particularly championed the poem and described hearing it among the Greeks of Asia Minor from sailors who: ". . . recited to me in childhood the song of *Erotokritos* with tears in their eyes."

CHAPTER 14

Ayios Nikólaos

Back in Liberty Square, having inspected the statues of Kazantzakis and Venizelos, we went down through the St George Gate to the shops and businesses of Icarus Street to find our car adorned with a parking ticket – we didn't take it personally, every other car in the street had one too. Rather sheepishly, we drove off through the crowded suburb of Póros, past the outer harbour and the airport. Even here, they found a Minoan tomb when excavating for building foundations. Further along the road, at the mouth of the Kairatos River, is Katsamba, once the harbour for Knossós, and where a vase with the cartouche of Pharaoh Tuthmosis III was found. A little later, we were bowling along the New Road to the east, past an area of brash coastal development which we didn't remember from our last visit, dominated by the great radar bowls mounted on the hills above by the nearby American airforce base. We slowed momentarily in the town of Mália with its banana plantations under polythene. Banana cultivation is new to Greece, and brought with it a series of jokes on the lines of "so now we're really a banana republic". Then we climbed into the mountains across the base of Cape Ayios Ioánnis, through twin-bore tunnels and into the narrow valley by Neápoli, whose roofs are scattered below the road, and then past the old windmills of Nikithianós. After only a few more minutes on the new highway, we reached the first turn-off for Ayios Nikólaos on the Gulf of Mirabéllo, and ran down into the centre of the town.

Venizelos Square, with its memorial to the Balkan wars of 1912 and the Asia Minor war of 1922, looked very little different after six years, neat and tree-shaded, and, like the rest of the town, rather middle-class. The traffic was a little busier and the strollers under the trees of Koúndourou Street at the beginning of the evening *vólta* looked a little more affluent, a little more cosmopolitan. However, as we drove on and parked by the inner harbour, we realised how much had changed. Gone was the little fairground with its roundabouts and swings to amuse the children and where the teenagers would gather to listen to *mantinádes*, and sometimes begin an impromptu dance for sheer fun. Now there was only room for one big civic car park and rows of cafés and restaurants jammed cheek by jowl all along the waterfront, with chairs and tables spilling on to the road.

This inner pool, Lake Voulisméni, or sometimes the "Bath of Athena", is, needless to say, reputed to be bottomless although Captain Spratt, in his survey for the British Admiralty, measured it at 64 metres. Another story is that an undersea passage connects it with Santoríni to the north. Legend aside, it is a strange geological feature, probably the outlet of a subterranean river draining these limestone mountains, for there is a constant upwelling of cold, fresh water. A channel has been built, crossed by a road bridge, connecting it with the main harbour and the sea, thus allowing the smaller open caiques to run into the shelter of the lake with its steep rocky cliffs behind. These gaily-painted craft seemed less numerous than before; none of the bold human eyes on the bows now, which superstitious Mediterranean fishermen used to believe would ward off the evil eye. We sat on the edge of the dock for a while, watching as a few fishermen refuelled their tanks and coiled the long lines ready for use at dawn the following day. Most were old now, possibly the young men had found more lucrative employment in the town's hotels and bars, or perhaps by entertaining foreign women. Does the "fish hook" operate here, as in Rhodes and Cyprus? The cars looked new and smart and the motorcycles outside the cafes were the latest Japanese models, instead of the ancient British and Italian relics which used to drip oil on to the warm asphalt. The corporation's pre-war American fire engine, which once stood in a quiet side-street, had finally gone, presumably to a museum.

The outer harbour had changed even more, the discotheques and pubs garish with English signs, and already the noise of competing juke boxes was ringing across the water. Was that restaurant on the corner the same "Vassilis' Place" where the proprietor had proudly cooked his special *moussaká* for us one winter evening, his shotgun and game bag leaning against the wall after his day's sport in the mountains, and no other customers to disturb our talk? Now, with its smart tables and decor, it seemed to have been transplanted from London's West End. Further round the harbour wall, the cheap bars where fishermen and seamen used to play cards and drink *rakí*, sometimes dance to the lyre music on the radio when the mood took them, had all disappeared. In their place, were a motorcycle hire business, a booking office for day trips around the gulf in a custom-built cruiser, and a very expensive-looking fish restaurant. Outside this last stood a brand-new BMW, locally plated, but with a BMW Park Lane personal export sticker in the back window – unheard of wealth by Cretan standards. There were still fishing caiques in the dock, but also a number of yachts and a beautiful schooner, converted for cruising. A Hellenic Navy patrol boat was tied to the outer wall where I used to watch the tramp steamer come in twice a week or so to drop off piles of gravel, building blocks, timber, sewage pipes, or whatever the town had ordered, before spinning round, almost in its own length, and heading out to sea again with no more fuss than a van driver delivering parcels.

There was once a Hellenic port on the gulf here, and Roman tombs have been found beneath the foundations of the town. The Venetians were here too, but there is no trace of them left; the entire modern town having been established in the late nineteenth century, as is apparent from the formally laid out square blocks of its buildings and streets. In 1904, it officially became the prefecture of the Lassíthi Nomós, although some of the government functions are still fulfilled by Neápoli, where the law courts are. Ayios Nikólaos has always had a bourgeois air and a reputation for stuffiness, but with a certain sleepy Italianate charm. The civil servants working in the offices of the Nomárchia, immersed in the reams of paper and red tape required to govern the eparchies, rural communes and urban districts into which Greek counties are sub-divided, helped to contribute to this impression of respectable inertia. Formally suited for the office, they would appear in the cafés and bookshops for the long lunch-hour of the afternoon before returning to the prefecture for the evening. Greek civil servants used to take 25 days' religious holiday each year. On these days, and on Saturdays and Sundays, the whole family would appear in the late afternoon, children buttoned into their best clothes, to stroll up and down and exhange pleasantries with acquaintances.

This is where organised tourism really began on Crete, with the building of the famous Minos Beach Hotel bungalow complex further round the bay to the west, in the 1960s. The charm remained for a long time – John Le Carré came and stayed to write a novel here – but eventually the development began to accelerate, and now the character of St Nicholas has just about been submerged under the gift shops, bars and hotels. It is still picturesque, but just another Mediterranean resort. Strangely, there is a strong Sfakian contingent in Ayios Nikólaos. Most arrived around the turn of the century, looking for work in a more prosperous part of the island, or because "family problems" had made the west of Crete too hot to hold them.

Some of these, keepers of *tavérnas* and bars, earned a reputation for scandalous overcharging in the early days of tourism, perhaps a kind of watered-down brigandage to keep their hand in.

Tied to the outer mole was a big ocean-going salvage tug, the *Creta Maris*, flying the Greek flag. We fell into conversation with an Asian seaman in a brightly-coloured sarong who was leaning on the rail and smiling at us as we sauntered along the dock. With his thin black moustache and red kerchief wound around his forehead, he looked like a Malay pirate.

"When do you get to go home?" we asked him.

"Indonesia?" He shrugged his shoulders and smiled ruefully. "I haven't been home for years. I am a poor man and I have to go where the work is. They don't pay us British union rates, you know."

"I suppose not. But this must be a good place to be docked. The Greeks are so friendly to strangers."

"Maybe to you, but not to us. They have the . . . what do you call it . . . colour bar here. They won't let me into a restaurant or a bar. See those two bastards there?" (He nodded towards an official car moving along the dock behind us.) "Those are the port police, never let me alone. Anyway, nice talking, come and see me again."

He disappeared down an open hatch as the cruising car of the *Limenikón Sóma* slowed beside us, and one of the occupants stared hard at his retreating back before the car accelerated away.

A spicy smell of cooking meats and rice pilaff drifted from the open doorways of the *tavérnas* by the harbour, doner kebabs turned on their spits and chicken sizzled in the pan. The kiosks were selling newspapers, cigarettes, paperback books and magazines, bars of chocolate, sunglasses and chewing gum. A rich smell of new leather – tanning, as might be expected, is one of the few traditional industries of Crete – came from the many shops selling shoes, handbags, belts and wallets. Joan found the lady who had sold her a favourite dress years before and began to look through her stock. The Agricultural Bank had closed, but they were holding a staff meeting; you could see them sitting in a circle surrounded by plate glass and white marble. The mechanics in the motorcycle repair shop were still working in their greasy overalls, spare parts in brightly-coloured boxes piled against the walls. In the barber's shop a last customer was being shaved in the old black leather chair, a week's growth of stubble succumbing in swathes to a cut-throat razor. Cretan barbers still have to work for their money.

The old Minos Beach Hotel is now virtually entangled in the outer suburbs of the town. We always had a soft spot for this hotel, with its scented flower gardens and wood fires which were lit on winter evenings, until all the white marble rooms smelled faintly of pine and olive wood smoke. Most of the rooms face east over the Gulf of Mirabéllo to the blue and purple mountains of Ornó towards Sitía. A little before dawn, a warm dry wind would spring up from the south, a hot breath of Africa, making the shutters bang, and which often woke me from sleep to sit on the balcony in the warmest part of the day, watching the rising sun illuminate those mysterious and distant peaks far across the water. In the summer, the *scirócco*, the notorious south wind, would bring clouds of dust and close, sweaty weather, but in winter the heat was magical.

The clientele in January was a mixture of rich Alexandrians taking a mid-winter holiday, English ex-colonial people of the kind who never settled at home, what used to be called remittance men, and widows just wealthy enough to escape from the English winter for several months at a time. I can remember a tweedy English matron with a piercing home counties accent, buttonholing a pleasant and rather shy Egyptian at his dinner table.

"I just want to tell you," she said, her voice ringing across the room, " how very much I admire your President." (Meaning Sadat, not Nasser.)

"Er, most kind," he spluttered and blushed, trying to swallow his mouthful of food.

On this occasion, we were booked to stay at a newer hotel, a few hundred yards further along by a little inlet of the sea. It eventually turned out to be run with such hilarious incompetence as to be a divertissement in its own right. However, the view of at least a corner of the gulf was a compensation. There are two islands out in the bay, the wild ibex reserve of Nísos Ayii Pántes, close at hand, and Nísos Psíra, a larger island over against the Sitía mountains near Móchlos. We unpacked and sat on our balcony, sipping an ouzo and listening to watered-down folk music from the loudspeaker behind us. The limpid water lapped quietly against the concrete piers by the tamarisk trees on the shore. Across the inlet, the great tawny hills towards Eloúnda rose steeply from the sea, looking dry and baked even at this time of the year.

CHAPTER 15

Kritsá, Lató and Eloúnda

As the sun came up the next morning, the quiet putter of a little diesel engine drifted through the open door to our room. As I moved out onto the balcony to see the hills already glowing in the ruddy light, a small caique from Ayios Nikólaos circled around by the hotel's tennis courts and the single occupant threw out a buoy. He controlled the tiller with his knee as he paid out the long line carefully coiled in a tub, a hook and bait every few feet, until he had laid several hundred yards. Then out with the marker buoy at the end, and the process was repeated with the next tubful. When he was well out in the inlet, he met with two other caiques who had finished laying their lines. The fishermen tied their boats together and drifted; I could see the flash as cigarettes were lit and the voices carried clearly over the shining sea as they waited. It is said that the sweepers had an easy job clearing the German and Italian mines from the gulf after the war, for the fishermen of Ayios Nikólaos had stolen the explosive already, in order to dynamite fish with it. By breakfast time, they had hauled their lines and gone.

Under a rather sad-looking *agrími* head and a muzzle-loading *kariofílis* rifle on the wall of the dining-room, we helped ourselves from an unimaginative buffet – no yoghurt and no honey – before driving into the town. At the top of the hill, we crossed the new road and followed the signpost for Kritsá and up into the foothills of the Dictean mountains.

The field workers were driving their mules to the olive groves as we came up the road, the tools and the cloths to be laid under the trees roped on either side of the wooden saddles. These animals are not overloaded. I cannot recall seeing a donkey or mule in a bad condition for the simple reason that they are far too valuable to be mistreated. Incidentally, I have noticed that in Crete, when a peasant couple have one riding animal, the man will usually gallantly walk while leading his wife on the animal's back. Elsewhere, the man will sometimes ride like an oriental potentate, while his wife follows meekly behind on foot. The reason for this, the men tell you slyly in the coffee shop, is that she does not want him to be tired when they reach home.

Just outside the village of Kritsá, there is a little wooden sign pointing down a track to the right towards the ancient site of Lató. You can drive down the track, but it is much pleasanter to leave the car on the asphalt road and walk the last four kilometres as we did. This was a pleasure we had been saving and anticipating for some time. The stony path leads downhill at first and crosses a little stream; even in the spring, this had already dried to a trickle. As we climbed the opposite bank, past pumps and irrigation channels leading into the olive groves, the large village of Kritsá came clearly into view behind us. The brilliant white houses cluster around the great square-domed church on a ledge under the steep cliffs of the mountain.

Kritsá is the archetypal Cretan village, the houses regularly washed with disinfectant, waterproof lime which is at first transparent, but then turns crystalline and white in the sunlight. As the layers build up, year by year, the angles and corners of the walls are smoothed and rounded. (The houses on Rhodes were whitewashed too, with the charming exception that when a daughter of the household required a husband, her parents would paint the house in a pastel shade as a subtle advertisement. Once a betrothal was arranged, the house would once more be painted as white as its neighbours.) The houses of a Cretan village huddle closely together for protection, and it is very rare to find an isolated farm away from the main settlement – such freedom is confined to those countries which have known centuries of peace and safety for their citizens. While a similar mountain village in Sicily or Andalucia would be a kind of hilltop fortress, to be held against brigands or marauding soldiers when necessary, here the philosophy of defence was different. The village was built under the mountain and was abandoned under serious attack, while the inhabitants climbed into the hills above and fired down on the enemy, who of course dared not follow the natives once they got among their familiar rocks and crags.

The olive groves were busy with women from the village; all smiled and exchanged a cheerful "Kaliméra" with us as we swung along in the sunlight towards the lonelier country beyond. The white crown daisies grew so thickly over the grass under the trees, that the ground appeared to be spread with drifting snow, though the dry parched look of the mountains which sternly dominate the landscape to the west spoke of hot sun and barren ground.

An old man sat on a stone by the side of the path, an outsized cap shading his lined nut-brown face from the sun. On seeing us he sprang up and pulled out from his pocket a little paper bag stuffed with the aromatic rosemary and thyme which grow all over the mountainsides of Crete. He seemed a little crazy and asked us for 200 drachmes – the nearest thing I have ever seen to begging in Crete. I had rather hoped that he was offering us the famous Cretan dittany, which grows on dangerously inaccessible cliff faces, and in pursuit of which a number of lives have been lost. *Origanum Dictamnus*, named after the nearby mountains, is known here as *díktamo*, or *stamatóhorto* or *erondas*. Cretans drink it as a herb tea; in classical times it was reported to expel arrows from wounds, and it was believed that the ibex could cure itself with the herb when injured by hunters. It is still used as a relaxant for women in childbirth, and if one goes so far as to take a bath in the tea it is supposed to have a powerful aphrodisiac effect – but I cannot speak from experience.

Many Greeks have a deep-seated faith in herbal medicine, and some plants have a mystical, symbolic significance, such as the squill, which will not wither when picked, and so is hung over the door for good luck. Basil, the plant named for a queen, is grown in pots everywhere and a visitor is sometimes handed a small piece on leaving. They say that the Empress Helena was guided to the True Cross by the beautiful scent of this herb, and so gave it her royal name. In winter, the shepherds on the mountain make a tea from marjoram sweetened with honey to keep out the cold. And marjoram, together with thyme, was once picked by young girls to pack between the sheets of their dowry, so that their marriage beds would smell sweet and fragrant. Every one knows that Orthodox couples are crowned in church when they marry – many women preserve their wedding crowns through the years until death, when they are placed in the coffin with them. But in the old days, according to Spratt, three crowns were also placed on a bride's pillow, to symbolise the attributes and qualities she would need and hope to find during her married life. A crown baked of bread expressed a wish for peace and prosperity, one made of orange leaves and myrtle for tenderness and love, and, a bitter touch, a crown of thorns would give her the strength to endure a long, hard life. This last she would surely need. On entering her new home she would take a pomegranate and throw it down on the floor, the scattering seeds symbolising all the worldly goods that might one day fill the house.

The country grew dryer and the olive trees smaller and spaced further apart as we walked on away from the irrigated groves. We meta shepherd whose flock of sheep were remarkable for their magnificent long white fleeces; excepting the gold, we felt that the Ram of Colchis must have looked something like these.

You come upon Lató quite suddenly: a cluster of ruins spread over a rocky crag and the saddle which joins it to the main hill. There is a breathtaking view of the valley and the blue Gulf of Mirabéllo showing between the hills to the north. It is my favourite of all the archaeological sites, purely by virtue of its situation. We found the guardian with his new pick-up truck at the end of the track, hauling up water with a rope and bucket from an antique cistern, in order to wash the car. A friendly and cultivated man who speaks excellent English, he made no bones about his enjoyment of the scenery and even the solitude which his vigil involves at times. This is unusual in a Greek, for their word *monaxiá* translates as either solitude or loneliness, the two being indistinguishable to a naturally gregarious people. In Crete, many shepherds and mountaineers are forced by circumstances to live isolated and solitary lives; when they meet a stranger these men are pathetically anxious for human conversation. There is the old chestnut about the shepherd who welcomes the traveller to sit by his fire, shares his food with him, and then prepares to be entertained, saying:

"Well now tell me all the news, any news is interesting . . . and if there is no news at all, well tell me some lies for God's sake!"

Lató was probably originally a Dorian settlement, well fortified on its lofty perch, but its heyday was in the Classic and Hellenistic periods, for most of the ruins date from the fifth to the third century BC. Sir Arthur Evans began the excavations, but handed over to the French, who continued to dig until the 1970s. The hill is steep, and we climbed up over masonry blocks and wild flowers to the circular threshing floor and storage cisterns on the saddle. Higher up, we halted in the shade of a carob tree which has established itself against the wall of the *agorá*, and looked out over the grassy pavements to the spurge-covered hillsides beyond. The inevitable eagle circled about half a mile away. The climb up to the *acrópolis* on the crag has to be made with care, for there is a sheer drop on three sides. When we were safely seated among the rocks of the summit, we could see for miles away along the ridge to the west where a single cloud in the blue sky hid the peaks around lonely Katharó. This is the 'Clean Plain' above Kritsá, a remote and silent place high in the mountains which the men of the village cultivate in summer. A big cargo ship had anchored out in the gulf, and was framed by the surrounding mountain slopes on an azure background. The only sound to be heard was of birdsong and a solitary tractor working the fertile, irrigated land of the Plain of Lakónia far below. We could just make out a hot glint of metal as it passed in and out of the rows of trees. The Church of the Archangel on the plain has a famous fresco showing the Emperor Constantine with his mother, Helena, and the True Cross.

The guardian smiled benignly at us as we rejoined him, pleased to see us enjoying his preserve. "Don't forget the Temple of Apollo," he said, pointing out the remains below the second *acrópolis* to the south. The temple is small with a *pronaos* and *cella*, or vestibule and inner shrine. Its charm lies in the twisted trunks of the trees which surround it and the wild flowers in which its white masonry is half buried. It is thought that the ancient shrine and oracle at Delphi was once devoted to Gaia, the Earth Mother who bore the Titans, and whose worship originated in Crete. Later Cretans landed on the Gulf of Corinth to bring the new cult of Apollo Delphinios to the shrine, together with its later name.

The walk back to Kritsá was delightfully relaxed and tranquil. We passed a German couple on their way out to the ancient city, weighed down by archaeology textbooks. The women from the village had left their work and were now seated, some of them on mule saddles placed on the ground, eating an early lunch in the deep shade of an olive tree.

On the main road, not far from the Lató turning, lies the Byzantine Church of Panayía Kerá, the Holy Lady, containing the most famous frescoes in all of Crete. The white church, surrounded by olives and cypresses, is unusual in that it has three naves, the oldest in the centre, dating from the fourteenth century. Many of the religious scenes depicted in the church may be unfamiliar to a West European, as they relate to the Apocryphal Gospels, including the life of St Anne, mother of the Virgin Mary. Among the martyrs and saints on the walls of the church are the faces of Theodoulos and Zotikos, two of the Ayii Déka, or Ten Martyrs of Górtyna; it is thought that the faces of the other eight have been erased by time. During the rule of the Roman Emperor, Decius, in the third century AD, these ten leading Christians were brought before the Proconsul of Crete and threatened with torture if they would not forswear their faith. The ten stood firm for thirty days and then were brought to the place of execution. The story tells that they joined hands in a ring, singing: "Mountains and peaks, plains and ravines, let fall drops of sweetness, because today ten Cretan men were united to bear witness with their blood to the blood of Christ."

In the church at Ambeloúzos, near Górtyna, is a slab of marble with the marks reported to have been made by their knees as they prayed before their beheading. The festival of these early martyrs is on 23 December, and it is interesting that the Roman Catholic, as well as the Orthodox Church, continued to recognise them after the Schism.

We drove the short distance to Kritsá, leaving the car at the bottom of the village under the watchful eye of the policeman, for parking restrictions had arrived since our last visit. One of the *kafeneíons* above the steep street used to serve marvellous *mezéthes* just with a glass of ouzo: olives, tomatoes, pickled fish, beans and *féta* cheese. Kritsá has been on the tourist map for some time, partly because of the famous church outside the village and also the proximity of Ayios Nikólaos. More than twenty years ago, the American film director, Jules Dassin (who later made *Never on Sunday*), filmed the Kazantzakis novel, *Christ Recrucified* here, under the title *He Who Must Die*. Many of the villagers acted in the film, which is memorable for its remarkable portrayal of peasant faces, "chiselled by work and weather". Ever after this, the village seemed aware of its photogenic qualities, although life in the winter months went on much as usual. Now it is a regular stop for the tourist coaches, and handicraft shops have sprung up all along the narrow main street, which was intended for donkeys rather than cars. Women beckon to the foreigners, to show them the lace they are making, where once only the priest and the elders could be seen whiling away the day outside the *kafeneíon* by the yellow-painted post office.

Our favourite little *tavérna* was still there, however. In the narrow triangle where two streets run together stands a general store, with just room for two tables and a dozen chairs outside the door, surrounded by a low wall and pleasantly shaded. The same friendly woman who presides over this establishment (the cool, dark interior seems to be an important centre for village gossip, although doubtless some business is also done), brought us wine and, as before, arranged for omelettes, fried potatoes and salad to be prepared for us in a kitchen a few doors along. When the food was ready, it was whisked down the street on a tray. I think I would as soon eat a meal on this little island in the middle of the lively chatter of the village, as in any restaurant I know. The food isn't exactly memorable, but you can sip your wine and eat black olives while the women's knitting needles click as they sit and gossip in their doorways and trays of fresh bread are carried past from the baker, who will still cook your dinner in his oven for a small fee. Perhaps the *pappás* in his tall black hat will exchange grave and courteous greetings with you as he rides past on his mule.

Long-staying visitors seem to fetch up here. I can remember past conversations with Australians who were "doing" Europe over six months in a Volkswagen Camper. They had started with Crete as it was winter, and after three months were still trying to talk themselves into leaving for the north. Then there were the Canadians who were camped down on the coast at Eloúnda in a giant, articulated Ford motor caravan which seemed to take up most of the village square. With a V8 engine, and beautifully finished in two-tone green, it was totally unsuitable for the roads of Crete, and the locals had never seen anything like it. However, it was equipped with two small motorcycles attached to the back and the Canadians had formed the habit of riding up to Kritsá for lunch. They too, had planned to move on months before, but were slowly falling asleep in the winter sunshine, sinking under the island's spell.

Michael had in fact fallen asleep immediately after lunch, the sun and perhaps the wine having produced its effect. Joan and I wandered through the doorway into the gloom of the shop, and the owner broke off from talking to the group of men and women seated on various boxes of merchandise around the room. I had seen one of those lemonade bottles of colourless liquid in the window, labelled by hand, "*Raki*: 100 drachmes". The assembled company grinned when I asked her for it. "No, don't take that one," said the shopkeeper, pulling an empty bottle from under the counter and filling it from the tap of an enormous plastic bulk container. The grins became broader.

"That's a good, strong healthy drink," said an elder with an enormous grizzled moustache. "You know what's gone into it."

The spirit is distilled from the crushed grapes after the wine juice has been run off and is very pure. Powerful as it is, the effect always seems to wear off without a hangover, unlike the strong black wines of the island. Once or twice, in the mountains, I have seen a still with yards of coiled copper piping being moved, strapped to a mule's back. *Raki* isn't moonshine, however, for it is quite legal for anyone owning a vineyard to make it, and in some parts of Crete this means almost everybody. The making of fiery spirits seems to be a general Greek skill. They say that in the bootlegging days of American Prohibition, the Italian gangsters organised the sales and distribution, but they used Greeks to actually manufacture the liquor. Greek peasants are generally rather abstemious in their attitude to drink, but this is not so true of Crete. The Cypriot maxim, "Early on the road and early home", applies here too, and the mountain people, especially the

shepherds, tend to be up and ready for their day before dawn. Breakfast is light; cheese and a few olives, a cup of coffee and one or two
glasses of *raki* "to kill the microbes", makes a good fortification
against the morning cold. When drinking is communal, they seem to
derive more fun from the social ritual than most people. It is essential
to clink glasses when toasting, which is done whenever anyone
drinks. This is guaranteed to make any occasion cheerfully noisy.
Moreover, when drinking wine, the glasses are always kept half full,
never more and never much less, by constant replenishment from the
bottle. It is amazing how this seems to increase the speed of
consumption. "Stiniyássas", (your health) is the most common and
straightforward pledge. "Of the dog that has bitten you, throw in
some of the fur", has a familiar sound to it. Apparently, in the
villages of Mount Kédros, they say: "May we become as rich as the
Sultan Amurath!" "May you always be happy", has great charm. But
the most Cretan toast of all must be: "May the All-Holy One scour the
rust from our guns!"

I have an Irish friend, a philhellene of long standing, who regards
raki with a kind of affectionate awe. "The extraordinary thing about
that stuff," he says, "is the way it gets to your legs. I mean you can be
sitting there, holding your own in conversation quite sensibly and
yet be totally unable to get out of your chair." He claims, incidentally, that the very best *raki* is always made by monks.

* * * *

A lazy afternoon seemed in order, and we drove back through Ayios
Nikólaos, and along the shore of the gulf to the north. We passed over
the bare brown hills which slope so steeply down into the sea here,
looking back over Mirabéllo to the blue mountains of Ornó miles
away in the east, before running down to the little port of Eloúnda.
The topography of this area requires some explanation. The mountainous coast runs north towards the point of Cape Ayios Ioánnis.
Near Eloúnda, however, a hilly peninsula, very nearly an island, and
known as Spinalónga (Long Thorn) is connected to an area of marshy
littoral by a narrow isthmus, and stretches for several miles parallel
to the coast towards the north, enclosing a sort of fiord. At the exit to
the open sea, rather like a loose stopper in a bottle, is a small island,
with a Venetian fortress, also confusingly known as Spinalónga, and
of which more later. On the seaward side of the peninsula is a long
islet known as Kolokýthia, (the Marrow). The flat, narrow isthmus
has been cut by a canal, reputedly dug by the French during the
occupation of the Great Powers, which allows caiques with a shallow

draught to gain the open sea to the south directly from Eloúnda, without being forced to sail around the point. A causeway has been built over the isthmus marshes, and the canal is crossed by a narrow stone bridge around which cluster a small group of windmills.

Before the war, the Gulf of Mirabéllo was a refuelling stop for the great flying boats of Imperial Airways on their long journeys out to Cape Town and India. The airline's base was here at Eloúnda, although there was apparently little more than a motor launch for ferrying passengers ashore, a petrol bowser and a generator for the flare path. Sir Arthur Evans made at least one of his later visits to Crete by flying boat. In June 1940 operations came to an end, and no trace remains now. Once a simple fishing village, since the 1960s it has made more profit from the tourists spilling over from Ayios Nikólaos and now has hotels of its own, while the outskirts are filled with signs for rooms and villas to let.

We took the track to the right on the outskirts of the town, signposted to Oloús, which leads down to the marshy land and the causeway. The old salt flats here were worked until quite recently, being filled up with seawater before the sluices were closed and the water left to evaporate off in the sun. Now it is a deserted and slightly mysterious place, with a couple of palm trees standing isolated in the flat waste.

We parked on the gravel causeway close to the windmills, disturbing a few egrets and then a heron which flapped slowly off over the sound like a ragged grey pterodactyl. The halcyon blue flash of a kingfisher flickered under the bridge. This place is something of an ornithologist's paradise, and indeed the whole island of Crete is remarkable for the number of migratory birds which use it as a stepping stone between Europe and Africa, exactly as the Straits of Gibraltar are used in the west. In the autumn, the cranes of Poland and Russia can be seen in their thousands, flying high over the Cretan mountains on their way south.

There was no one in sight as we walked across the bridge, carrying swimming costumes and towels, before making our way along the shore to the right. This is the site of ancient Oloús, the port of Dréros near modern Neápoli. In the post-Minoan era, this city was powerful enough to conclude a treaty with Rhodes, and it survived through Roman times. There were once temples to Zeus and Britomartis, or Artemis, remaining above ground, but the country people took the stones to build the low walls which divide the fields of Spinalónga. This part of Crete is gradually sinking with each successive earthquake, and much of the harbour of Oloús now lies beneath the sound. By a white chapel, close to the shore, the foundations of an ancient wall can be seen running into the water. The boys and I put on our costumes and, while they paddled on the edge of the wall, I gingerly lowered myself in, trying to avoid treading on the numerous sea urchins, and swam out into deeper water.

At first, I could not make the mask I had brought fit properly, but the sea was not too cold and as clear as glass. It rapidly became obvious that the stones littering the bottom had been squared and shaped, but I could not define the outlines of any recognisable structure. Then, as a depth of twelve or fifteen feet was reached, there were cracked flagstones, the remains of a level pavement and low shelves, covered in marine growths, which might once have been walls. These are believed to have been the shipberths of the old city. At one point, I came across a large block of stone, projecting far enough above the seabed for me to stand on it with my head clear of the water: a pillar perhaps, or part of a tower? I was interrupted from these musings by a loud splash as Steven fell off the wall into deep water, much to his surprise and annoyance, and was fished out by the others amid general confusion. The water did not seem so warm now, and I abandoned my amateur archaeological dive in favour of a dry towel and clothes.

Michael and the boys were still happily annoying crabs in the rock pools when Joan and I walked a little way along the dry-stone wall to a threshing floor, amidst lush knee-high grass speckled with pink and purple wild pea flowers. These circular stone areas must presumably once have been cobbled, like those of Spain and Italy, but most of those in Crete seem to have been modernised with puddled concrete, which at least indicates their continued use. The sight of grain being husked by dragging a heavy sledge over the floor and winnowed by hand-tossing in the ever-present Cretan wind, as the chaff blows off to one side, brings home how little some aspects of the peasant's life have changed here. These biblical scenes would have looked the same, one thousand, two thousand or three thousand years ago. It does not seem possible that they can continue very much longer, for surely this generation and the next will not be prepared to undertake such backbreaking, if picturesque labour.

About 100 yards inland, among the meadows, a mesh fence encloses a mosaic floor and part of an early Christian basilica, all that now remains on land of ancient Oloús. The mosaic depicts swirling fish surrounded by geometric designs, the fish being the very first symbol used by the followers of Christ.

The shadows were growing longer now and the sun, sinking closer to the mountain tops, was turning the calm sea to gold. The handful of peasants who farm the peninsula fields were slowly making their way over the bridge and along the causeway to Eloúnda. An elderly couple passed us, the man leading the mule on which his wife rode amidst sacks of potatoes roped to the wooden saddle, while a long-haired white goat, hobbled head to hind leg, wandered behind. The only sounds as they crossed the bridge by the windmills in the evening light, were the clip-clop of the hooves, the intermittent tinkling of the goat's bell and the slow murmur of their voices. We decided to follow, and left Spinalónga to its ghosts for the night.

CHAPTER 16

The Plain of Lassíthi

The old road to Iráklion follows the twists and turns of a narrow ravine. I knew we had to turn left somewhere for Ayios Konstantínos, but we became confused by the signs, and what appeared to be a new improved road to take coaches up to Lassíthi, not shown on our old map. We found ourselves bumping along dirt tracks through more of Crete's thirteen million olive trees. We stopped in a little hamlet to consult a group of old men with superb waxed moustaches, who were pruning the vines and loosening the earth around the roots. They scratched their grey heads and seemed as puzzled by the map as we, handling it reverently as if it was immensely precious. They advised us to go on to Neápoli and then turn up into the high mountains there.

On one of a series of hairpin bends climbing up a sun-drenched hillside, we stopped to stretch our legs for a moment and noticed a middle-aged woman shaking her fist at a donkey some fifty yards away. The animal had broken away from her and was skittishly trotting back and forth through the olive trunks, trailing ropes and a length of netting from the saddle. It kept a roguish eye on its furious owner and made sure to keep a good space between them.

"You devil," she shouted, "I'll make you pay when I catch you! I'll beat the evil out of you!"

The epithet may not have been chosen at random, for Cretan peasants used to believe in the *anáskelos*, the "upside-down one", a donkey possessed by Old Nick himself, capable of human speech and of expanding at will to an enormous size. If you are unwise enough to climb on this donkey's back at night, he will take you straight down to Hell. At the very least, a donkey is likely to house a soul sentenced to Purgatory. All this seems rather a slur on the character of these beasts, which are normally so docile and hard-working. The only protection when meeting the Devil in the guise of a donkey is to make the sign of the Pentalpha, Solomon's five-pointed star, and to pray to the Virgin.

Neápoli has a rather high-brow reputation, possibly stemming from the famous son of the town, Peter Philargos, born in 1340 in what was then the little village of Kares. After studying in European universities, he entered the Roman Catholic Church and was eventually elected Pope Alexander V in 1409. His reign was short, for he made too many enemies by his agitation for the reunification of the divided churches. After only a few months, he died in mysterious circumstances, probably poisoned. He had done his bit to put Neápoli on the map, however; not every little Greek town can boast a Catholic Pope. There is a modern technical college on the road into town, a library (and it must be said that the country people of Crete are not normally great readers), together with a little museum. Apart from these intellectual achievements, Neápoli is famous for the number and quality of its almonds, a tree which reached Greece from western Asia at a very early date. We parked on the wide square outside the gates of the large and impressive town church.

The eight hundred or so Byzantine churches of Crete are all really quite small, many no more than tiny chapels. From the nineteenth century on, Cretans have delighted in building the largest and most imposing churches the community could afford, and this is a good example. Behind its protecting wall and bulbous palm trees, the broad steps lead up to an ornate façade of grey stone and primrose yellow stucco. The twin bell towers each have a large clock under a red-tiled roof. Inside, the gloom is relieved by tall, stained-glass windows, which cast their coloured light on to great chandeliers, hanging from the cupola. The church is heated in cold weather by two enormous wood-burning stoves, whose enamelled flues run for many yards to emerge from the side windows. The acrid smell of incense still hung in the air from the last service. An old lady shuffled in as we left, crossed herself backwards in the Orthodox manner, and went to add her candle to the battery that were burning before the iconostasis.

A short distance from the town, behind the New Road, lies the archaic site of Dréros, already mentioned in connection with the associated port of Oloús. The tarmac road runs out after a while and you must climb up to the *acrópolis*, high above the narrow pass in which Neápoli lies. French excavations before the last war uncovered bronze statues and a temple to Apollo, but the most significant finds were inscriptions in Greek and the mysterious Eteocretan language, which is not yet fully understood. There is evidence that after the fall of the Minoan Empire and the Dorian invasion, the remaining Minoans retired to a reduced kingdom in the east of the island. Archaeologists have termed these people Eteocretans, or indigenous Cretans. In those much quoted, though lovely lines of the Odyssey, Homer describes the peoples of Crete at the time of the Trojan War:

Out in the wine-dark sea there lies a land called Crete, a rich and lovely land, washed by the sea on every side, densely peopled and boasting ninety cities. Each of the several races of the isle has its own language. First, there are the Achaeans; then the genuine Cretans, proud of their native stock; next the Kydonians; the Dorians with their three clans; and finally the noble Pelasgians.

(Homer, *The Odyssey*, Trs. E.V. Rieu)

We know that the Achaeans of Mycenae on the mainland had a long association with Minoan Crete and that some of them were probably settled on the island by 1500 BC. The name of Kydonía still exists in modern Khaniá; the people of this ancient western city seem to have been racially separate from others on the island, according to Homer. We know that the Dorians overran much of Greece from the Balkans, and the Pelasgians were a people who settled many parts of the Aegean and Asia Minor. Is it reasonable to assume that Homer's "genuine Cretans", speaking their own language and proud of their ancestry, were the last of the Minoans?

In the Dorian period, however, the people of Dréros seem to have been a remarkably bloody-minded lot involved in a long-standing feud with the neighbouring city of Lýttos. Citizenship involved the taking of the following venomous oath: "I shall never be well disposed to the people of Lýttos by any device or contrivance, neither by night nor by day, and I shall strive as far as lies in my power to do ill to the city of Lýttos."

There is something tense and dramatic about the journey from Neápoli, past the Kremastón Monastery, up towards the Oros Díkti; the manner in which the changing scenery gradually unfolds seems theatrical, and there is the feeling that the best is saved for the last. Each little village, Vríses, Amigdáli, Zénia, Argiró Neró, Exo Potamí, Mésa Potamí (the Village of the Fountains, the Village of the Almonds, the Village of Strangers, the Village of Silver Water, the Village of the Outer Streams, the Village of the Inner Streams), has a different character. Each is that much higher, that much colder, that much more secretive than the one before. Mile by mile, as the snows draw nearer, the trees and plants of northern Europe seem to have been transplanted here to this far southern outpost of the continent. Many of the rough grey-stoned houses are empty, or the roofs have collapsed; their occupants have emigrated and will not return to the hard life of these narrow valleys, beautiful as they are in the morning sunshine and ice-cold air.

I remember coming down from the mountains on a chill, cloudy January morning and entering the strange, dark village of Mésa Potamí, the place of the Deep or Inner Streams. The single, narrow street, lined with a double row of poplar trees, was deserted, the house roofs on either side stacked with winter firewood. The lichen growing on the grey stone of walls and pavement seemed unfamiliar in this warm, dry land. For once, no wind blew and a sort of blue autumnal haze hung around the brooding slopes which tower above, and dead leaves had drifted into odd corners. No one seemed to be about, until we found a shy, smiling woman inside the tiny *kafeneíon* who brewed us some coffee and seemed fascinated by our two fair-haired boys, then little more than toddlers. She made them sit next to her as she cooked them jacket potatoes in the embers of the stove and stroked their heads constantly. She was expecting her first child, she told Joan, patting her belly, and the whole smoky room filled with her happiness and contentment. I wondered about her on this day, but there appeared to be no *kafeneíon* sign here now.

There are all sorts of old stories about the evil eye and the bad luck which comes from over-complimenting a good-looking or healthy child – rather spit upon it for its own protection. It was part of that all-pervading, fatalistic belief that wealth, strength, good looks, any happy attributes ostentatiously displayed, would of themselves attract the dark legions of ill-fortune or Cháros himself, like moths to a candle flame. Even blue eyes were considered unlucky. The precarious life of the village, protected by church and mountain chapel, was nevertheless threatened, for the superstitious, by black and frightening forces all around: ghosts, vampires, the *kallikántzaros*, nereids and lesser spirits of mischief; the Angel of Death himself made his dark journeys through these valleys. The villagers speak circumspectly of "He who dwells beneath the wilderness", i.e. the Devil.

Somewhere up above the village, snow-covered crests begin to show above the dull green of the scrubby mountainside, and then a bend in the road, at the high point of the pass, quite suddenly reveals Díkti in its full height and breadth. The mountain forms a barrier ahead of grey rock and dazzling snows, while the pale green plain of Lassíthi lies like a lake at its foot. We stopped to take in the sight, and again further down by the village of Mésa Lassíthi, where the almond trees on the bends of the road were covered with an explosion of white and pinkish blossom framing the views of the mountain and the plain. In Mésa Lassíthi, the vines are trained up to the tops of the flat roofs to give summer shade, but now the gnarled branches were still bare against the backdrop of distant snow. The village is surrounded by lush grass, for the land is good, and the street was full of tractors and pick-ups. The plateau is basically circular in shape, but a little extension runs into the mountains here.

After another kilometre or so, we were down on the rim of Lassíthi proper. The name "Lassíthi" is used for the entire eastern prefecture and is a corruption of the Venetian *La Sitia*, their city at the eastern end of the island. The plain is six or seven kilometres in diameter and about 900 metres above sea level. Over the millennia, the alluvial deposits eroded from the encircling mountains have produced a thick soil, and the land is traditionally among the richest in Crete. In a hard winter, the snow sometimes covers the plain, but it always thaws by March. If the spring rains and snow melt are heavy, the lower, western part of the plain floods to a depth of several feet until the waters gradually drain out through a *katavóthras* into the limestone below. The land is planted with apple trees, potatoes and grain, but in order to maximise the use of the fertile ground and to avoid the floods, the twenty odd villages and hamlets are all built in a circle on the higher ground at the circumference. Only the thin lines of mule tracks and irrigation ditches criss-cross the green of Lassíthi in geometric patterns, for the motor road keeps to the periphery as it runs from one village to the next.

"You promised me," said Michael as we looked down on the plain, "that there would be ten thousand windmills. I can't see any."

Yet they could be seen everywhere as we came closer, standing like gaunt skeletons of rusty iron and wire, unused during the winter. As the hot spring sun dries out the land, the water table sinks, until in May the white sails are set on the mills which begin to turn the clanking pumps and bring the water gushing to the surface. At the last count, there were indeed more than ten thousand windmills on Lassíthi, where a man's wealth is measured by the number he owns. There are diesel pumps now too, but wind power still drives most of the machinery.

The system of drainage and irrigation ditches is very ancient, perhaps constructed by the Romans as part of their project to make Crete a granary for the Empire. Traces of their occupation, together with those of earlier periods, have been found all over the plateau. The men of Lassíthi have always tended towards independence, aided like the Sfakians by their isolation amidst these mountains, for the passes are easily defended. Following a revolt early in the Venetian occupation, all the inhabitants were forced away from the plain, their villages burned and the fruit trees torn from the ground. In an unusually cruel edict, even by Venetian standards, any man who dared to cultivate the plain or pasture animals there risked death or dismemberment. As a result, the land lay fallow for more than a century, the only interruption in thousands of years' continuous cultivation and an extraordinary waste of such a valuable resource. During this major revolt led by the Kallergis family in 1365, numerous rebels from Ierápetra, Sitía and the villages of Mirabéllo took refuge in Lassíthi with all their families and flocks, defying Venice for three years until a large enough army could be found to force the passes. It is sometimes claimed that the Turks rarely penetrated this mountain fastness, though this is certainly untrue. As already mentioned, even the Sfakians were subject to household and capitation taxes. Nevertheless, the people of Lassíthi were doubtless isolated enough to retain a certain freedom of spirit. The motor road up to the plateau is relatively recent; it was not so long ago that you could only get in on foot or by mule.

Near the entry point to the eastern end of the plain, stands the Monastery of Kroustallenia on a little mound of limestone. It is still occupied, although the Turks sacked it twice for revolutionary activities. We drove through the settlements around the southern rim, Ayios Konstantínos, Ayios Yeóryios, which now has a little hotel, Koudoumaliá, Avrakóndes, Kamináki and Magoulás. The next village, Psychró, meaning 'Ice-Cold,' is right under the flank of the big mountain which actually has three major peaks: Díkti, Lázaros and Aféntis Christós. Psychró obviously gains a large part of its income from tourism nowadays, but there was no sign of life at the Zeus Hotel today, and chickens were pecking at the ground in front of the shuttered restaurant. We drove on to the little car park which marks the beginning of the track up to the Diktaean Cave. Something had changed, but I couldn't immediately place it. Only when I looked at an old photograph later, did I realise that a new *tavérna* had been built on the hillside beyond the old one, and that the iron wind pump which had once stood there now lay rusting on its side among the rocks.

A smiling man with a brown face walked up to greet us. I thought I remembered him from years before; we had eaten a memorable lunch of bean soup, bread and cold beer together, out on the stone terrace, with all the sounds of the plain funnelled up to us through the winter sunshine. A pedlar had just acquired a cassette player for his pick-up truck, and drove it from one village to another, blaring lyre music through a loudspeaker on the roof, much to everyone's delight. You could hear it clear across from the far side of the plain. He had spent some time leading Joan's mother up to the cave on a mule and, holding a very small Steven by the hand, had conducted us into the depths of the earth, illuminated by the flame of three or four candles. He couldn't be expected to remember us from so long ago.

"Kaliméra sas. Deutsches?"

"Kaliméra. Ochi, Angloi."

"Oh welcome. We see all people here, but the English are special to us. My father fought for three years up there with an Englishman." He jerked his thumb over his shoulder at the peak of Aféntis Christós and I thought of Sandy Rendel, who had organised the resistance in these mountains for the SOE.

"My name is Peter," he said, shaking hands with Michael and myself before embracing Joan heartily and planting a large kiss on each cheek. We introduced ourselves by the first names which the delightfully informal Greeks tend to give and use at once without inhibition.

"We came here in 1979; I think you guided us to the cave then."

"You've come back to us! Wonderful!" Another embrace and kisses for Joan. "Things have changed up here a lot. Every day so busy. The cave has been made safer with railings and steps. You won't need me to guide you if you have been before. Look under the large stone to the right of the entrance and you will find where I keep my candles – help yourselves. You want lunch? Come to my *tavérna* and order before you go up the mountain and we'll have it ready for when you come down. You know the story of the cave of course?" he continued, taking Joan gallantly by the arm and leading her towards the steps of the *tavérna*. We did, but it would have been a shame to interrupt the routine.

"Cronus was once master of all the gods and Lord of the World, but he was afraid that one of his children would take his place. So whenever his wife, Rhea, had a baby, he ate it. But when she had a boy child, the little Zeus, she gave Cronus a stone to eat, wrapped in the baby's clothes, while she hid Zeus in the cave up there. The baby was protected by the *Curétes* who clashed their weapons on their shields to hide the baby's crying from his father outside. When Zeus became a man, he overthrew Cronus and gave him salt and mustard, so that he vomited up first the stone and then Zeus's brothers and sisters. The people of Mount Ida say Zeus was born and hidden in *their* cave, but in Psychró we know better!" This with a broad grin – well they would, wouldn't they?

"Of course, these old stories aren't necessarily exactly true. You

185

don't have to believe in the old gods to like the cave, you can think what you like; it just depends what you want to believe."

"I don't think that she believes in anything at all," said Michael mischievously. Peter dropped her arm in surprise.

"What, not anything!" he gasped, visibly shocked, "not even God?"

"Well," Joan began uncertainly, "I'm not sure what I really believe. I'm what the English call an agnostic, of no formal religion."

"I see," said Peter, looking at her warily, "what would you like for lunch?"

While Peter went into the *tavérna* to organise lamb cutlets, salad and fried potatoes, we began to climb the stony path through the stunted ilex and oak trees. As we gained height, we could see more and more of the pale green plateau below, until we seemed to be suspended above a great dish, faintly marked with a tracery of paths and with a patchwork of squares, all slightly different in hue. Where the hills rose abruptly at the perimeter, a pencil-sharp line separated the green of the irrigated land from the pale grey of the rocks and the dull khaki of the maquis. The wild bees were still nesting at the mouth of the cave, where once the men of Psychró had waited with mules. We found the candles easily enough, and left the warm sunlight to follow the steps down into the dim green light of the opening below.

The cave was certainly known to the ancients, but it was lost or forgotten for many centuries. The entrance must have been partially blocked, for the villagers found it by chance in 1881. When Professor Halbherr and Hadzidakis came riding by, they made a preliminary exploration and Sir Arthur Evans also investigated it in the last years of the nineteenth century. In 1900, British archaeologists, helped by the men of Psychró, cleared various blockages with dynamite, and later the French also excavated. They found large numbers of votive offerings, including Minoan double axes and bronze statues. It should be remembered, of course, that Zeus would have meant nothing to the Minoans, who worshipped an earlier Mother Goddess, and for whom these offerings must have been intended. The Olympian Zeus must have arrived in Crete with later Greeks from the north and have gradually been assimilated. The remains from the Mount Ida cave make it plain that the worship of Zeus eventually succeeded the Mother Goddess cult there. The actual story of Zeus' overthrow of Cronus, as recounted by Peter, was first described by Hesiod in the eighth century BC.

The newly-cut steps and handrail only slightly detract from the adventure of clambering down the steep slope – the cave is another limestone swallow-hole, and so follows the usual Cretan pattern of a sharp descent from the mouth. As in most deep caves, the temperature varies very little, remaining cool all the year round. It can, however, be very wet at certain times. Candles are somehow more fun than torches – you need four or five in a bunch to get a decent light – and reveal the features more progressively and dramatically. Various stalactites can, with a great deal of imagination, be likened to divine form; there is one known as the "Mantle of Zeus", and I was once shown a formation supposed to resemble the little god in his cradle. The bottom of the cave is quite extensive, and you progress in a sort of circular tour among the mounds and piles of rock on the floor, occasionally stepping in a puddle of icy water in the dark, until the steps lead up again towards the daylight filtering through the diagonal cleft above.

At the entrance, the boys finally and reluctantly blew out their candles. We strolled leisurely down the mountainside, looking at odd shrubs and flowers, while the boys ran on ahead. They found Peter waiting on the terrace with a large carafe of light red wine which he placed on a table.

"You like to eat outside? And now you believe me when I say we have lunch ready as soon as you come down?"

His teenaged daughter served the food, while he excused himself and hurried off to greet another small group of tourists as they arrived in the car park. His daughter, smart and modern in jeans and sweater, smiled indulgently at his retreating back. As Michael said, they seemed to have found the perfect formula for success and prosperity. "Of course, the story isn't necessarily true . . ." I heard him saying, as he led his little party up the track.

The wine was local – I think Peter said it was his own – and apart from the famous estate-bottled names, it was the best we found on the whole trip. A delicate, fresh young red, rather like some of those of Portugal, it was a treat after the rather rough and acidic wines we had often been drinking at lunch-time. The day was warm, in spite of the altitude and the proximity of the Diktaean snows. As so often happens, lunch developed into a long drawn out affair, as we enjoyed first the wine with olives and *féta* cheese, and then lingered over the lamb.

A very battered and dusty Volkswagen Camper came up the road, with surf boards lashed to the roof rack. A long-haired, bearded man got out and walked slowly up the steps talking to Peter's wife in fluent but heavily accented Greek. He sat at the other table with a beer, and stretched out his sandalled feet with a sigh as if he'd had a long hard day. The wine had chased away our natural British reserve and made us as inquisitive as any Cretan. We guessed he might be German.

"Do you live in Crete?" we ventured.

"I am here ten years now. But . . . very little contact with the people."

We felt instantly sorry for him. He was about our age, probably born after the war – was he still ostracised? In which case why did he stay?

"Where do you live?" we wondered.

"In Móchlos. A little village by the sea on the Sitía road. I used to live in the west, but they put up the rent of my house."

"Do you work here?"

"Yes, I have a workshop. Gold. I make . . . what do you say . . . jewellery, and I sell it each year at the Christmas Fair in Frankfurt."

"You seem to have discovered the secret of a happy life," we told him. He gave a wry smile.

"I don't know. I came here because it was cheap to live, but not so much now. Ten years ago, you could rent a house for maybe two thousand drachmes a month – but not now."

We left him to his beer and dreams of a magic land where you can still live in the sun for ten pounds a month, and went back to our car. Peter was up in the cave again with more tourists. We drove down to the plain and on to the village of Pláti, past a track leading up to the lonely valley of Aféntis and a long circuitous path down to the lowlands. There is a chapel near here, on a grassy mound covered with piles of dry stones and almond trees. We walked up to the little white-painted building, wrapped in warm pullovers, for the sun was now covered by cloud and an icy wind had begun to blow, shaking the almond blossom on the branches. Some of last year's dead leaves still clung to the apple trees, and they shivered and rustled in the grave-yard over the white marble tombs. The oil lamps were lit before the *iconostásis* in the chapel, showing the armed Angel Gabriel, the Virgin and Child, Christ carrying the Cross and the Ascension, in strong glowing colours against the cold white walls. These walls were so thick that the soughing noise of the wind could not pene-trate the calm of the interior.

There is an Orthodox tradition that men may pass behind the side doors of the *iconostásis*, but women may not. This inhibition puzzled me until I heard the explanation that women might be in an unclean state, i.e. menstruating, and thus offend the holiness of the inner sanctum. This surely must be a direct inheritance from Judaism and the restrictions defined in Leviticus 15.

We continued on foot towards the centre of the plain, past iron windmills, pumps, tanks and the litter of old irrigation pipes running along the ditches. It was a populated landscape, with workers every few hundred yards hoeing and weeding, or repairing the concrete cisterns. The growing season was about to begin, although the apple and pear trees still looked dormant and winterbound. Not a fresh green shoot could be seen among the coarse, rank grass, and virtually no wild flowers, for over 900 metres of height above sea level delays the spring up here. The cold wind blowing unhindered across the flat lands makes the climate seem even harder than among the surrounding mountains.

Somewhere between Ayios Charálambos and Káto Metóchi, as we drove slowly through the fields, a figure in an old blue sweater and faded jeans beckoned to us frantically.

"Ela, ela, come here, come here," he shouted when we stopped, waving a half-full bottle of *retsína*. We walked to him through the long grass of the old vineyard he was hoeing. A mule stood patiently in the background, waiting until the time would come to carry his master and his tools home again, together with a great bundle of prunings which lay on the ground. The man was short and middle-aged with a twinkling eye.

"Kalós orísate," he said, "welcome. Are you English?"

"Yes. Good to have found you. Is this your land?"

"Yes, it's mine."

"You speak very good English – how did you learn it?"

"I talk to people who come here. In the summer. I make this wine, try it."

We passed the bottle from hand to hand, drinking from the neck, and he made a point of offering it to Steven, who in his shy, polite way pronounced the wine to be good. We introduced ourselves and Joan offered the man a cigarette.

"Thank you, no, Kyría Ioanna. I must not smoke now, no good for me. I was smoking forty cigarettes each day. Doctor says no more. Have you been in Lassíthi before?"

"Yes, but in the winter."

"Ah, that is not a good time. Like now. Next time come in . . . what do you say, June? June, and all the mills which are now still will turn with white sails like ships on the sea," he finished in a sudden burst of eloquence.

"This is good land?" we asked.

"Maybe once. Now it is tired. Men work the ground here since the old Greeks and the goodness is all gone."

Lassíthi is close to the maximum height at which vines will grow, and too high for olives. The vineyard was ancient and did not seem to have been cleared of weeds for years. Some of the twisted vines were almost as thick as a man's thigh. He was carrying the kind of mattock that one sees in Asia, swinging at the ground as with a pick-axe. Michael, meanwhile, had made friends with the mule who presumably wasn't used to such attention and stood gently nuzzling his shoulder.

"What's his name?"

"Oh, he's Yeoryios."

"Do you make much wine?" we asked.

"Enough for myself and my friends. Much wine," he smiled, the epitome of *philoxenía*. He looked sad when we waved goodbye to him as he turned back to his lonely job.

Beyond the Vidianís Monastery, we turned on to the road which leads out of the plateau to the north-west towards Iráklion. We wanted to look at the stone windmills which hold a lonely vigil at the very summit of the pass, four or five oval sectioned stone towers on either side of the road, facing into the blustering wind like a V-formation of wild geese. These are not water pumps like those of the plain, but flour mills in varying states of decay, although the mechanism of several is well preserved. A couple of them are locked up, and may work to this day for all I know. It must be said that compared to the great and technically sophisticated English and Dutch windmills, these Cretan mills are extremely crude. Unlike the modern iron water pumps below on Lassíthi, there is no mechanism to turn the sails to face changing winds, either manually or automatically. The towers have simply been built to face into the prevailing wind at the narrowest and highest point of the pass. The wind on this day was certainly blowing steadily and powerfully square at the bare creaking poles, making them quiver and oscillate slightly as we walked under them, and whistling through the rusty bracing wires. The axle on which the sails are mounted carries a large wooden-toothed wheel inside the tower which directly drives the single pair of stones via a vertical shaft and spur. It appeared that the mill could only be stopped by loosing the sails, and there was no sign of automatic hoppers or any machinery to control the supply of grain into the stones. Everyone knows the beautiful Greek windmill sails, for they appear in every holiday brochure: six to tentriangles of white canvas, mounted on wooden spars, braced with rigging wires around the circumference and secured to a central sprit protruding from the main axle. The system was simple, and cheap to manufacture locally in comparison with the giant sweeps of northern mills.The same design can be seen in Andalucia and elsewhere in the Mediterranean.

The road to the north twists its way out of sight among the mountains towards the coast, but we retraced our steps down to the plain and continued around the rim to the village of Tzermiádo. We passed a man riding a massively constructed push-bike, the kind an English district nurse might once have bestrode, and a rare sight in the mountainous terrain of Crete. Tzermiádo, or Tzermiádhes (named after the Venetian family which once held it), is the largest village on Lassíthi, with two small hotels and much rural charm, but no pretensions. A large sow was being driven down the muddy street, followed by a sounder of piglets.

Beyond Tzermiádo lies a smaller plateau, where in 1896 Sir Arthur Evans discovered the "Cave of Trapeza". It would appear that the turn of the century was such an exciting time for archaeologists on Crete that they hardly knew where to direct their efforts first. Trapeza was not systematically excavated until 1936, and then a jumbled collection of sealstones and pottery was recovered, together with over one hundred bodies, some buried in sarcophagi. The confused nature of the finds makes it extremely difficult to date them; the current theory is that the cave was used for burial from Neolithic through to Minoan times.

Perhaps more interesting is the story of the British archaeologist who carried out the excavations: the romantic, quixotic John Pendlebury. This intelligent, quick-tempered young athlete had a spectacular, though stormy career: student of the British School at Athens followed by visits to Knossós, where he so impressed Sir Arthur Evans that in 1929 he was appointed Curator. Here he settled happily with his new wife at the annexe to the Villa Ariadne, alternating seasons in Crete with winters digging at Amarna in Egypt. When his duties at Knossós permitted, he hiked all over the island in an attempt to inspect every known site, covering stupendous distances at a time and often sleeping rough. His schoolboy enthusiasm for sports had turned into a virtual obsession with physical fitness, and it has been said that he was one of the very few foreigners who could outwalk, and indeed outdrink, the Cretan mountaineers. Something about the Cretan style appealed to the romantic side of his nature, and he made many friends in the hill villages, who remembered him for his sense of humour and his glass eye (he had lost one eye as a child).

The fiery temper made itself more apparent in the professional side of his life. An example of this was the blazing row with Professor Marinatos, then Director of the Iráklion Museum, who virtually accused Pendlebury and the British School of being implicated in the illegal export of antiquities from Greece. The police and the newspapers were involved and the whole scandal was the talk of Iráklion for some while. There was of course nothing in the story; Pendlebury demanded and received an apology from the Ministry of Archaeology, while he and Professor Marinatos later became the best of friends.

Pendlebury resigned his post in 1935, but continued his independent explorations. He first visited the cave at Trapeza in that year, and in 1936 he began serious excavations, based at Tzermiádo. Later, he excavated a second site, high on the peak of Karphí (the Nail), 1,100 metres above sea level on the rim of the plateau. This mountain can be climbed from the windmill pass described earlier, and seems to have been the refuge of an isolated and beleaguered post-Minoan community at the time of the Dorian invasion.

In 1939, Pendlebury went to Tzermiádo alone for the first time, leaving his family in England. When war finally broke out, he returned to England to enlist; by the summer of 1940 he was back in Crete working for Military Intelligence with the rank of captain, but ostensibly a civilian Vice-Consul under the famous Elliadhi. It is most unlikely that this ruse deceived either the Greek authorities or the German agents, who were equally active at the time. His job was to contact potential guerrilla leaders, and to help them lay the foundations of a resistance movement in preparation for an occupation by the Axis Powers. When Greece joined the war in the autumn and the Albanian campaign began, Pendlebury's office in Iráklion became a meeting point for men of wild and nefarious appearance. Pendlebury himself spent most of his time tramping the hills, his glass eye discarded for a pirate's black eye patch, a rifle and bandoliers on his shoulders and carrying a swordstick. As might be imagined, this greatly endeared him to the *pallikária* of the mountains. Pendlebury felt a personal pride in the performance of the Cretan Division in Albania, and was convinced that the irregular Cretan *andártes* would be of great value to the Allies, if only they could be adequately armed. But London did not share his conviction at this stage, and the "ten thousand rifles for Crete" which he requested were not forthcoming.

As the mainland fell and troops were evacuated to Crete, the situation grew more and more confused. John Pendlebury became associated with Mike Cumberlege and the crew of HMS *Dolphin*, an armed caique charged with reconnoitring remote inlets and beaches on the south coast, suitable for landing commandos or supplying guerrillas by night. Together they planned a raid on Kássos in the Italian-occupied Dodecanese to the east, in order to ascertain whether preparations were being made there for the invasion of

Crete, and possibly bring back prisoners for interrogation. *Dolphin* had been occupied on the south coast, and was due to rendezvous with Pendlebury at Iráklion; by the time Cumberlege had made the voyage around Cape Sídheros, they found the swastika flying over the city and fighting in the streets, so rapidly had the German airborne invasion proceeded. *Dolphin* was forced to put to sea again, and Pendlebury effectively disappeared. It was not until years later that the story could be pieced together little by little, and the details are still less than certain.

When the German attack was at its height, Pendlebury left his office with a rifle and a small group of *andártes*, with the aim of making for the hills. At the Khaniá Gate, he parted from his friend, the guerrilla leader known as Captain Satan, with an agreement to rendezvous on the slopes of Mount Ida. He continued for about a mile along the road until he came upon a Greek company under heavy attack from a fresh wave of parachutists. Rather than turn back into the city, he left his car and driver, climbing alone up the hillside to try and fight his way through. The Greek unit were ordered to withdraw, but for some reason one of the machine gunners remained in position. After the war he told of a strange officer who appeared and fought alongside him, killing several parachutists at close quarters with his revolver, until he was himself wounded by a bullet through the right breast. He was still conscious, however, and encouraged the machine gunner to continue firing until the ammunition ran out and both men were captured. The Greek was separated from the wounded officer and did not see what became of him. But a Greek woman, Aristea Drosoulakis, who lived in a nearby house, testified in 1947 that a group of German soldiers asked for a blanket and then brought in a wounded man, an English officer shot through the right side of his chest. He was able to speak and she realised that he was John Pendlebury, for her husband was connected with British Intelligence and had spoken of him. On two separate occasions, German doctors called at the house, bandaged the wound and treated the injured man honourably and kindly, promising that he would soon be collected for hospital treatment. But the fighting continued, no one came for Pendlebury and on the following day, while searching for the German doctor, Aristea and her companion, Theonymphe, were forced to leave the area of battle for a temporary internment camp.

Pendlebury was left wounded and alone, until another German patrol broke into the house. There was even a Greek witness to the end of the story, for after the war Calliope Karatatsanos made the following statement, to be found in the Cretan police records:

I declare that I know about the execution of the officer
Pendlebury by the Germans at Kaminia that on Wednesday at
eight o'clock in the morning when they put him outside the door
of a house when they asked him where are the English forces he
answered No No No they gave the order Attention and shot him
in the chest and head and he fell.

(Trs. Dilys Powell, *The Villa Ariadne)*

In Crete, the Englishman with the glass eye had become a legend –
"Blebbery" they called him, for Cretans never could pronounce his
English name. The seeds he had sown bore fruit during the years of
the occupation, many of his Cretan friends serving their country and
the Allies with distinction.

Antonios Gregorakis, known as "Kapetán Satanás", was a famous
example. All sorts of stories are told about him; as a boy he had
fought against the Turks, and he had abducted his wife by force in
the time-honoured Cretan fashion. Once, after some particularly
heavy gambling losses in an Iráklion bar, he is said to have pulled
out his revolver and shot off his right forefinger, with the remark
that "you will never roll the dice again." "Satan" became one of the
three main *andárte* leaders of central Crete and was much admired by
the English officers who met him. George Psychoundakis describes
him about to embark for Egypt, kissing his silver-plated Turkish
Mauser and handing it to another guerrilla with the old Turkish/
Arabic word *tesilimi*, meaning consignment in trust or bestowal, and
begging him "not to shame it". Such men created quite a stir when
they reached Egypt, although the British authorities took care to
disarm them for the duration of their leave. Satanás never returned
to Crete, for he died in Cairo.

Shortly after Tzermiádo, we reached our original entry point near
the Kroustallenia Monastery, having completely circled the plain.
We made our way down the long winding route we had followed
during the morning, and by the time we emerged in the main square
of Neápoli, felt in need of refreshment. We walked along past the
shops and newsagents' kiosks in the early evening bustle, looking at
the newspapers and magazines. As at Khaniá and Iráklion, we noted
that pornography seemed to have arrived in Greece with a rush since
our last visit.

Neápoli is renowned for *soumádha*, a drink made from almond
syrup flavoured with orange blossom water and served hot or cold,
according to the season.

"That sounds delicious, just what I need," said Michael, hopefully
marching up the street, trying to find an open *kafeneíon*.

"You'll be lucky," we said cynically, "how often do you find a local speciality which is actually available when you ask for it?"

We found a tiny threadbare bar run by an old couple who cooked *mezéthes* and brewed coffee on a little stove at the side of the room. It was the kind of place where tourists are greeted with friendly surprise. Two Sfakians from the west were there for some reason; big, burly men with oily ringlets of black hair, they were putting away glasses of *rakí* at an alarming rate. A couple of games of backgammon were in progress. No, they were sorry, there was no *soumádha* – we had the impression that nobody had asked for it in years, rather like asking a Spanish bar away from the regular tourist routes to make *sangría*. We settled for coffee and *rakí*, watching the very fine coffee grains being put with plenty of sugar and very little water into a *bríki*, a narrow-necked Turkish coffee pot, and just brought to the boil before being poured into the cups and served with a glass of water to clear the palate between sips. Greek coffee is usually served *métrio*, or medium-sweet, unless you specifically ask for it *skéto*, or plain. If you don't like your coffee this way, you must ask for Nescafé, and instant coffee is usually what you get. The old lady had chestnuts roasting on the stove, a pleasant reminder of winter evenings in London as a child. Poor Michael was disappointed on this occasion, but we subsequently came across *soumádha* in Cyprus, and served hot, it is the most soothing drink for a cold or a sore throat that can be imagined.

CHAPTER 17

Ierápetra and Ano Viánnos

The road south from Ayios Nikólaos winds along with pretty views of the Gulf of Mirabéllo to the left and mountains ahead. There is a low marshy place where salt water wells up from underground, before running into the sea, and delightful secluded areas of sandy beach below the road. A turn to the right leads up to the village of Kaló Chorió and lonelier places beyond under the Diktaean range. On our first visit to Crete, we had returned from Ierápetra that way one strange windy afternoon, on dirt and gravel roads past white mountain-top chapels, and through villages so isolated that every-one, including the priest and the schoolchildren, came out to meet us. The architecture, the people and the landscape were so unfamiliar to us that we seemed to be in another continent, another century. I remember that I was concerned lest we ran out of fuel, and learned that in remote areas one can buy it in cans from the village shop.

We had no time for such diversions this morning, and drove on past the turn which leads up to the Convent of Faneroménis, on an eminence above the sea, and also the sign for "Gourniá Antiquities", of which more later. After a little pass through the rock, we picked out on the right the large villa built by Richard Seager, a rich young American archaeologist who excavated in this area at the beginning of the century, and apparently entertained on a lavish scale. Basing himself here, above the village of Pachiá Ammos, Seager assisted the remarkable Harriet Boyd in her excavation of Gourniá, and in 1903 began work at Vasilikí, a short distance to the south, not far from where the New Road now runs across the narrow neck of the island down to Ierápetra. This site is early Minoan, about 2500 BC, and is perhaps best known for defining the striking red and black pottery type known as Vasilikí flameware, which can be seen in the Iráklion Museum. More work has been carried out here recently, proving Mycenaean and even Roman occupation of the same area.

Later, Seager turned his attention to the island of Psíra (the Louse), further along the shore to the east. This is waterless and deserted now, but is believed to have had a good spring in Minoan times, for the remains of a well can be seen. The anchorage is sheltered, and it is thought that this little port traded with Egypt and the Middle East. Seager also excavated Móchlos, an island opposite the modern village of the same name (home of our German acquaintance up at Lassíthi). Móchlos is only an island today due to the steady tilting which has occurred over the centuries. Areas of western Crete have been raised by as much as 8.5 metres since prehistoric times, the centre has remained roughly stable, while the north-east has sunk, resulting, for instance, in the sunken harbour at Oloús. It is known that in the Minoan period, Móchlos was joined to the mainland by an isthmus of solid land, whereas it is now isolated by 200 metres of sea. Seager found tombs containing vases made of marble, breccia, alabaster and steatite. He did not neglect his own village of Pachiá Ammos, where he found Minoan tombs along the littoral, the bodies crammed into great burial jars.

His own death was slightly sinister. After serving with the Red Cross during the First World War, he went on to Egypt, and in 1923 was one of those present when Tutankhamun's tomb was opened. He became ill on the journey back to Crete, and died in Iráklion in 1925. Evans attended the funeral, and described him as "the most English American I have ever known," which one suspects was his ultimate accolade. The house was used by the local German commandant during the last war.

Pachiá Ammos (Thick Sands) is a thriving little town with a good harbour and a fertile plain renowned for its tomatoes. In the days when Crete had no road system to speak of, it grew prosperous in the coastal shipping trade. The town was severely damaged in the last war, but has been rebuilt, and there always seems to be activity in its narrow main thoroughfare. Just beyond the town, while one road follows the mountainous coastline to Sitía, another branch turns off southwards across the narrowest part of Crete, towards Ierápetra and the Libyan Sea. The isthmus of Ierápetra is an almost flat plain of fertile land, several miles in width, which completely splits the great blocks of highland to the east and west. It is the only break in Crete's rocky spine, the height of the watershed being just 125 metres. The gap allows the winds to whistle through, and for once the weather systems of the north and south coasts meet. When a northerly blows in summer, the cooling *meltémi*, or honey wind, from the Aegean relieves the sultry heat of Ierápetra and the south coast. But when the dreaded *sciócco* blows up from the south, clouds of

Sahara dust push through the gap into the clear skies of Mirabéllo, the weather becomes close and thundery, tempers fray and surfaces are covered with fine powder.

The new Ierápetra road is broad and straight, cluttered with three-wheeled pick-ups and lorries running up and down with the produce of the market gardens and plastic-covered hothouses on either side. A shepherd in a brown *capóta* and carrying a long machete was moving his flock along the edge of the road and looked out of place among all these modern agriculturists. To the left, the old road to Monastiráki runs to a great gorge in the Thriptís Mountains. The village of Episkopí has a little Byzantine church to which a carved wooden *iconostásis* was added in the fifteenth century, while Káto Chorió, a little further on, has an interesting Turkish fountain. But we kept to the New Road, soon entering the outskirts of Ierápetra, the only major town on the south coast.

The ancient city of Ierápytna very probably existed as a port in the late-Minoan period, trading with Africa and Asia. It is said to have been the last city of Crete to have been captured for Rome by the Consul Metellus (who was subsequently allowed the title "Creticus"), but very little in the way of Roman remains have been found, with the exception of a strange bronze statue of a boy which was found in the sands here, and which is now in the Iráklion museum. The Venetians built their usual fortress, the towers of which still stand by the harbour, while the Turks contributed a minaret and a fountain in the old part of the town. There is also a house where Napoleon is said to have spent the night on his way back from Egypt in 1798.

When we first visited Ierápetra, we gained the impression of a town just awakening from a long sleep. It claims to be the southernmost town in Europe, although the citizens of Tarifa by the Gibraltar Straits would argue the point. Even winter afternoons tend to be hot, and with an average of 340 sunny days a year, the heat can be enervating. On the sultry afternoon of that first visit, the streets were deserted during the siesta, except for a policeman in a soiled white leather jacket and cap leaning against the saddle of an old American Harley Davidson motorcycle of enormous dimensions. The sea trade with Egypt and Syria had long died away, and the harbour was silting up, used only by fishermen now. Even their catch of under-sized fish looked mediocre as they unloaded by the old Venetian walls. No wind disturbed the dusty palm trees then as the water lapped with oily calm against the long promenade. It certainly looked like the last town in Europe, a quiet backwater overcome with lassitude. We liked it enormously.

Nevertheless, Ierápetra was changing, and quickly. The surrounding plain has always been fertile and capable of growing vegetables all through the year, but the isolation of the town from the potential markets of Northern Europe put paid to any possibility of exploiting the winter sunshine. Now, with the great ferries plying regularly between Iráklion and Piraeus, giant air-conditioned Mann and Mercedes diesel lorries were beginning to make the long haul up to West Germany, packed full of tomatoes, cucumbers and lettuces, grown under polythene in the middle of the winter. I had a long talk with the young driver of a truck marked "Germanía-Hellás Fruit Company" or something similar, one of dozens parked on the waterfront waiting to be loaded up for the gruelling drive to begin, while he explained the mechanics of the operation. There was no doubt about it, local agriculture was buzzing and money was being made, even if the surrounding countryside was now littered with torn, opaque pieces of dirty polythene. For so many years Germany has been the richest market for Greek produce, and has employed emigrant Greek workers in her factories. It is certainly ironic to recall that it was Germany which provided the Cretan Kazantzakis with his first real experience of poverty, when he was shocked by his encounter with starving children in the Berlin of the depressed 1920s.

Apart from the new agriculture, hippies from Northern Europe discovered Ierápetra during the 1960s and stayed for long months, enjoying the wide sandy beaches, cheap prices and sweetish red wine. Some of these outstayed even Cretan hospitality and there was a distinct clash of cultures to say the least. The physically modest, deeply religious and conservative Cretans found them incomprehensible. I rather like the story told by Peter Greenhalgh, who encountered some American draft dodgers staying in a lonely Cretan village in 1968:

For a long time the locals simply refused to believe that the young men actually preferred not to fight; when they were finally convinced, they all manifested the most withering contempt, except for one splendidly moustachioed old warrior who produced his own, more credible theory. "Of course they wanted to fight," he confided in a stage whisper, "but they were not allowed to. They have flat feet, perhaps, or bad eyes. They do not look strong. And they have come here to hide their shame, the ill-fated children."

(Peter Greenhalgh & Edward Eliopoulos, *Deep into Mani*)

Now there was talk of developing the town properly for real tourists with money to spend, and a complex of hotels was planned for the outskirts. As we sat on those hot days outside one of the waterfront *tavérnas*, eating spicy chicken and drinking wine drawn from a great hogshead, most of the other customers were fishermen, farm workers or lorry drivers. None of them seemed to feel any urgent need to get back to work as the long afternoon wore on under the tamarisk trees. There was plenty of time to play backgammon or cards, or simply stare out to the east at the mountains above Koutsounári.

Today, the shops of the town centre were the first noticeable change. The plate glass and modern façades had multiplied, and many of the signs for the new souvenir shops were in English or German. The immense promenade with its rows of shady tamarisks was still the terminus for the refrigerated trucks, but large numbers of modern cars were here as well. The fishermen's antique motorcycles had given way to lines of Japanese machines for rent to tourists. Our old *tavérna* was still there, looking rather overwhelmed by the competitors which had sprung up on either side. As we walked along by the sea, their owners importuned us as if in some gastronomic red light district, even though it was barely eleven o'clock in the morning. One young entrepreneur of about twenty, in black shirt and trousers and festooned with gold pendants and bracelets like a caricature of a lady's hairdresser, was particularly insistent:

"Where are you going to have lunch? Eat with me, I will cook you *moussaká*, *souvlákia*, whatever you like. Good price, cheap." His two waiters, who looked as though they should have been in school, lounged by the door of the empty *tavérna*, idly watching the performance.

Spyros, the barber, has for years decorated his shop with all sorts of macabre and curious oddities of the sea brought in by the fishing boats. Now it has been entirely turned over to the sale of curiosities. Here you may see the shells of the hawksbill turtle, leathery tails of tuna fish and thresher sharks, giant lobster claws and gaping sharks' jawbones with jagged, inward pointing teeth. Today, the owner stood before his emporium, under the ghastly skeleton of a vulture nailed over the facade, to which a few feathers still clung. The fishermen who keep him supplied with his marine monstrosities were mending their nets, stretching the mesh with their bare toes. Someone had hung an octopus up on a nail to dry out in the sun and it flapped overhead in the breeze like a malevolent chamois leather. Octopus is a delicacy, but they say the sea here has been ruined by overfishing and illegal dynamiting. There was a time, so it is said, when the fishermen on this coast would throw a stick of dynamite with a short fuse at anything large they saw moving in the water, and the accident rate was such that most of them had at least a finger or two missing.

The children were still playing football on the dusty patch of ground under the Venetian walls by the harbour, as if the game had never stopped. To the east, across the blue waters of the bay which curves like a great bow, the town straggles along with its blocks of flats and chimneys under the purple mountains, wisps of cloud drifting in front of their peaks. At the far end of the conurbation, hotels and beach bungalow complexes are still under construction. In the hazy sea to the south is Nísos Chrisí, the Golden Island, which is sometimes less glamorously known as Gaidourónisi, or the Donkey Island.

A dredger was at work deepening the harbour, manoeuvring itself back and forth with a series of winches and wires attached to the sea wall, fishing out great weed-covered blocks of stone with a draglink. We watched, fascinated to see what might emerge from the mud of such an ancient port: a Turkish cannon? The anchor of a Venetian galley? Amphorae, or the keel of a Roman ship? At the same time, the outer side of the sea wall was being strengthened by the addition of enormous precast concrete tripods, like the jacks which children play with on the pavement. The stench of the open sewer which runs on to the beach here mingled with that of dead fish and lay heavily over the oily water. A tall, arched clock-tower, with an open iron staircase spiralling up to the mechanism, stands looking over the harbour and the fleet of brightly-painted caiques. The great clock under the surmounting cross seems to be permanently stuck on twenty past six.

There once used to be gipsies encamped on the road out of Ierápetra to the west; some had travelled all the way down from Roumania and Bulgaria to escape the winter. They were not the scrap-metal merchant kind of English travelling people, but the real gipsies you still see in Portugal and Spain sometimes; buying, selling and breaking horses. The men wore earrings, while the brown, colourfully-dressed women and children went barefoot. There was no sign of their camp this year, but only the warehouses of agricultural co-operatives and dusty fields of polythene sheeting to mark the border of the town. As we drove along the edge of the Libyan Sea, the plain became narrower and the dry whitish-coloured mountains moved closer, until we reached the point by a chapel where the early Minoan site of Trouli, or Fornou Korifi, can be reached by climbing up from the road. There is not very much to see of this 4,000 year-old settlement, but in fact archaeologists discovered a great deal about the lives of the hundred or so people who lived and farmed here. Their houses were destroyed by fire and never reoccupied.

The village of Mírtos lies on the coast, a little off the main road. It is one of the many on Crete which had a bad war; the Germans razed it and executed most of the men and boys during a reprisal. Now it is making money from intensive vegetable cultivation, and is a good base for visiting several ancient sites. Apart from Trouli, you can see the bricks of a Roman villa by the coast path to the west, together with some fragments of mosaic. On the summit of the hill across the Kriopótamos river from the modern village, with a superb view of the sea and north to the Diktaean massif, is the ancient settlement of Pýrgos. The earliest remains date from about 2200 BC, but most impressive is the 1600 BC villa, a country house built in the Minoan palace style whose staircase, courtyard and pavements can be clearly seen. The interesting feature of this particular site is that volcanic ash is scattered among the ruins and that it appears to have been destroyed in about 1450 BC. This, of course, fits in neatly with the "Santoríni explosion" theory for the destruction of the great palaces.

These southern slopes of the Diktaean mountains are dry and barren, the crystalline rock bright and glaring in the sunlight. We came to an area devastated by a fire the previous season; the destruction was on a massive scale and the blackened olive trees went on for miles. It appeared that some of the olives might recover, but the vineyards were obviously a total loss. The burned-out land was unbearably bleak, haunted by eagles gliding close enough for the shadow of their great wings to run ahead of us on the scorched road, which deteriorates considerably, although it does eventually connect through to the Messará. The builders of the New Road seem to have run out of energy or cash at the end of the great project. We didn't stop until the small town of Ano Viánnos, perched high on the mountain's flank, not so very far for a soaring eagle from Lassíthi, but a severe journey indeed on foot, even for a Cretan shepherd. We parked the car to the side of the single street, close to where a track runs down towards the coast at Arvi. As we got out of the car, conspicuous with our cameras and fair-haired children, we became aware of the staring of a group of men in the street outside the *kafeneíon*. Their eyes were hard and unfriendly. They wore the long boots of mountaineers; one seemed to have just come off the hill, for he wore a dirty sheepskin jacket and a long-barrelled gun was propped against the wall beside him. We wished them good morning;

they nodded without smiling and continued to stare while we walked up the narrow street. I noticed that many of the houses were daubed with the red hammer and sickle of the Greek Communist Party, KKE.

In the dusty shop we bought a bottle of wine and a few oranges. The girl who served us couldn't wait to be rid of us. We walked back to the *kafeneíon*: was there somewhere we could have lunch? One of the men, tall with hard-bitten features, jerked his head at a scruffy little *tavérna* around the corner out of the sun. You could have cut the atmosphere with a knife. Conversation stopped in the *tavérna* as we walked in, and an unshaven, middle-aged man asked what we wanted.

"Kaliméra sas. Can we eat here please?"

He nodded guardedly, then he came out with it. "Deutsches?"

"Ochi, eímaste Angloi."

The tension vanished quite suddenly and smiles were in order. I heard the word "Angloi" repeated outside in the street. Ano Viánnos is one of a number of towns in Greece whose scars are taking a long time to heal. The guide books will all tell you that an atrocity took place here – yet the town with its long memory is part of a broader pattern with many disparate threads, which has been fifty years in the making and is still evolving today.

When Venizelos retired from politics, following his abortive coup of 1935, a national referendum, held under highly questionable conditions, voted for the return of the monarchy in the shape of George II. Shortly after the King had resumed his throne, General Metaxas seized control of government with the aim of modelling Greece on the lines of the fascist states of Italy and Germany. King George acquiesced in the rule of the illegal military regime, confirming the chief ministers in their positions. This toleration of the dictatorship by the monarch resulted in his alienation, not only from the Communist KKE, but also from Venizelist liberals and many other Greeks, apart from the extreme right.

Metaxas himself was an interesting man. His military training took place in Germany, and German technical and administrative efficiency made a great impression on him. Greece under Metaxas had many of the objectionable features of a fascist state: press censorship, police torture of prisoners, concentration camps, and many restrictions on personal freedom. It is also true that he instituted some valuable reforms in areas that Venizelos and others had neglected, particularly with regard to the pay and conditions for factory workers. Perhaps most important for Greece, he was familiar with German militarism and had shrewdly assessed Hitler's

intentions. Other markets were sought for Greek agricultural produce to reduce financial dependance on Germany, and the Greek
Army was modernised as rapidly as possible.

During the early days of the Second World War, Metaxas attempted to maintain a strictly neutral stance. During this period, British
Intelligence were forming an undercover network of agents in
Greece, in preparation for the possibility of invasion by Germany or
Italy. This was totally without the knowledge or connivance of the
Greek Government, and inevitably the men recruited were opponents
of the regime. Many were Venizelists, but some were Communists,
and these men formed the core of the later resistance organisations
and the seed of so much dissension.

Italy, which had already occupied Albania, began to apply pressure. On 15 August 1940, an unknown submarine torpedoed the
Greek cruiser *Elli*, on a courtesy visit to Tínos harbour during that
island's famous religious festival. Although no hostilities had been
declared, it seemed obvious that the Italians were responsible. It was
a crude and brutal message to the Greek Government. Shortly afterwards there were scenes of extraordinary pretence, as leading Greek
ministers were asked to a reception at the Italian Legation (including a performance of *Madame Butterfly*), while the Italian army were
preparing to invade Greek territory. Finally, at 3.00 am on the
morning of 28 October, Count Emilio Grazzi, the Italian Ambassador, called personally on Metaxas with an ultimatum from his
government. In effect, Italy wanted unconditional free passage for
her forces across Greece, in order to attack the British in the Middle
East. The popular story is that Metaxas opened the door in his
dressing gown, looked at the note, uttered the single laconic word:
"Ochi" (No), and shut the door on his visitor. A more likely version is
that Metaxas asked the ambassador in and, after reading the note,
turned white and said: "Alors, c'est la guerre. " Whatever the truth,
28 October, or "Ochi Day" as it is called, is now a public holiday in
Greece.

As already described, the Greeks fought a courageous campaign
through the winter, and forced the Italians to retreat into Albania.
Nevertheless, they and the small British expeditionary force were
totally unable to resist the mechanised German advance which
Hitler finally ordered in April 1941. Metaxas, perhaps fortunately,
died before the worst excesses of the German occupation. As the
Allies retreated to the isthmus of Corinth, preparatory to evacuation to Crete, Koryzis, the new Prime Minister, signed the surrender
of Athens and then committed suicide. The sentry on the Acrópolis
was ordered by the Germans to lower the Greek flag. Having done so,

he wrapped himself in the material and flung himself over the precipice.

Some 300,000 Greeks died in the great famine of that winter. The resistance began to form as a series of separate, self-contained units, varying from small bands of guerrilla fighters to sophisticated political and military organisations. Communication was so difficult that many of these groups were initially unaware of each other. When they did meet, they were often hostile and suspicious. Allied Intelligence had great difficulty in making contact with the various guerrillas and ascertaining their political aims.

The Communist Party, KKE, together with other supporters of the Left, formed an organisation called EAM, the Greek Liberation Front, whose military wing, ELAS, or the National Popular Liberation Army, was much the strongest of the resistance groups on the mainland. Officers of the Allied Military Mission formed the opinion, perhaps erroneously, that ELAS had close links with Soviet Russia, and was at least as concerned with taking over power in Greece on liberation as actually fighting Germans. Relations with the Military Mission became strained, and ELAS was frequently unwilling to commit men to projected combined operations – on the other hand they were very anxious to receive air drops of arms and equipment. Towards the end of the occupation, ELAS actively attacked the weaker resistance groups of the Right (EDES) and of the centre (EKKA) in order to occupy the most strategic areas and to be able to move rapidly into the cities as soon as the Germans withdrew. (This is the conventional account of the confused fighting which took place in the mountains of northern Greece. In fairness, it should be stated that this interpretation is hotly contested by supporters of EAM/ELAS, who firmly insist that the aggression began from the Right.) Meanwhile, anti-monarchist feelings grew stronger, and it appeared less and less likely that the exiled King and his government would be accepted back into Greece. In spite of the British Government's wishful thinking, there was overwhelming evidence that a majority of Greek public opinion favoured the policies of EAM/ELAS.

A private agreement between Stalin and Churchill, followed by a Russian Military Mission to ELAS, probably restrained the left-wing guerrillas at this point. The Germans withdrew from mainland Greece in September 1944, but in December EAM/ELAS attempted to seize control of Athens, and heavy fighting lasted for two months until British troops restored order. Churchill and Eden were sufficiently concerned to make a visit to Athens in order to reassure the Greek Government.

By the end of 1945, the brief honeymoon between Stalin and Churchill was drawing to an end, and left-wing forces in Greece were once more receiving some Soviet support. Guerrillas were trained and supplied by Albania, Yugoslavia and Bulgaria. In 1946, a referendum favoured the return of King George, and elections, supervised by the Western Allies (the Soviet Union declined to participate), elected the Populist Party, led by Constantine Tsalderis, to power. The Left, who opted to boycott the election completely, found themselves at the mercy of a growing campaign of terrorism from the forces of the extreme Right and turned to arms once more. Tsalderis appealed to the UN for assistance in the "fight against Communism", while Britain announced that she could no longer afford the role of military and financial supporter which she had undertaken. The United States stepped in, and the "Truman Doctrine" evolved, the principle of general aid to any country "threatened by Communism". Even with US backing for the Government forces, the civil war dragged on until 1949 with all its peculiar horrors and atrocities: forcible enlistment of women fighters and the *pedomásoma*, the abduction of children from guerrilla-held areas for indoctrination as political cadres in Eastern bloc states.

The situation in Crete had been very different, mainly because the original guerrilla bands were patriotic rather than political. Before the emergence of politically-motivated groups, the bands had been dominated by the personality of each individual leader. In the east, the most powerful captain was Manoli Bandouvas, who had taken to the mountains with the nucleus of his band immediately after the Battle of Crete. A heavily moustached and powerfully built figure, with a forceful and dominant personality, he exerted immense influence over his followers. It is said that, being nearly illiterate, he employed a scribe to write his messages. British agents admired his undoubted courage, but deplored his lack of judgement and tendency to hot-tempered and rash decisions. Tom Dunbabin had serious trouble with him on one occasion over the distribution of stores following a parachute drop.

Lassíthi, the easternmost nomós of Crete, had been occupied, not by German but Italian troops, the Sienna Division commanded by General Carta. When Marshal Pietro Badoglio's provisional government surrendered Italy to the Allies in 1943, there was a race to fill the vacuum the Italians would leave. The British agent, Patrick Leigh Fermor, contacted the Italian General at Neápoli in order to persuade him to hand over his troops' weapons to the guerrillas and leave for Egypt, or even to enter the hostilities directly against the

Germans to the west. Bandouvas and his guerrillas were to hold themselves ready to take over the Italian arms and equipment on Leigh Fermor's word. But for some reason Bandouvas convinced himself that the surrender of Italy implied an imminent Allied invasion of Crete. He therefore decided on a head-on clash with the enemy, and on his own initiative attacked a large German force near Ano Viánnos and killed over a hundred. Muller, the German commander, reacted with fury, executing some 400 innocent civilians, 100 in one day at Ano Viánnos, and burning the nearby villages of Ayios Vassílios, Káto Sími, Péfkos, Krevetás, Kefalovríssi, Kalámi, Vachós and Amirás. So intense was the German drive to capture Bandouvas and his followers that no one dared shelter them, and they had to be evacuated to Egypt. It is perhaps understandable that there should have been a backlash in the Viánnos district against the rightist guerrillas' provocation of the Germans, and a subsequent turning to EAM/ELAS and the Communists.

Liberation came to Crete later than the rest of Greece. British agents had with difficulty kept the rival factions apart; perhaps naturally, they showed favouritism to EOK, the National Organisation of Crete, which could be described as Liberal/Venizelist in political character, anti-Communist and pro-Allies. At the same time, arms were denied to EAM. Tom Dunbabin held a meeting of guerrilla leaders in an attempt to resolve their differences; it was a colourful and stormy occasion. Even the retreating Germans were concerned by the Communist influence. There is a story of a convoy of German trucks on their way into the Khaniá enclave, and the soldiers throwing rifle ammunition to a group of EOK guerrillas. "Nationalisten," they shouted approvingly.

One of the first EAM leaders on Crete had deserted Bandouvas' original group after the massacre at Viánnos. Iannis Phodias, a young man from a family of Asia Minor refugees, seems to have struck everyone who came into contact with him as dangerous, even psychopathic. As the Germans pulled out of Iráklion, rival groups of guerrillas raced to take over control. Phodias rode into the city on a horse garlanded with flowers, while Petrakoyiorgis commandeered a German car. The confusion was such that liberators and retreating German transport actually mingled in the streets, but somehow the peace was kept amidst general flag waving and jubilation.

In the case of the German retreat from Réthymnon on 14 October 1944, EAM and EOK had made a bargain in advance to share the responsibility for the town. But in January, EAM/ELAS set up road blocks outside the city and refused to remove them. In the ensuing fight with EOK, EAM was defeated and lost control of the area.

While the mainland was in the throes of the civil war, there were isolated outbreaks of violence in Crete, although it is sometimes difficult to decide whether these were politically motivated or merely the normal family feuding. Iannis Phodias' band murdered a group of right-wing Albanians in Ierápetra, and this brought them into conflict with Bandouvas, now returned to the island. During a battle on the slopes of Mount Ida, Phodias was shot while hiding in the branches of a pine tree. A right-wing guerrilla carried his severed head through the streets of Iráklion.

After the civil war ended with the defeat of EAM/ELAS in 1949, many who had fought on the losing side were forced into exile behind the Iron Curtain. Sad little communities were founded as far away from the Greek homeland as Tashkent in Central Asia. Membership of the KKE was made illegal in Greece, and the remnants of the party went underground. As the years went by, a steady trickle of refugees made their way back over the borders from the Communist countries to the north – children who had been abducted by force, and those whose involvement had been slight enough for them to feel safe in returning. Many returned to Greece in 1974 with the fall of the Colonels' Junta and the legalisation of the KKE. In Crete, two ELAS guerrillas came down from the mountains after thirty years in hiding. Communist Deputies were returned to the Chamber, and the people of such villages as Ano Viánnos could paint the hammer and sickle on their white walls without let or hindrance. In Greece, there is a thirty year time limit on prosecutions for serious crimes, including murder, and this too, has resulted in the return of many exiles. Recently there have been accusations that history is being rewritten. There are young people in Greece who claim that there were no atrocities – it is all propaganda. But most older Greeks are in a mood to forgive and forget – very few of those involved on either side during that cruel, fratricidal war can claim to have clean hands.

Ano Viánnos neither forgives nor forgets its innocent dead, to whom there is a monument on the main road. It seemed to us that they could just bring themselves to speak to what had appeared to be a party of young Germans – but only just.

The group of men outside the coffee shop all smiled and said hello as we passed after lunch, as if to make up for their earlier unfriendliness. We idled in the sun too for a while, watching a group of black-garbed women washing clothes in the rocky bed of a stream which ran below the glowing fruits of lemon trees before disappearing under the road. The scene would have had great beauty, were it not for the discarded plastic fertiliser bags and tin cans lining the banks.

The stream looked shrunken and inadequate, but there are a number of disused water mills which it must once have been able to drive. Beneath a great stack of firewood on a stone platform, the women bent painfully over the water, pumelling the garments and laying them out to dry on the bank.

We had parked our car by the new church, but there are also two Byzantine churches, the fourteenth-century Ayía Pelágia, with its fresco of a fallen woman being devoured by snakes, and the fifteenth-century Ayios Yeóryios. They are kept locked, and you must enquire in the village for the keyholder. The steep track leads downhill from the village street, heading directly south towards the coast. Side turnings lead off to various vineyards and olive groves. As the land levels out below the village, the water trickles along the side of the road, and black plastic irrigation pipes run in all directions. The white daisies shone in an unbroken sheet under the dull green of the olives, which shivered and occasionally showed the silvered underside of their leaves in the freshening breeze. Looking back at the Diktaean mountains, we could see that dirty weather was blowing in from the north, for thick black clouds covered the summits and were evaporating in the sun as they rolled down the southern slopes. The houses of Ano Viánnos were spread over the foothills like the wings of a white bird, with the little hamlet of Loutráki showing separately higher up. The writer Kandylakis was born in this district in 1861, fought the Turks, and lived to write *Patouchas*, a description of country life in Turkish days.

The dirt road remained fair until we stopped at the little, crouching church of Ayios Yeóryios, with its barrel roof and massive stones, to which we had not, of course, the key. We peered through a tiny window while the boys played under the almond trees by the roadside. When our eyes grew accustomed to the gloom, there seemed to be St Georges slaying dragons on every wall. St George is a busy saint, constantly concerning himself with human affairs and problems, and usually good for a posthumous miracle if approached in the right way. There is a famous story of one Theophistus, a Cappodocian farmer of the fourth century, who lost a pair of ploughing oxen. He prayed to St George for help in finding them, desperately throwing in the incentive that if they were found, he would kill and roast one of them and ask the saint to dine, presumably in the form of a spirit, for George had been martyred at Nicomedia in 303 AD during Diocletian's persecution of the Christians. When the oxen turned up, Theophistus decided that his offer had been unnecessarily generous, and no doubt the saint would be quite happy with a kid. That night St George appeared to Theophistus in a dream and chided him for the broken promise. Nevertheless, in the cold light of dawn the farmer still could not bring himself to sacrifice a valuable ploughing ox, and slew a sheep and a lamb instead. Finally, St George lost his temper and let Theophistus know that if he didn't slaughter every head of cattle that he owned, he would very likely find that he, his family and everything they possessed would be burned in righteous fire. Poor Theophistus was terrified, killed and roasted his entire herd, and asked the priests and the poor of the district to sit up and feast through the night with him while he waited for his guest. Finally St George arrived, in the guise of a knight with a group of richly dressed companions, and joined in the eating of every last morsel of meat. At the end of the feast, the saint ordered all the bones to be piled in a heap before him and he blessed them. In a trice, they had all become fully fleshed live cattle again and three times the original number. St George disappeared before Theophistus could even stammer his thanks.

Michael was continuing his search for scorpions, which have some inexplicable fascination for him. None here, but a harmless skink, a sort of lizard which has lost the use of its legs and squirms its way through the stones, trailing its limbs behind.

This track would be no problem in dry weather for any ordinary vehicle. After the spring rains, however, it had deteriorated in places to a chain of puddles of uncertain depth. Our car became plastered with mud as we slowly made our way as far as the white painted Ayía Monastery on the left of the road. Although the low buildings appeared in good repair and the gardens well kept, there was no sign or sound of life within, although the distant figure of a monk could be seen working in the fields below us. We seemed to be approaching an enormous cleft in the mountains towards the sea, but the track turned away to the west and then passed under a vast pyramid of limestone with sheer crags at the summit: the 600 metre high Keratókampos. Occasionally, through the clouds which obscured the peak could be seen a ruined arch: a tiny silhouette traced against the disturbed sky – who would be mad enough to build up there? It is the remains of the Keratókastello, and if the climb can be made safely, the view must be a fine reward. At the base of the rock are traces of post-Minoan occupation.

The road now begins to wind down steeply through terraced olives towards the blue Libyan Sea. We stopped again to look at the ruins of a long-deserted village and a couple of threshing floors overgrown with asphodel, that tall, slightly sinister plant which always seems to grow where man has disturbed the ground. Grazing animals will not touch it although, according to Theophrastus, the ancient Greeks ate parts of it. There was once a belief that the asphodel provided food for the spirits of the dead, and so it was encouraged to grow in graveyards.

With the reduction in height, the afternoon had grown hot again, and unfamiliar butterflies, one very large and white, were fluttering over the flowering bushes of gorse. The valley narrowed; the road did not improve and seemed to be about to peter out altogether. Then, without warning, we came across a polythene-covered greenhouse, full of the lush growth of banana trees, half-ripe fruit already showing. Round the corner were several more, and suddenly we emerged by the line of buildings which forms the tiny village of Arvi, squeezed between the mountain and the sea, isolated and famous, even in Crete, for its tropical microclimate.

The water which irrigates the gardens runs out of a gorge, the entrance to which we had seen from the north on the track from Ano Viánnos. The sheer walls of the canyon are 300 metres high, and when the winds blow hard through the gap, or the stream is in flood, the little village below is said to shake with the thunderous roar. According to legend, Zeus struck the mountain to create the fissure. Pashley travelled here, and claimed to have found an ancient pagan temple to Zeus Arvios, on the site of which the church is now built. He also acquired a sarcophagus, which is now in the Fitzwilliam Museum in Cambridge. It is a most lovely thing, engraved with reliefs of the Triumph of Dionysus. The Greek suspicion of foreign travellers during the eighteenth and nineteenth centuries as being treasure hunters was not entirely unfounded; indeed the black market in Minoan articles continues to thrive even now. To be quite fair to Pashley, however, he claimed that the sarcophagus was lying derelict on the seashore, already broken into pieces.

On this day the wind was blowing, as almost always in Crete, but no terrifying rumble could be heard from the mountain. This really is a small place, just a short row of buildings by the water, with the track running behind them and a few boats pulled up on the black sand of the narrow beach. The only inhabitant in sight hailed us as we crossed the stream by a fringe of giant reed, and parked on the bank; in spite of the warm and humid weather he was dressed in a heavy suit and tie. He was waiting for a friend to drive him into Iráklion and he wanted to know all about us.

"Arvi", he said, "is the warmest place in Greece. Did you see the bananas? We grow them all year." He felt in his coat pocket and brought out two small but perfectly ripe bananas for us to sample. We realised that he had taken the fruit for his journey, but, typically Cretan, had given them away to strangers without a second thought.

"We don't seem to see bananas like this in England."

"No, they all go to Athens. They fetch a high price there."

Steven was making a show of enjoying his piece of banana, although I know it is the one fruit he cannot stand. I began to wonder whether we had met the mayor of the village, so keen was he to extol its virtues.

"You come here for a holiday next time, come and stay in our hotel, the Ariadne. It's cheap. Stay two, three weeks, we'll make you a special price for a room. The sun always shines here, the beach is nice.

I think if I were very tired, I might be tempted to disappear from the world behind the bananas and do nothing at all for a week or two. No place to write or work though; the whole atmosphere is far too soporific.

By the side of the gorge is the Arvi Monastery, one of Crete's smaller, poorer religious houses. It was once the custom for Orthodox families to give the second son to the Church, but predictably, the religious life in Greece has suffered from the impact of Western ways and living standards. Monasteries which once housed hundreds of monks and thrived through their labours in the vineyards and olive groves, often are now left with only a handful of elderly occupants, who manage to do little more than preserve the sacred relics and continue the traditions and daily prayers as the ancient building slowly crumbles around them. The practice of monasticism came originally from Egypt, and became widely established in Greece during the fourth and fifth centuries. Its crowning glory is the Holy Mountain of Athos, that extraordinary time capsule from the Byzantine world, a statement of faith which has survived all the vicissitudes of the centuries.

In the old days, more colourful characters found their way into holy orders. There was a time when brigands who were getting a little old for the open-air life in the mountains would find a religious house a safe haven for their old age. Many Cretans entered monasteries to avoid military service under the Venetians – a service overseas from which few returned. The fiery, militaristic monks took a leading part in resisting the Turks. The isolated, fortress-like monasteries were natural rallying points, and the monks secretly and illegally taught the Greek language to the children of the nearby villages. This active role taken by past religious leaders in political, as well as religious matters, has lasted to some extent to the present day. The Turkish Sultan's decision to rule the Greeks through their own religious hierarchy compounded the situation. In times of rebellion, the heads of the bishops were often the first to roll. The obvious modern example is Archbishop Makarios of Cyprus, who was elected as *ethnarch*, leader of the people in both secular and religious affairs.

We took the easier road back, via Amirás. A little beyond Péfkos is a road leading to the north as far as the village of Káto Síme. If you climb for another six kilometres and 1,000 metres higher on to the border between the nomes of Iráklion and Lassíthi, you will, aside from gaining an insight into your state of physical fitness, find yourself at an ancient and sacred site, close under the Diktaean peaks. There is a spring and a plane tree by this sanctuary, once dedicated to Hermes and Aphrodite. It is interesting that worship continued here until the third century AD, when Christianity was superseding the old gods in Crete. (The Emperor Theodosius offici-ally forbade pagan rites in the fourth century, although remote areas such as the Máni are said to have clung to the old religions as late as the ninth century.)

There has been much speculation as to the survival of the old beliefs in the folklore and religion of modern Greece. The issue is confused by the mass of romantic literature and poetry lavished by Western European writers on the gods and heroes, long after the Greeks themselves had lost their belief in them. In fact, the ancient Greeks' relationship with their gods was a practical and phlegmatic one. The gods were powerful, short-tempered neighbours; it was unwise to anger them. If one inadvertently did so, a suitably gener-ous present would put the matter right. It was all a matter of persuasion and appeasement, inducing the gods to be one's allies and not one's enemies. Love did not enter into the equation, nor did sin, beyond the fact that any action which offended a god would require a major sacrifice to avoid divine displeasure. The gods, for all their power, were essentially human in their nature: vain, jealous, quick-tempered, and highly partisan in their championing of indi-vidual human beings. It is fair to say that this attitude of bargaining and appeasement is very much that of the modern Greeks' accommo-dations with their favoured saints. One goes to different saints with different problems; St Menas of Crete, for instance, specialises in lost property. It is difficult to refute the argument that the Greeks have always been polytheists by nature.

The early Christians shamelessly borrowed and adapted from the older religions. The obvious example of a pagan survival in Northern Europe is the Christmas celebration – which seems to bear even less relationship to Christianity recently, as is invariably pointed out by some eminent churchman every year. In Greece, there are many more, from obscure customs such as the hanging of garlic over

doorways on May Day, the throwing of the cross into the sea at
Epiphany, the censing of houses and the green boughs of Palm
Sunday, to the boys and girls who still leap through fires at the
summer and winter solstice in some areas. As already mentioned,
the custom of making little votive offerings in the form of silver arms,
legs and other afflicted parts of the body – these hang in every
church – goes back to the sanctuary of the healer Asclepius at
Epidaurus. The most important Greek festival, the Easter celebration of the death and resurrection of Christ, has strong similarities to
the myths of Adonis, Persephone and the Eleusinian mysteries.
Charos, or Charon the ferryman to the underworld, still plies his
trade, sometimes known as St Charon. Artemis changed her sex to
become St Artemidos, as did Demeter to become St Demetrius, still in
charge of ripening crops. Zeus, father of the gods, became God the
Father, still seen as a bearded patriarch. Dionysus as St Dionysios
continues to concern himself with the fermentation of wine, and
Hermes now carries his messages in the guise of the Archangel
Michael, although his wings are now on his shoulders and
have grown out of all recognition. Is there a connection between
Hephaestos, the gods' smith and armourer, and the armed knight St
George? Does the Virgin now occupy the position once held by
Athena?

The thinnest disguise of all is worn by Zeus's son, Apollo, who in
Greece was commonly known as the driver of the fiery-horsed chariot
which drew Helios, the sun, daily across the sky. A glance at a
detailed map of Crete, or any part of Greece, will reveal numerous
mountain-top chapels dedicated to the Prophet Elias (Greek for the
Hebrew Elijah). The Prophet Elias is appealed to in time of drought;
perhaps he can be persuaded to remain behind the rim of the world
for a day or two and allow the rain to fall. On the shortest night of the
year, great fires are lit on these lofty peaks in honour of Elias, while
the people stay up to welcome the rising sun.

Pan, the god of shepherds and animals who revealed himself in the
heat of midday, was originally a minor deity of Arcadía in the
Peloponnese, but perhaps he would have found the pastoral countryside of Crete to his taste. He appears in the Bible as the "noonday
demon", and is the author of the "panic" which comes for no reason
on people in lonely places, or occasionally makes flocks scatter and
run with no visible cause. Ovid wrote of the "weirdness of noonday":
"Grant we meet not the Dryads nor Dian face to face, Nor Faunus,
when at noon he walks abroad."

Pan has not ensured his immortality by the ruse of joining the
Christians, but he still haunts the Greek landscape in the form of the

kallikántzaros, literally the "good centaur", a little cloven-hoofed spirit who turns milk sour and makes bread go mouldy. Sometimes he urinates down the chimney to put out the fire. He hasn't lost his habit of pestering young girls, and tends to be accused of causing miscarriages. This is as far as his mischievousness goes, and he can be placated by leaving out a small offering: some milk or a little cake.

There is a legend in which Pan comes to represent all the old gods rolled into one, and in which all the survivals discussed here are denied. This tells that at the very moment that Jesus of Nazareth died on the cross, cries of lamentation were heard in the woods and over the sea: "Pan is dead", for the power of the Nazarene was stronger than the old magic. Thus the world passed from a heroic age of mystery and enchantment, to a newer, harsher reality, in which heaven and earth were clearly defined and separated. Aféntis Christós is the name of the great mountain which dominates the Viánnos district, "Christ the Lord", or "Christ Effendi". But men must once have had another name for it.

CHAPTER 18

The Palace of Knossós

The new highway to Neápoli cuts through the Selinári Gorge, a place reputed to be haunted by demons. There used to be old water mills along the riverbed but they were obliterated to make way for the road. High above, to the north of the road, is the Monastery of Selinári, where travellers traditionally stopped in order to pray to St George for a safe journey and drink from the spring. Once, every busload would pull off the road to do this, and there is still a great pilgrimage here on St George's Day, 23 April. The monastery is now used as an old people's home.

We were approaching the most developed part of Crete, leaving aside Ayios Nikólaos. The next village of Mália is, of course, famous for its Minoan palace, but the fine beach has attracted a string of hotels and pensions, together with the attendant *tavérnas* and bars. Mália is fortunate to lie on a fertile plain, watered by windmill pumps in the dry season. With the income from tourism and growing bananas, the village is doing nicely.

The Minoan site is signposted towards the sea before modern Mália and, I suppose, could be said to rank third of Crete's palaces, after Knossós and Phaestós. The Cretan Hadzidakis began the excavation, but it was continued by the French School who are still working here. As with Phaestós, the palace has not been reconstructed to any major extent, and the site is a beautiful place, between the mountains and the sea. There was a Neolithic village here once, but the first palace was built in about 2000 BC, and a second, larger building replaced it in about 1700 BC. As with the other palaces, it was destroyed in about 1450 BC. Legend, as opposed to archaeology, assigns Mália to King Sarpedon, brother to Minos of Knossós and Rhadamanthys of Phaestós.

The basic features of the palace are very like those of Knossós and Phaestós. An excellent guidebook is sold at the site, and so it seems

The isthmus of Spinalónga, near Eloúnda

Windmills on the pass above the plain of Lassíthi

Knossós: the Cupbearer Fresco in the South Propylaeum

Knossós: the west portico of the north entrance

unnecessary to describe in detail the great courtyard, the storage magazines and the throne room. There are a few features unique to Mália, such as the sacrificial pit in the courtyard and a large *kernos*, like a millstone, which may have been an offering table. A series of little hollows is believed to have been provided for samples of all the different grains and crops in cultivation at the time. Also, a great tomb was found between the palace and the sea where the kings were buried. Robbers broke into it many centuries ago, but enough of the royal treasure remained for it to have been named the *khrysolakkos*, or "pit of gold". Illegal diggers flocked to the area in the nineteenth century when word of the treasure leaked out, and one man was killed by an earthfall. Another strange find was the "acrobat's sword", a weapon believed to have been set in the ground, point upward, in order that acrobats might perform a back somersault over the blade.

The next village of Stalída, with its wide beach and pleasant palm trees, is largely given over to tourism with a cluster of hotels and restaurants. Liménos Chersonísou has become a totally modern beach resort. Irákliots, as well as foreigners, tend to use it as a refuge from the noise and heat of the city. In fact, this settlement is very ancient; the Minoans were here, and in the Classical period the town was the port for Lýttos, the Dorian city further inland near Kastélli, and there are remains of the harbour in the water around the headland. The Romans built a little fountain which can still be seen, and the foundations of a fifth-century Christian basilica are visible on the headland. At that time, the town was important enough to house an archbishop's palace. Since then, Chersonísou has gradually declined to become merely a pleasant fishing village, with more than its share of ancient coins and pottery sherds buried in the sand, until tourism brought about the present revival.

We passed the turn which leads inland, eventually to the northern entrance into the Lassíthi plateau, and the smaller road marked to Goúves. Beyond Goúves lies Skotinó, where the villagers will show you another of Crete's giant caves; it was a place of worship through Minoan, Classical and Roman times. This is a busy section of the New Road, and some remarkably ugly development is taking place along the margins, fuelled by the nearby aviation base as well as the tourist boom. All the same, there is much to see if you have the time to look. Near the modern village of Cháni Kokíni is the *mégaron*, or great hall of Nírou Cháni. You will have to find the caretaker to show you this house of a Minoan lord or priest, which contained many religious objects: bronze double axes, vases and tripod altars, all now preserved in the museum at Iráklion. Some distance to the west at Ayii Theódhori are the remnants of a Minoan harbour, where Evans traced the bases of columns under the sea.

The same caretaker holds the keys to the "Cave of Eleíthiya", marked by a fig tree a short distance up the side road to Episkopí. Hadzidakis and Halbherr made the first serious exploration, although the people of the area had always known of it. The use of the cave as a shrine dates back to the Neolithic period, even before 3000 BC, which makes the later Minoan occupation seem almost recent. Eleíthiya was believed to have been born to the goddess Hera in this cavern, and the worship is thought to have been directed at her as the patroness of women and childbirth. The cave is mentioned in the *Odyssey*, and so it can be assumed that its fame was widespread in Homer's day. A little further down the main road towards Iráklion, and almost bordering the airport, lies the ancient port of Amnisós, also mentioned by Homer as the embarkation point of King Idomeneus and his Cretan army for the Trojan war. It was here, in the 1930s, that Professor Marinatos first found the pumice stone which led him to the theory that the eruption of the Santoríni volcano had overwhelmed the Minoan civilisation.

On our last visit to Knossós, we had stopped first in the walled city of Iráklion, to eat an al fresco lunch of kebabs in a street of old wooden-balconied Turkish houses. Today it was still early, and we pressed straight on, taking the road south out of the city, through the heavy traffic of the suburbs, until the houses began to give way to gardens and vineyards. Some visitors, who have dreamed for years of their visit to the Minoan palace they have read so much about, make a sort of pilgrimage to Knossós on foot from the centre of the city. A road to the left leads to Ayios Ioánnis, where Evans unearthed a domed Minoan burial house, the Tomb of Isopata, which was destroyed during the Second World War. Above the valley of Knossós, the main road passes a great sanatorium, built with American money after the same war. All sorts of post-Minoan, Roman and Christian remains have been found in the surrounding fields, including the Roman Villa of Dionysus, with mosaics still visible, part of the colony of Julia Nobilis which was founded by army veterans after the conquest of Crete. A little further, and one comes to the Villa Ariadne, the house Sir Arthur Evans built for himself, and which was taken over by the German Commandant of Crete during the war. It is quite easy to drive past the entrance to Knossós, for all that can be seen from the road is a car park and a line of cafés on the far side of the road.

During the Roman occupation of Crete it was said that the ground opened up near here, presumably during an earthquake, and a tin box was found full of tablets covered in writing which no one could understand. The find was sent to the Emperor, and it was decided that the strange writing was an account of the Trojan War. In the nineteenth century, ancient remains were constantly turning up in this heavily-populated district south of the city, most of them Roman. Pashley, Raulin and Spratt had surveyed enough of the surface of the island to make it clear that remarkable finds might await a serious excavation. But the suspicious and uncomprehending attitude of the Turkish administration was a great hindrance to the archaeologists of the time, and must have considerably delayed the uncovering of the Minoan civilisation. Much credit must go to the amateur Cretan historians who persisted in trying to expose their island's past.

One of these was the middle class merchant and enthusiastic spare-time archaeologist, Minos Kalokairinos. In 1878 he was digging amongst the olive trees when he uncovered something which seemed much older than the Roman masonry nearby. He excitedly dug further to find the remains of extensive walls, some of the stones still showing the marks of the masons, and the enormous storage jars or *píthoi*, which are now so familiar to us. He had in fact broken into the storeroom of the Minoan palace. Kalokairinos, naturally enough, was bursting to tell someone. The man he rushed off to consult was W.J. Stillman, once the American consul and also a keen archaeologist. But before they could proceed much further, they came up against the resistance of the authorities and the Turk who owned the land, who was unwilling to sell it or have it extensively excavated, presumably being more interested in olive production.

Stillman wrote up their finds, however, although without understanding their full significance, and the paper was widely read among the international scientific community. The great Heinrich Schliemann read of the discovery and felt that it might prove the answer to his personal quest for the Mycenaeans, the Greeks who had set out to conquer the city of Troy which he had uncovered in 1870. In 1886 he came to Crete, and made determined efforts to buy the land and commence a full-scale excavation. He was unable to persuade the owner to sell, however, and eventually had to leave, frustrated.

Arthur Evans was from a wealthy English family of paper millers: he had a passion for travel and wandered all over Europe, particularly the Balkans, where he was special correspondent for the *Manchester Guardian*. He developed a particular affinity for the nationalist aspirations of the people of Bosnia and Herzegovina, whom he knew first under Turkish, and then Austro-Hungarian rule. At this time, he lived in the ancient city of Dubrovnik, until the Austrian authorities first imprisoned, and then expelled him as an undesirable alien. Back in England, he married, and was appointed Keeper of the Ashmolean Museum at Oxford – indeed he virtually created the modern museum over ten energetic years of fighting for funds – and built his wife a beautiful house, Youlbury on Boar's Hill, though she died before its completion. When he came to Crete, still only 43 years old, his life had reached a kind of natural crossroads.

Evans' interest in Crete was stimulated, so it is said, when he came across ancient sealstones being offered for sale by curiosity dealers in an Athenian market; when he asked their origin, he was told that they came from Crete where peasants found them in the ground. In fact, Cretan women used to wear them as milk charms. These sealstones have now been found in enormous numbers at many Minoan sites, and are thought to have been pressed into soft wax in order to identify the ownership of a bale of trade goods or a jar of oil or wine. Some of the designs are very beautiful, depicting such subjects as a leaping ibex or a stag delineated with fluid and expressive lines. Stones have been found showing animals (wolves and horned mountain sheep) which are now extinct on Crete.

Evans' archaeological speciality was the study of prehistoric picture-writing languages. He had been to Mycenae and met Schliemann, who had just astonished the archaeological world by his proof of the existence of a Cycladic civilisation, a race of Indo-European origin and the progenitors of the Greeks of antiquity. It should be remembered that before Evans and Schliemann, Greek history was assumed to begin with the first Olympic Games in 776 BC. Everything before that date was regarded as insubstantial myth and better left to the poets and romantics. Both Schliemann and Evans were, of course, romantics themselves; there is a breed of modern archaeologist which delights in criticising these nineteenth-century men as hopelessly unscientific and subjective. Evans, in particular, had in later life a tendency to hold on to his pet theories in the face of overwhelming evidence to the contrary. Yet their instinctive approach served them both well, and the discoveries speak for themselves.

In 1894, the hill of Kephála at Knossós was still virtually untouched, although the digging carried out by Kalokairinos had earned it the new name of "the Place of the Jars" among the local Cretans. And the old legend of King Minos, the Minotaur and the Labyrinth was still associated with this mound, covered in wild flowers and odd pieces of ancient stone. Evans surveyed many of the lesser sites of Crete, but he was convinced of the importance of

Knossós and determined to buy it. He persuaded the Turkish owner to sell him a quarter share before Crete slid into bloody revolution again and the Great Powers took control. Evans took to writing on the Cretan situation for the *Manchester Guardian,* as he had previously done in Dalmatia. It was not until the rule of Prince George, and a more sympathetic administration, that he was able to buy the rest of the land. With a mixed Muslim and Christian work-force, in the interests of harmony, and backed by his considerable personal fortune, he began to excavate in 1900. Some of the men fell sick with malaria due to the proxmity of the Vlychiá stream which runs into the Spiliopótamos (the ancient Kairatos river) underneath the hill. For this reason Evans abandoned his first headquarters, the Turkish Bey's house by the water, and moved to Iráklion, then still known as Candia, where he lived for five years, before building the Villa Ariadne.

As the treasures were one by one revealed to the astonishment of the world, the resulting publicity can be imagined. Evans gradually realised that as the palace was built on a number of different levels it would not be possible to show the true form of the building without a certain amount of artificial reconstruction. This was eventually carried out on a large scale with reinforced concrete, and the ethics of this decision have been the subject of controversy ever since. Evans spent most of the rest of his life and practically all his fortune on the project, and work still continues.

The palace stands on a flat-topped hill in the valley with the Vlychiá stream running around its base, although the hill does not stand as proudly as it originally did, due to the excavated earth which has been packed on the west side. It is not generally realised that Knossós is one of the oldest sites in Europe, for beneath the Minoan palace lies a Neolithic settlement dating back to 6300 BC, or the very first human occupation of Crete from Asia Minor or North Africa. These men used tools of stone or animal bone, made simple clay pottery, and after initially living in caves, eventually built crude clay brick houses. The little idols they have left in the ground indicate that they worshipped a female fertility symbol, a mother goddess. The great palace visible today dates from about 1700 BC, when it replaced the earlier building which is presumed to have been destroyed by earthquake; 1450 BC is, of course, generally given as the date of destruction for the later palaces, although it will be seen that Knossós was less damaged than those at Phaestós, Mália and Zákros.

It has been estimated that the palace was the centre of a great city, perhaps as large as modern Iráklion. The word "palace" may not be the best description, for this focal point of the city was certainly the seat of the ruler, but was also the administrative and religious centre, and the storage area for large quantities of trade goods. It is remarkable that there appear to be virtually no fortifications or defensive works – in what we always imagine to have been a hazardous and violent age, they felt secure. There have not been many periods in the later history of Crete, even to the present day, when the arts have been able to flourish in an atmosphere of such tranquil prosperity. The Minoans apparently lived well; it seems that they hunted red deer, ibex and hares; they kept goats, sheep, pigs and cows; they had no chickens, but they may have kept a domestic Egyptian goose; they grew corn, barley, broad beans, peas, lentils, olives, figs, quince, apples and pears; they fermented wine, gathered wild *hórta*, as Cretans do today, and were accustomed to the use of herbs as flavouring. They enjoyed all the range of Mediterranean seafood – and the fishing was surely better then; they had no refined sugar, but used honey as a sweetener; no potatoes, tomatoes or citrus fruit of course, but they did use salt and, surprisingly, pepper. The valley of Knossós is particularly fertile, and to this day is intensively cultivated with olives and grapes.

The crowds of summer seemed far away as we walked under the purple bougainvillea hanging from the pergola which shades the pathway from the entrance to the bronze bust of the grand old man, forever under a hot Cretan sun at the edge of the West Court: "Sir Arthur Evans – The People of Iráklion, in gratitude." It is hard to know why he was generally liked. He could certainly be very distant and autocratic; when he travelled he had a large retinue of servants and invariably camped in the countryside rather than staying in the villages. It is said that he never learned to speak Greek well. Yet Cretans who worked at Knossós spoke of him with affection and when the bust was unveiled in 1938, he was "very touched" when 10,000 people turned up for the ceremony.

The boys, as always, ran to explore the intricate passages, their heads full of stories of the Labyrinth and Minotaur; Joan and Michael shouldered their cameras and followed them. A class of schoolchildren chattered excitedly as they went with drawing boards and paper to sketch the ruins. I was left idling at the highest level, the "Piano Nobile", taking my bearings from the surrounding hills.

Personally, I cautiously approve of the partial reconstruction. Remember that an ancient traveller approaching the palace would have seen a great building, four or five storeys in height, crowning the hilltop: something most men of that day would never have seen or dreamed of. It would be beyond the capability of most casual visitors to extrapolate the appearance of the complete palace from the evidence of levelled walls, courtyards and pits. The socket where a pillar once stood may be all the evidence an archaeologist requires – but I need to see the pillar. When I first saw the impression of the Phaestós palace by the artist Costas Iliakis, my breath was taken away by the massive presence of the structure. Even allowing for a little artistic licence on Iliakis' part, I do not believe that I could have worked this out for myself in an afternoon spent among the low walls of Phaestós. Evans' "halfway stage" is enough for my imagination to make the leap, whatever the archaeological purists may have to say about it.

Today, cypress trees cluster around the walls of the palace, the dark sombre green of the foliage contrasting with the pale yellow earth of the vineyards on the surrounding hillsides. To the south, across the Vlychiá, lies the Gypsades Hill, and beyond, the rather eerie cone of Mount Ioúchtas pushes above the horizon. Our Minoan traveller might have approached on the southern road from the Messará and crossed the stream on a "Viaduct" after passing the "Caravanserai". Here, surrounded by frescoes of partridges and hoopoes, he might have stopped to wash his feet in a stone bath through which the spring water still runs, before climbing up by the "Stepped Portico". The Minoan route to the coast continued roughly along the course of the modern Iráklion road, but an official leaving the palace on business at the port would have joined it by initially travelling down the remarkable "Royal Road" from the theatre at the northern end of the West Court. This sunken corridor, overhung now by shady trees between its deep stone walls and in almost perfect condition, is 130 metres long and one of the most atmospheric parts of the palace. It was excavated quite recently and is often, justifiably, referred to as the oldest road in Europe. Just beyond its junction with the road to the coast is a building known as the "Little Palace", and beyond that is what Evans described as the "Unexplored Mansion", in that there was no time to deal with it until the late 1960s. Excavation here was difficult, for the Minoan dwelling had later additions from the Mycenaean period, and there were Roman and later remains above. Archaeological maps of these rolling hills are scattered with Minoan sites. To the north-east, near the village of Makritíchos is the "Royal Villa"; beyond the Gypsades Hill to the south is the quarry where the Minoans obtained gypsum for the interior of their buildings (for Crete has no marble), and on the road to Archánes is the "House of the High Priest" and the "Temple Tomb". It should be remembered that these names are largely conjectural and owe much to Evans' romantic streak.

Knossós is a complicated and intricate network of staircases, rooms and courtyards, with none of the carefully chosen proportions of Classical Greek architecture. To some extent, the appearance of the palace complex must have evolved as additions were gradually made over the years. Nevertheless, there is an overall design which has not been obscured. Moreover, there are a number of details which show the skills of the architect. One is the manner in which vertical shafts and courtyards are left open in order to allow light to penetrate to the lower floors, often incorporating elegant staircases. The drainage and water system is extraordinary; nothing as efficient was seen in Europe until the nineteenth century. At the East Gate of the palace, towards the Spiliopótamos, are a series of steps alongside which runs a rainwater gulley, the channel being obstructed in such a way as to control the flow and prevent splashing, while there are settlement tanks to remove silt. The Minoans had some idea of how to make buildings resistant to earthquakes, in that wooden beams were often strategically employed in order that their resilience would withstand the tremors. This was not always successful, for on the site are several private houses of the ancient city, clustering by the palace wall. One of these is known as the "House of the Fallen Blocks", for it was destroyed by giant stones, some of them weighing over a ton, which fell from the palace during a violent shock. The great square stone pillars used on the lower floors are mostly original, but the more elegant outer columns, tapering to a narrow base, which Evans has replaced with concrete coloured a deep, dull red, were originally the trunks of trees from the island's cypress forests. It is thought that these were mounted upside down to prevent rotting or sprouting from the roots.

The palace must have amazed a visitor from mainland Greece, or perhaps an ancestor of Ulysses might have seen it and felt something of a country bumpkin, fresh from the simpler pleasures and ruder comforts of such an island as Ithaca. Homer still spoke with admiration of the Cretan civilisation of his day. It seems quite credible therefore that the ruler of Knossós employed a great architect, a Daedalus, whose skill seemed almost magical to his contemporaries. Did the legendary craftsman fall out with his ruler, and was he imprisoned together with his son? Where could the extraordinary story of man's first attempt at flight have come from? It made us smile to hear that modern Greek Air Force officers graduate from Icarus College, and that aircrew are popularly known as *icarians*.

Minos himself is an enigmatic figure: son of Zeus and Europa, together with his brothers, Sarpedon and Rhadamanthys, a mixture of blood and ichor flowing in his veins. At one level, he is a cruel tyrant, exacting his tribute from Athens and the other subject states, sacrificing youths and maidens to his monster, the Minotaur. At another, he is renowned for his wisdom and justice in administering the law, eventually becoming immortal as a judge in the next world. The throne of the Knossós palace is still there, made of gypsum, and the oldest in Europe, but we don't even know if Minos ever occupied it. It may have been used by a high priestess of the Minoan Mother-Goddess cult. The whole problem with the Minos legend is that all the evidence indicates that people at that time worshipped goddesses, not gods, and that the Aegean states were in fact matriarchies, the king being no more than a symbol, privileged lover of the queen, who was sacrificed at the year's end and his blood and flesh ploughed into the land to ensure its fertility. A time must have come when the role of the king became more important and a substitute or an animal died in his place. But the very name Minos may not refer to one man, but be a general title for the ruler or king. It seems unlikely that we will ever learn more than the old legends reveal or conceal.

Theseus, the hero who challenges and bests Minos, seems to be more closely grounded in history. After the Minotaur's death and the flight with Minos' daughter, Ariadne, he returns to find that his father, Aegeus, has cast himself into the sea now named after him. As king of Athens, many more stories are told of his adventures; he was said to have been one of the Argonauts who went to Colchis for the Golden Fleece. (A very prosaic explanation is now given for this legend, and it has been reduced to a piratical expedition in about 1200 BC to rob the Armenians, who used sheepskins to wash gold dust out of the river silt.) Theseus is said to have died on Skíros in the Northern Sporades, for he owned land there which the King of Skíros coveted, and murdered him for it by pushing him from the top of the *acrópolis*. Another version is he died accidentally, falling while drunk after dinner.

His memory was certainly held in great reverence by the Athenians for centuries. At the Battle of Marathon in 490 BC, many soldiers swore they had seen his armoured ghost charging with them at the Persian army. After the Persian Wars, the Oracle at Delphi ordered the Athenians to search for his bones on the island of Skíros and bring them back to his native Attica. The story becomes blurred again, but it seems that in 470 BC the Athenian commander Cimon had been sent to suppress Skiriot pirates, which he achieved by selling off the entire population as slaves and replacing them with colonists from Athens. As Cimon searched for the remains of Theseus, it is said that he saw an eagle raking at the ground with its talons. When they dug in this place, the Greeks found an enormously tall skeleton, armed with a bronze sword and spear, which was reverently brought back to Athens and housed in the Theseion.

Was the Minotaur – half bull, half man, eater of human flesh – Minos' creature or Minos' curse? Supposedly, it was the result of Poseidon's anger, for in another version of the legend in which Minos fails to sacrifice the superb white bull to the Earthshaker, Poseidon causes the queen, Pasiphae, to become enamoured of the animal. She persuades Daedalus to construct a full-sized model of a cow in which to conceal herself (surely his strangest commission) and the intercourse results in the Minotaur. The Athenians had killed a son of Minos and so he demands a tribute, seven youths and seven maidens, every nine years, to feed the monster with which the god has cursed him.

The bulls shown in Minoan carvings and frescoes seem familiarly natural enough: wild bulls caught in nets or, with human figures, in the famous *Toreador Fresco* found in the "School Room". The beautiful bull's head from the "Little Palace", now the pride of the Iráklion Museum, is a wonderful study of an animal's nobility and strength, but there is nothing magical or sinister about it. An enormous fresco of a charging bull can be seen, copied and reconstructed by the Gillérions, a Swiss father and son who undertook most of this work for Evans. The fresco is back in its original position in the West Portico above the Northern Gate, where it may have been visible among the ruins well into Classical times and thus have given impetus to the old legend. There is evidence enough that the Minoans played some sort of game involving gripping the bull's horns and leaping, something like the modern *corrida* of Portugal or the Landes district of France perhaps. Did it have a religious significance, or was it just for sport? Was the Minotaur no less than the Earthshaker, Poseidon himself, living in the form of a huge bull deep below the palace and shaking buildings to the ground when rage overcame him?

Visitors are sometimes disappointed to find no maze of passages or chambers which might form a labyrinth, suitable for imprisoning a monster. There is a complex of caves near Górtyna which has a better claim to be a labyrinth; Cretans hid there from the Turks in 1867. The archaeologists patiently explain that the pre-Hellenic word *labrys* meant double axe, the religious symbol which appears throughout Knossós and the other palaces. Another ancient word-ending *nthos* (as in Corinthos) simply implied house or place. Therefore, *Labrynthos* would mean "House of the Double Axe", a likely name for the palace, which in view of the size and complication of the building, might eventually have come to mean any place with many rooms and corridors. A clay tablet of Linear B script has been found quite recently which refers to "Our Lady of the Labyrinth".

The marks of fire from the burning olive oil in the magazines at the time of the palace's destruction in about 1450 BC can still be seen. John Pendlebury conjectured that: "A strong south wind was blowing which carried the flames of the burning beams almost horizontally northwards." But the Minoan civilisation would not have ended suddenly and catastrophically, for undoubtedly the palace was repaired and reoccupied to some extent, and society continued on a more modest scale as the Achaean influence grew. When the Mycenaean Greeks sailed to Troy, the Cretans of King Idomeneus of Knossós were respected and powerful allies, even if Crete's commercial influence in the Mediterranean had largely disappeared. Knossós even outlasted the Dorians who came in the twelfth century BC, and in the Classic and Hellenistic periods was once again, like Górtyna and Kydonía, an independent city state, though now of only provincial importance. In the Classical period, Crete was quite eclipsed by Attic/Athenian culture. Nevertheless, this culture had been heavily influenced by the earlier civilisation in art, religion and myth. As already mentioned, the first priests at Delphi are said to have come from Knossós. The Cretan reputation in the field of law and justice was famous, and Lycurgos, the lawmaker of Sparta, was said to have come here to study. Some time before the Roman occupation, the old name and city finally declined and disappeared, to be rediscovered 2,000 years later. It is interesting that in its later years the city of Knossós issued marvellous coins, some of which show the Labyrinth and the Minotaur, so the story is old enough to keep us wondering whether something lies behind it.

The Villa Ariadne has acquired enough ghosts during this century to rival any shades of the long dead Minoans which remain attached to Knossós: the powerful character of Evans and the tragic John Pendlebury; Mackenzie, the first Curator, whom Evans suspected of drinking and hypochondria; Humfry Payne, the excavator of Eléftherna, and Manolis Akoumianakis, Evans' foreman at Knossós for many years. Akoumianakis had come from the Amári village of Gerakári as a boy to sell cherries in Candia at the time when Evans was beginning to dig; on an impulse he asked for a job. He proved to have a natural talent for the work and a kind of nose for what lay under the ground, guided partly by a countryman's knowledge of the local vegetation. (Certain plants, the deep-rooted wild fennel for instance, like to grow where the soil has been disturbed by man, even if the disturbance took place thousands of years before. Asphodel tends to do the same.) Manolis Akoumianakis was eventually put

227

in charge of the whole work force, a calm, respected figure who habitually wore traditional Cretan dress. He was able to afford to educate his children, his oldest son, Micky, being trained as a lawyer.

When the Germans invaded Crete, Manolis Akoumianakis was fifty-eight years old, and, as might be expected, had joined John Pendlebury's undercover organisation. He received the news (inaccurate, although he never knew it), that Micky had been killed in Albania. Another son, Minos, was in the Greek Navy, probably a prisoner of war. Akoumianakis was left in charge of the Knossós site, where his wife and younger children remained for protection until he could arrange for them to travel to a safe village in the hills. On 21 May, the day John Pendlebury was wounded, he wrote Akoumianakis a letter, asking him to rally the men of Skaláni in the vineyards to the south-east, and to deny the Germans the high ground across the Spiliopótamos to the east of Knossós. In fact, by this time the Germans were already established on the ridge, but on 28 May Akoumianakis led a party of Cretans to assault the position in unison with a group of British soldiers, a desperate attempt in which most of the attackers were slaughtered. Manolis Akoumianakis' body was found by his daughter some days later, the Germans having forbidden the burial of Cretans who had resisted. He was still dressed in the Cretan waistcoat and sash, the loose breeches and high boots, while the straw hat which he habitually wore during excavations was in his hand. Pendlebury's letter and the keys to the Villa Ariadne were in his pocket. Forty-four days after his death, four more days than prescribed by the Orthodox Church for the memorial service, his son, Micky, reached Knossós after a perilous voyage from Albania. The body was secretly removed to the little ruined Byzantine chapel of Ayía Paraskeví nearby, a site which Manolis himself had found and excavated, and there buried.

Micky, like any Cretan in such circumstances, had a debt to pay. He became an active British agent, gathering all the information he could about the German dispositions in the Iráklion area. When the Germans requisitioned the Villa Ariadne to house their commanding officer, he made a point of cultivating the staff there, particularly the general's driver. There seems to have been a genuine element to this friendship, but the information Micky acquired was later to prove invaluable. Meanwhile, the Greek archaeologist Nicholas Platon was in charge of Knossós and the Iráklion museum during the occupation; he protected the more vulnerable parts of the Knossós site as best he could by packing them with earth.

It was in the Villa Ariadne that the German surrender of Crete was finally signed in May 1945.

CHAPTER 19

Archánes and Mount Ioúchtas

When the boys had tired of running up and down the steps and passageways, we continued south towards Archánes, a town whose name on the map at least appears mysterious, and the capital of the most renowned grape-growing district of Crete. Shortly after Knossós, where the road bends sharply, we passed a large aqueduct built in 1838 across the gorge of Spília, apparently designed by a Cretan during the short period when the Egyptians ruled the island. Its purpose was to supply Iráklion with spring water from Mount Ioúchtas.

The vines growing on these hillsides actually produce the superb *rosaki* table grape. Nevertheless, many fine wines of great variety are made in Crete. The *aliatico* is now the most famous wine grape, but in 1817 there were apparently more than sixty different strains under cultivation. Wine was the main export during the Venetian period, and it is recorded that the town of Réthymnon used to export 12,000 pipes – some one and a quarter million gallons – each year. The Cretans boast that Prince Henry of Portugal insisted on using Cretan vine cuttings to plant the island of Madeira (although the Cypriots claim the same for their famous Commandaria wine). The malmsey wine of Crete (the word is a corruption of *Malevísi*, the wine-growing eparchy south of Iráklion, although some relate it to Monemvasía in the Peloponnese) was famous in England. The first consul England ever appointed abroad was a man named Balthazari, whom Henry VIII entrusted with the vital task of ensuring a steady supply of Cretan malmsey to his court. Today the quality varies, but the better ones are very good indeed; rich, dark and powerful reds, some of them almost black, are sold locally at extremely reasonable prices. They tend to be kept to quite a considerable age, and it is nothing unusual to find oneself drinking an excellent red that has been fifteen or so years in the bottle, at a very modest price, in quite ordinary restaurants. These aside, the local tendency is to drink the wine light and young. The monasteries are reputed to make the best wine of all. Sadly, there is not a large export trade and I never seem to see Cretan wine in England, although I understand that this may soon change. The *sultanína*, or dried grape, is by contrast an important commercial crop, the growing of which was introduced during the 1920s by the refugees from Asia Minor. The island's raisins, distinguishable by the short stalk left attached, are delicious, and a major export. They may be seen drying on great nets spread in the vineyards under the autumn sun.

I cannot resist relating the story told of St Dionysus, the patron saint, and indeed the first fermenter of wine, a saint who seems very little changed from his earlier persona as the pagan god of wine. This holy man was travelling from a monastery on Mount Olympus to the island of Náxos, and sat down for a while to rest his feet. His eye alighted on an attractive little plant with large green leaves and it struck him that it would look nice in his garden. So he uprooted it, and in order to protect the fragile plant from the hot sun he put it inside the hollow bone of a bird which he found on the ground. He continued on his journey, but when he became sufficiently tired to stop again, he found that the plant was already growing – indeed it had outgrown the bone of the bird. The bone of a lion was lying nearby, and so he put the plant and bird-bone in that and set off once again. On his next halt he was amazed to find that the plant had grown even larger and so he cast about until he found the legbone of an ass and put the plant with its two previous containers inside this, before finishing his journey to Náxos. Here he found that the plant had become so entangled around the bones that he planted the whole assembly in the ground and was delighted to find that it grew into a large vine with a crop of fruit.

St Dionysus crushed the grapes to make a drink and by accident the juice became fermented. The saint sat down to try the result of his labours. He drank a little and was quite pleased with the taste. After a little while he was surprised to find that he could sing like a bird. He continued to sip in between verses. By and by, an extraordinary feeling of confidence came over him, such that he felt himself to be as strong and courageous as a lion. But, sad to tell, St Dionysus drank even more and, before he fell asleep, he became as foolish as an ass.

There is a crossroads beyond the Spília valley, where we took the right fork for Patsídes and Archánes on to a rougher, narrower road. It is a pleasant and rural place, and no doubt General Karl Kreipe, newly-appointed commander of all the German forces in Crete, was enjoying his drive on a spring night in April 1944, when two men in the uniforms of military police corporals flagged down his car. He had spent an agreeable evening playing bridge at the divisional headquarters in Archánes, and the comforts of the Villa Ariadne were but a short distance away. Thus began one of the most audacious undercover operations of the war, for the two corporals were the Irish guardsman Patrick Leigh Fermor, and William Stanley Moss, who later told the story in his book *Ill Met by Moonlight*. Many other brave men were involved, including Manoli Paterakis from Koustoyérako and Micky Akoumianakis, who gave the warning signal of the car's approach.

Leigh Fermor, who had lived disguised as a shepherd in the mountains after parachuting into Crete, took the General prisoner at revolver point. The partisans took their captive to a cave near the village of Anóyia, not far away on the north flank of Mount Ida, having driven in the General's Opel through a whole series of checkpoints and right through the middle of Iráklion. After avoiding a massive German drive, and moving the General from one hide-out to another, over Mount Ida to the Amári and on to the south coast, he was finally spirited away to Egypt by a powerful motorboat. It was quite a coup and Patrick Leigh Fermor was awarded the DSO.

They had thought to capture the loathed General Muller, who had presided over various atrocities in Crete, but during the planning stage he was replaced by Karl Kreipe, a straightforward regular soldier fresh from a command on the Russian front. When they came to know the General, they quite liked him, Leigh Fermor and he quoting Horace at one another. From Cairo he was sent on to Canada from where he did not return to Germany until 1947.

Unfortunately, the Germans somehow learned later of the district in which Kreipe had been concealed. Their humiliation made for particularly harsh reprisals and General Muller was recalled to his old command. He began by annihilating Anóyia and executing all men found within a one kilometre radius. The razing of the villages of Amári on the far side of Mount Ida occurred at the same time, just as Lochriá, Kamáres and Margarikári had been punished in May. In the case of Anóyia the stories conflict; some say that many of the men had escaped, as even those not involved with the resistance had formed the habit of sleeping rough in the hills during periods of German activity. It would seem that about two hundred were caught and executed, together with a number of old and infirm women, by a force of 5,000 Germans, who, on 13 August 1944, burned every house in this large village. Women and children were held back as dive bombers completed the destruction. Anóyia (the name means Upland) stands high on the mountain slope at 750 metres above sea level, surrounded by ancient terraces. Sherif Pasha burned it during the 1821 rebellion against the Turks, but on this occasion, out of nearly a thousand buildings, only the church was left standing, and of this the Germans had destroyed two out of its three naves, and stabled their horses in the remainder. Today, Anóyia is built of stark, new concrete, there is a proud, bitter quality to the inhabitants, and German tourists are definitely not welcome.

There is something very uneasy still about these injured communities, a suspicion which extends to all strangers, and a melancholia which passes on down the generations. Perhaps the worst example is Kalávrita on the mainland, which lost 700 dead according to evidence at the Nuremberg trials, but 1,200 according to the survivors. After the war, Germany made direct reparations to such villages, and visits were made by philanthropic figures such as Baroness Von Thadden, in an effort to mend the damage where possible. In truth, not much could be done to heal the mental scars, and the gifts from Germany were received uncomfortably. What could be said, in the circumstances?

There is a tradition in the mountainous parts of Crete of marriage by abduction, a tradition which is not quite dead. The negotiation of a marriage is a long and complicated matter, with dowries and settlements to be discussed, engagement and wedding ceremonies to be formally held. A young mountaineer might lose patience with all this, and when he sees the girl for him – why not simply steal her and take her into the hills with him for a week or two? The idea is that on their return, the girl's parents will not have much choice but to retain the honour of their family by quickly allowing the marriage on favourable terms. In practice, it has often resulted in a bloody vendetta. After all, the Trojan War was fought over an abduction.

In 1951, Kostas Kephaloyiannis, a young man from Anóyia, fell in love with a girl named Tassoula, the beautiful daughter of Petrakoyeorgis, the resistance leader from the Iráklion district under whom he had served during the war. It should be explained that the girl's family were of the Venizelist party, while the boy's were Royalists, an explosive mixture at that time. In time-honoured fashion, he kidnapped her with the help of a friend and carried her off to a cave on Mount Ida, apparently the one in which General Kreipe had been held after his capture. Petrakoyeorgis arrived at Anóyia with a large band of armed and aggressive companions, and threatened to burn the village all over again if Tassoula was not given up at once. The Anóyiots, equally well-armed and quite ready to fight it out, told them what they might do. The situation between these Montagues and Capulets became very tense for some while; the whole island took sides, and the story reached the international press, but eventually the men from Iráklion backed down and searched the mountainside for days looking for the couple. Strangely, they failed to look in the cave, the most obvious place. The two lived there undisturbed for two weeks, and, according to local gossip, the boy did not touch the girl and told her she could leave whenever she wished. She stayed, and eventually they escaped to Athens, supposedly to live happily ever after. But this is not quite a modern fairy story, and I believe the couple were later divorced. Even today, the honour of unmarried girls is fiercely guarded by their fathers and brothers in the mountainous districts, and a relatively innocent assignation might be misconstrued and even turn out to be dangerous.

Archánes, among its poplar trees, is a large and well-to-do place, full of tractors and lorries, like the towns of the Messará. The town concerned itself with little other than growing grapes until about twenty years ago, when it came under the close scrutiny of the archaeologists, particularly Ioannis and Eti Sakellarakis. Evans had always believed that there were Minoan remains in this area, but was too preoccupied with Knossós to give them much attention. Now, there are three important sites nearby. On the hill of Phourni, reached by turning off the main road to the right at the beginning of Archánes and walking up about a kilometre, are tombs dating from about 2500-1500 BC. Some of the earlier ones appear to have been made by people whose artefacts showed them to be connected with the Cyclades. The greatest find was the sarcophagus of a Minoan princess, surrounded by jewellery and the remains of a bull and a horse sacrificed at her funeral. Within the modern town itself is the site known as "The Palace", normally locked up, although the walls of a large Minoan house can be seen through the fence.

The town is dominated to the west by Mount Ioúchtas, at 811 metres hardly a giant by Cretan standards, but impressive nevertheless, by virtue of its striking outline and isolation from the surrounding lowlands, the lower flanks covered by olives, carobs and ilex. A track leads north from the town, past the rubbish dump, on to the north flank of the mountain where there are a number of caves eroded away by wind-blown grit, known as the Anemospilia, the "Caves of the Wind". Beyond this place is the Minoan site now called the "Temple of Human Sacrifice", again normally kept locked, though the spectacular scenery makes it worth a visit. An expedition following the course of the old Minoan road found a heavy concentration of remains close to the surface at this place, and detailed excavation revealed what appears to be a temple, with a corridor connecting three rooms. Almost 400 vases and other sacred objects were recovered in the various compartments, while in the corridor was the skeleton of a man who was apparently crushed to death by the building's collapse during an earthquake. He had been carrying a vase with a bull painted on its side, possibly to be used as a libation vessel during the sacrifice of a bull. In the western room were the remains of three people: a woman lying on her face, killed by the falling roof beams, a man wearing an iron ring (a rarer and more precious metal than gold at that time), who is believed to have been a priest, and a young man curled up on his side on a table or altar. Such is the sophistication of modern archaeological techniques, that chemists have been able to establish that most of the blood had already left his body at the moment the roof collapsed. A large bronze knife was found lying across this last skeleton. The obvious conclusion is that a human sacrifice was in progress to placate the god or gods thought to be causing the earthquake at the moment the fatal tremor struck. If so, it is the first direct evidence of this custom in Crete. The quake is thought to have occurred in about 1700 BC, when the first palaces were destroyed.

We drove out of Archánes on the southerly road, by Fountain Square, past a *tavérna* packed with working men watching the local election coverage on the television, and on to the track which leads to the fourteenth-century Church of the Archangel Michael at Asómatos (the keys are kept at the *tavérna* and the frescoes are famous). After some distance, we turned right, up a badly marked dirt road towards Ioúchtas, asking the way from a blushing courting couple in a pick-up truck. The road runs from the lower vineyards right up to a little shelf, just under the peak of the mountain, from where Archánes appears to be a group of toy houses jumbled together among its patchwork of fields. The older, Cretan Zeus is said to lie buried in one of Ioúchtas' caves, and yet the later, Classical Zeus is immortal and presumably reigns on Olympus still. The Greeks of the mainland were upset by this Cretan blasphemy, and, perhaps for the first time, pronounced the Cretans to be liars. Finds in some of the caves revealed them to have been used in the Neolithic period, and Sir Arthur Evans identified a Minoan sanctuary on the summit.

The highest point is not far above the little space where we left the car, but has to be climbed with care, as the rocks fall away sheer on the western side. These cliffs are one of the inaccessible habitats of Cretan dittany, and the business of harvesting it at the end of a long rope must be extremely dangerous. Once safely esconced like nesting eagles amongst the grey boulders, some of which seem on the point of toppling into the abyss, we had a view for many miles in the clear spring air. There are great mountain ranges to the west, south and east, but the land below consists of rolling, cultivated hills, the ribbons of dusty white roads curling sinuously among the rows of vines and occasional outcrops of rock. To the north, the land falls towards Iráklion and the Aegean, although the view is rather spoiled by the radio transmitter mast on this side of the summit.

On the peak is a white-painted chapel to the Lord of the Transfiguration. Inside, the olive oil lamps were lit and the painted and carved crucifix in front of the *iconostásis* was freshly garlanded with white and purple anemones. The splintered glass of a smashed vase crunching underfoot seemed incongruous in this beautifully-kept shrine. The Feast of the Transfiguration on 6 August is kept in style by the people of Archánes, who climb the mountain to enjoy the view and celebrate under an awning rigged on steel supports over the little courtyard beside the chapel. They take care, I hope, to avoid the sheer drop to the west. Nearby is a giant wooden cross, sited where it can be seen from the town below and covered with light bulbs – it must be visible for many miles at night.

The main road, if such it can be called, continues under the flank of Mount Ioúchtas to the south, until after a few kilometres a little sign to Vathípetro, the Deep Rocks, points away to the right. We turned off down a track so narrow that the vines rubbed the side of the car, and disturbed a falcon from the ancient stone walls of the site. It flew away towards the distant grey hills of the south, amidst rays of sunlight shining from behind the clouds of the late afternoon in a Jacob's ladder of diagonal golden bars. It was an enchanted moment, and we subsequently sat for a long time on the stones, eating oranges and gazing over a pastoral scene which the light had made a Byzantine painter's vision of Heaven's Gate.

The ruins of Vathípetro are the walls of a country manor house, only occupied for about fifty years, in about 1600 BC. In this lovely, immutable place, the builders constructed a courtyard and great hall, with various ancillary rooms. The interesting finds are unfortunately locked up in the covered lower rooms, for an olive oil press, a wine press and part of a weaving loom were found: an early example of rural activities which have altered very little.

The track beyond Vathípetro is poor, and it was some time before we emerged at Choudétsi and parked by the *kafeneíon* for a coffee. The air was unexpectedly chill sitting outside under the great plane trees by a trickling fountain. Inside, a group of elderly countrymen, their faces lined and sculpted by decades of sun and weather, were drinking and smoking, playing cards noisily and happily, while the *tsikoudiá* bottle was rarely still and the coffee bubbled in the pot.

Later, we passed the Monastery of Spiliótissas, off the road to the north and the village of Ayios Vassílios, famous for its thirteenth-century church of St John the Baptist, before turning east on to the main road from Iráklion to Kastélli. This town was named after a Venetian castle of the thirteenth century, of which nothing now remains. It once had a mainly Turkish population, and the Germans built an aerodrome here during the Second World War. We noticed a number of greenhouses in the area growing carnations for export. Close beneath the Lassíthi mountains lies Pigí, meaning "Spring" or "Source", which was famous in Classical times for the curative powers of its water. There is a very old Byzantine church here, with some of the earliest frescoes on the island, although it is difficult now to make them out. The builders borrowed what they could from the ancient ruins of the area and incorporated them into the walls, and whereas the columns inside the church are for the most part without capitals, one has been constructed entirely of purloined ancient Greek capitals, piled on top of each other.

This was a lovely drive in the evening, for the straight road runs across the plain of Pediádas through magnificent avenues of eucalyptus towards the mountains of Lassíthi, like a snow-capped wall in the distance. The great trees, the olives and orchards of the plain, and the far-away snows were tinged with the glowing light of the dying sun, until the green of the turf sprinkled with yellow ranunculus began to fade as the light waned.

CHAPTER 20

Gourniá and Sitía

On a warm, bright morning, we made a later start than usual, and thus left after the hotel's tour bus, which preceded us through the town, past the lime kilns and the factory which turns crushed olive pulp into fuel bricks, and eastward along the shores of the gulf. The heat was great enough to produce a haze over a sea the colour of bright steel, and the lines of a Hellenic Navy patrol boat showed indistinctly against the grey of the Sitía mountains, when glimpsed through a frieze of tall reeds. On this occasion, we took the right-hand turn marked to "Gourniá Antiquities", and parked behind the bus. The low ridge of limestone, covered with walls and the ruins of buildings, was crowded with tourists from the hotel, led around by a young Greek woman who explained the site in conscientious detail. We sat on a wall at the bottom of the hill, waiting for them to finish and drive on – selfishly we wished to savour the very special beauty of this place on our own.

I could not help remembering our last visit in mid-winter, a halcyon day, just as warm and sunny as this one, when we saw no one all morning except three men hunting partridges on the bare rocky slopes far above. I had walked up to meet them with Steven riding on my shoulders, knee-deep in fragrant herbs and yellow ranunculus, disturbing butterflies from the lush vegetation as we passed. Standing above the little hill, we could look out over the Gulf of Mirabéllo to the bare hills of Cape Ayios Ioánnis, from which streaks of white cloud trailed in the wind. The ancient, dry-walled town sprawled over the hill like a maze of geometric shapes, occasionally relieved by the dark, wind-distorted forms of wild carob trees. Today, those distant hills were almost invisible in the warm haze, although the wind still blew, as it almost always does in Crete. The yellow flowers of that distant January day had been joined by purple, pink and white anemones, and white daisies which flourished improbably, despite the dry and stony nature of the ground.

Many archaeologists must have passed along the coastal road to Sitía in the later years of the nineteenth century, without any idea of what lay concealed a few yards away. It was a remarkable and determined American woman, Harriet Boyd, who eventually made the discovery and undertook the excavation. Miss Boyd, as a student in Athens, reasoned that Crete would provide fertile ground for a young archaeologist to make her mark. The archaeological establishment were generally rather discouraging, except for Evans with whom she discussed her plans. Crete, in 1900, was a tough environment for a young gentlewoman to tackle, for the Turkish forces had only just left after widespread violence and civil unrest, while disease and brigandage were quite usual hazards for the traveller. Harriet Boyd, with her mother in tow as chaperone, was not in the least daunted by these risks and seems to have rapidly won the affection of the Cretan peasants. She engaged a foreman and a band of workmen for her excavations; I have seen a photograph of them, the foreman in the traditional *fustanélla* kilt and pom-pom shoes of the mainland, with a great hat shading his face, while the workers look very Turkish in short cross-over jackets with exaggerated lapels and loose-fitting breeches. Miss Boyd stands modestly at the side of the picture.

In 1901, while she was excavating at Kavoúsi, a little further along the coast, a peasant told her of a place where pottery sherds and the stones of buildings could be found. On the very first day of digging, dramatic finds were made, and after three years, and with the assistance of Richard Seager and Miss Hall, a complete Minoan town had been uncovered. The energetic Miss Boyd had also managed to write up and publish her findings over the same period – remarkable celerity by archaeological standards. Her description of her life in eastern Crete during the excavation makes interesting reading, together with her discussion of the merits of various systems to reward workmen for their finds – she favoured collective rather than individual bonuses. The pride of these uneducated men when bringing her a find of importance is most touching. Although they did not appreciate the full implications of the work, they knew that having just obtained their freedom from centuries of Venetian and Turkish rule, they were now discovering their own past.

Gourniá is an open site, although a guardian is often present to watch over it nowadays. This was no great palace, but a town of small, cramped houses clustered together, very like a modern Cretan village. The name Gourniá derives from *gourní*, little troughs for watering domestic animals, which were among the earliest objects unearthed here. The original, ancient name is unknown; there are no legends or classical literature referring to the site, which had been totally buried and forgotten. It is believed that in early Minoan times, ships would have landed their cargo for overland carriage across this narrowest part of the island to Ierápetra as a preferable alternative to the long sea passage around Cape Sídheros to the east. Gourniá would have been the northern terminal of this route, but not exactly a harbour town, as the ships would have been beached in the sandy bay below. There is a small palace, perhaps a governor's villa, once three storeys in height, close to the *agorá*, or public square, at the top of the hill. There is also a sanctuary, which revealed the usual evidence of mother-goddess worship: double axes, tripod and doves.

More interesting are the surrounding streets and houses, like a smaller, older version of Pompeii or Carthage, even to the position above the sea. The lower walls which remain are of stone; the upper parts of the houses were of sun-baked clay, while the roofs were originally reed-thatched. One can still climb up and down the narrow streets where these provincial Minoans once walked, see the paving stones worn by their feet and the corners where they must have stopped to talk. In the houses and shops were found such artefacts as a carpenter's tool kit, a smith's forge and moulds for casting bronze tools, vats for olive oil, pestles and mortars, all now to be seen in the Iráklion museum. In about 1450 BC, whether burnt by pirates, destroyed by the Santoríni explosion, or drowned by a tidal wave sweeping up from the sea, the town was abandoned quite suddenly, and forgotten. It is difficult to believe in the Santoríni explosion/tidal wave/earthquake theory when confronted with Gourniá – surely there would have been more damage?

The long thick grass behind the old walls was still wet with dew, and so full of flowers that we crushed them at every step. A few areas were marked out with pegs and string, so it seems that work still continues. The carobs grow wild everywhere here, their bunches of fruit like twisted, swollen green fingers, full of sugar. Sometimes the carob is known as St John's bread, as St John the Baptist is believed to have survived in the wilderness by eating them. Carob was very extensively grown once, and is still an important crop in the east of Crete, being used as animal fodder and providing a cellulose gum used in curing tobacco, and for photographic products and paper-making. Nowadays, a very pleasant and healthy substitute for chocolate is made from it. Everyone knows about the *keraton*, the little horn-shaped bean which was the standard measure used by the ancient Greeks for gold and precious stones, still in use with jewellers as the carat. However, quite recently a scientist carefully weighed several hundred carob beans and found that their weight varied by up to 20 per cent, the average being somewhat less than the modern carat. Buying and selling gold and jewels, using carob beans as measures, would thus seem to have been a rather uncertain business.

The road beyond Pachiá Ammos along the north coast to Sitía has gained the uninspired title of the "Cretan Riviera", probably at the instigation of the National Tourist Organisation. It is in fact a most charming drive, as the road switchbacks around the spurs and ridges thrown out by the mountains in their fall to the sea, little inlets and bays appearing here and there among the rocks and cliffs. These are the mountains which look so beautiful from Ayios Nikólaos across the gulf; seen close they seem a great deal more solid, and must have caused the road builders some difficulty. Up and down through the gearbox and winding hard on the wheel at the hairpins, it is all great fun until one is forced to crawl behind a lorry labouring up the gradients, for there are few passing places.

The villages perched on the mountainside are somewhat self-consciously bedecked with flowers, and the occasional roadside *tavérna* is often signed in English, for this is a popular tourist route. First Kavoúsi, beneath Aféntis Stavromenos, the highest peak, then Sfáka, where the road leads down to Móchlos by the sea, and then Exo Mouli020á, famous for its red wine. Chamézi is one of the two rival birthplaces claimed for the poet Vincenzos Kornaros, author of the *Erotokritos*. Then, after Skopí, the road cuts across towards the bay of Sitía, and descends towards the city past various industrial and agricultural buildings on the outskirts. We parked on the waterfront, the sun now blazing hot, making the sea and the glaring white of the apartment buildings stacked on the hill above painful to the eye.

La Citía is the name the Venetians gave their town, intended to become the fourth great city of Crete. In its corrupted form, Lassíthi is now the name for the whole eastern prefecture of the island. The Venetians built a large fortress and walled the city, but these fortifications did not prove strong enough to withstand a severe earthquake in 1303, and again in 1508. In 1539, the great Turkish corsair, Barbarossa, successfully attacked the city and sacked it. At this point the Venetians gave it up as a bad job, and in 1651 dismantled most of the stronghold in order to use the cannon elsewhere. The population virtually abandoned the city and what was left decayed further under the Turks, until in 1870 a planned reconstruction was carried out, resulting in the regular streets and blocks of the modern town. Today, Sitía makes its money by growing raisins on land irrigated by the River Pantelis – for the water short-age in eastern Crete is particularly acute – and shipping them out by lorry on the New Road.

Sitía is well-known for its sharp-tasting red wine, but we sat on the waterfront drinking cold beer and watching a fisherman standing in his caique below us, patiently coiling a long line into its basket, the row of hooks systematically imbedded in the rim. If anything, the town seems even sleepier than Ierápetra in the heat of the day – and, hard to say why, somehow lacking the vigour and robustness of the rest of Crete. The town was founded by Italians; this part of Crete was occupied by Italians during the last war, and somehow the air of *dolce vita* lingers on. The people are easy-going, romantic, even somewhat immoral according to the opinion of the sterner, western parts of Crete. "Khaniá for arms, Réthymnon for book-learning, Iráklion for drinking and Sitía for fornication" to complete the tag, although I really don't know what the justification is for the last section. The mountaineers of the west, with their long boots and riding breeches, are noticeably absent from these streets. All the men here are now *makrypantolonades*, "long trouser wearers", to use the old derogatory term. Even the dog which befriended us at our table, an amiable black labrador, seemed to belong to another species from the fierce sheepdogs of Sfakiá. The Cretan music playing along the waterfront was of the languid and romantic kind, rather than stirring and dramatic as in the White Mountains.

Sitía is the home town of the famous lyrist Ioannis Dermitzakis, whose records sold everywhere. Several travellers have written of how, with very little provocation, business in his draper's shop would come to a stop as he would take up his instrument and play for anyone there to listen. He may still be there today; we have always meant to ask after him when passing through the town, but somehow never had the time. Pandelis Prevelakis is interesting on the con-struction of lyres, the instruments "with which the Cretans are accustomed to settle such of their passions as cannot be settled with a knife." The wood is important: elder for the body, limewood for the cover and rosewood for the neck.

There is a delightful folk story as to how a merely good lyre player may become a real artist. The aspirant must go at midnight to a crossroads and mark out a circle with a black-handled knife. As he sits playing in the circle, nereids will gather round him and try to entice him out with their beautiful singing. If he gives way and leaves the circle, he will never be seen by mortal man again. "Come out," they say, "and we will teach you to play so that the very rocks of the hillside will dance." But he must stay safely seated and continue to play. One of them may ask for the lyre and, as he passes it across, he must be careful not to allow his hand outside, or the nereids will surely cut it off. The nereid with the lyre will play it as he has never heard the instrument played before and then pass it back – but he must still be on his guard. So the long night will pass as they try to trick him out of his life, until finally the cock crows before dawn and the nereids must leave. If the lyrist wishes to purchase their knowledge, he must do so now and pay them something, and so, very carefully, he exposes the tip of his little finger outside the circle. The nereids cut it off, and in a moment they have taught the man all their skill and are gone before the daylight comes. Ever since I heard this story, I find that I have an absurd impulse to check that the ends of lyre players' little fingers are both present, and I sometimes wonder about Dermitzakis, or the other famous exponent, Xylouris of Anóyia.

We left Sitía drowsing by a sea like a sheet of glass, and drove east again, towards the bare hills of Cape Sídheros, the Iron Cape, projecting far to the north into the Aegean towards the islands known as the Dionisiádes. This far eastern end of Crete is a high plateau of barren limestone, with few villages and even fewer trees. The dry, uncultivated hills, crystalline and painful to look upon in the bright sunlight, are desolate and oppressive. At Ayía Fotiá, which is the only village on this long stretch of road, a series of early Minoan tombs were found quite recently; the contents are not at Iráklion, but in the museum at Ayios Nikólaos.

The modern village of Palékastro, Old Castle, has a dusty little square and a bus-stop by a large *tavérna*. The only other occupants, were the local chief of gendarmerie and his small son, eating large plates of macaroni. The wine came from Archánes, there being very little made locally.

In ancient times, the east of Crete must have been a good deal more lively than this quiet backwater, for the map of the whole district is littered with Minoan and Hellenistic sites. A narrow track runs down from the village, through the olive groves to a fine beach by ancient Palékastro, near the hill of Kastrí. This was an important Minoan harbour, unusual in that it was rebuilt after the disaster of 1450 BC. The site was excavated by the British in 1902, and a paved street, houses and shops, together with the remains of a palace, can be made out. There is also a Minoan shrine at Petsofás, further along the coast to the west, a Hellenistic temple and a memorial column or *stele*, now at Iráklion, inscribed with a hymn to the Cretan Zeus. This is dated from the third century AD, the very end of paganism in Crete.

242

The road south out of Palékastro leads through the mountains to Ano Zákros, and then past a deep ravine containing Minoan tombs, locally known as the "Valley of the Dead". Beyond the modern village of Káto Zákros, where olives and bananas are grown and one can stay at a small *tavérna*, the track comes to an end close to the sea by the ruins of the fourth great Minoan palace of Crete.

The actual site is not a new discovery, for the Englishman, D.G. Hogarth – who was later associated with T.E. Lawrence in Arabia – began to dig in 1901. Finding a few small dwellings, he concluded that this was no more than a small settlement, perhaps a watering place for trading ships, and he turned his attention elsewhere. The first hint that he had overlooked something came from an Iráklion physician, Dr Giamalakis, a private collector of Minoan art, whose collection is now housed in the Iráklion Museum, having been purchased by the Greek Government. Giamalakis, incidentally, later distinguished himself during the German occupation by attending to wounded guerrillas.

During the late 1930s, Dr Giamalakis received a message in Iráklion, urgently calling him to the bedside of an old man in the remote village of Ano (upper) Zákros. Many years before, he had operated on this man and made no charge; the message said that there was something important for Giamalakis' collection. The doctor arrived late in the night, on the back of a mule, surely exhausted by the roads of that time, to be shown objects which had been carefully hidden for many years: a beautiful golden bowl, a gold diadem and pendant with the head of a bull – all unmistakably Minoan. They had come, said the old man, from Káto (lower) Zákros. The obvious conclusion was that Hogarth had not rewarded his workmen well enough, for one of them had found this treasure and concealed it for his own profit. The doctor's feelings as he viewed these objects in the lamplight can be imagined, and fumbling in his pockets he brought out his gold watch, some Greek money and a few English sovereigns as some kind of recompense.

Very shortly after this, all archaeological activity ceased due to the Second World War, and did not recommence for some years. Much later, Dr Nicholas Platon, the Greek archaeologist who had cared for Knossós and the Iráklion Museum during the occupation, was involved in a survey of the sites in eastern Crete and found enough at Káto Zákros to convince himself that further excavations should be carried out. In 1961 he began a limited dig, and then encountered a wealthy American couple with an interest in archaeology, Mr and Mrs Pomerance, who, falling under the spell of the prospect of discovery like so many before them, offered to finance a major excavation. The partnership was successful as the great palace was then uncovered and, with the backing of both the Pomerances and the Greek Government, work still continues.

Apart from the palace itself, all the expected remains of a major port have been found around the bay, large and small houses lining paved roads running down to the sea. The harbour itself is curiously missing, possibly because of the subsidence of this coastline over the centuries. The port was founded as early as 2600 BC, and there are the remains of an earlier palace below the ruins now visible, which are from about 1600 BC. There is no doubt that this settlement was powerful and important; the palace had 300 rooms and probably three storeys, while the foreign goods found within, such as Cypriot copper, ivory and gold from Egypt and Syria, indicate the extent of its trading activity. The palace is very similar in construction to the other three, with the extra innovation of a reservoir to hold the spring water welling up under the building, and conduits to distribute it to various points. As with the others, the palace was destroyed almost completely in 1450 BC, and here there is definite evidence that something occurred quite suddenly, for the inhabitants were able to escape with their lives, but without removing all their possessions. The inexplicable aspect of this disaster is that none of these possessions were removed or plundered from the ruins by the people who lived on the surrounding hillsides during the succeeding centuries. When the palace was uncovered, large quantities of valuable jewels, weapons and ornaments lay as their owners had left them. Did some kind of religious taboo apply to the site of the catastrophe, as if the gods' wrath lay upon it and the place was cursed?

CHAPTER 21

Vái and the Toploú Monastery

We drove out of Palékastro to the north on a dry and lonely road, and took the right fork for Vái, amid scenery which looked more North African than European. Here, we suddenly found ourselves driving beside a forest of date palms filling the valley of a little stream which trickles through the sands towards the sea. There are 5,000 trees thickly clustered together amidst a jumble of fallen trunks and debris; once there were many more, but the farmers, and particularly the monastery which owns much of the land, felled many of them. The forest is unique in Europe, for although ornamental palms are common enough in the Mediterranean lands, they are always individually planted and large numbers of natural trees are not to be found. Fortunately, the value of the forest has now been recognised, and the authorities have fenced off most of the area into a reserve. The local legend is that an army of Roman soldiers camped here; each man was issued with a meal of dates, dropped the stones on the ground afterwards, and hence the trees. It is also possible that the Arabs introduced them during the ninth century. In 1968, I understand, another small grove was found in a remote location, somewhere on the south coast.

At the end of the track we parked our car in the shade of a palm, finding it hard to believe that we had not somehow arrived in one of the oases of southern Tunisia or Morocco, and made our way across the sand under the trees, out on to a delightful beach. We walked along under the palm fronds, kicked off our shoes when the sand got into them and found a quiet glade a few hundred yards along the shore. Feeling among the razor-sharp branches above our heads, we found that most of the trees were bearing edible fruit, although the dates were small and pithy. We put on our swimming costumes and, while the boys ran up and down the sand, I swam out a few yards into a sapphire sea, the ferry to Rhodes showing far on the horizon as it rounded the Iron Cape out of Sitía. I floated on my back and tried not to think of returning to work in three days' time and the cold rain of an English spring. Although the sun was hot, the Cretan wind was blowing again, and, donning a shirt, I wandered up to a sort of freshwater lagoon, formed where the stream runs out of the forest to filter through the sand of the beach. It was full of tadpoles and shoals of small fish darting through the warm shallow water. The croaking of adult frogs could be heard everywhere among the clumps of reeds, until one approached too closely, when they would clam up and sit quietly until the threat had passed on.

Lying just beyond the reach of the waves was a large sponge, torn up by the winter storms, evil-smelling and full of black mud. There are still a few sponge boats working out of Crete, but nothing like the great fleets of Kálimnos and the Dodecanese which sailed annually to Libya and Tunisia to make their precarious living. The best sponges in the world come from the eastern Mediterranean, and they have been gathered since ancient times. The earliest known contraceptive, incidentally, was apparently a shaped piece of sponge soaked in olive oil. The Greeks, in spite of their general dislike of entering the sea, were the first people to learn the art of diving. In 460 BC, Xerxes, King of the Persians, engaged the Greek diver, Scyllis, to recover treasure from wrecked ships. When Alexander the Great was besieging Tyre in 333 BC, he made use of divers to remove the booms which had been erected against his ships. The days of harvesting sponges from the shallows with a long pole are over, thanks to over-fishing, and the gathering of the prize from deep water is a hazardous occupation. At one time, every Greek seaport had a few old, or not so old men, crippled by the bends.

Beyond the stream's mouth, the palms end abruptly and the bare hillside begins again. Walking around the point, we could see no sign of human influence at all, just dry, rugged limestone mountains, washed by a shallow, bright blue sea stretching away towards Cyprus and the Middle East. Strange butterflies moved over the low bushes of cistus, the rock rose of Crete. This is the source of the drug laudanum, which was once gathered with the help of goats. When they were driven to feed on the plants, the laudanum gum would stick in their beards which would regularly be cut. There is a species of violet from North Africa found near here; perhaps it arrived with the palm trees. This part of Crete, presumably because of the extreme shortage of trees, to which the forest at Vái is a notable exception, is even drier than the rest of the island. In spite of a wet winter, the ground was already baked hard and cracking; when the summer came the dust would blow like a powder over the land.

It was time for us to move on, and we emptied the sand from our shoes and drove back along the edge of the forest. We took a wrong turning for a couple of kilometres on to a bad section of road being resurfaced by a team of men with an ancient roller. With their help, we found our way to Erimoúpolis, the "deserted city" of ancient Itanos. There is not much to see in this lonely spot; part of an *acrópolis* from the Hellenistic period, the plinth of a Roman statue and the walls of a Byzantine Christian basilica. Although the settlement was originally Minoan, it did not become important until much later. At the nearby monastery of Toploú is preserved an ancient inscription describing a treaty between Itanos and Ierápytna in the second century BC. Now the site has virtually returned to natural mountainside and our eyes kept turning to the sea, deep here and coloured a rich Oxford blue. Three little boats were drawn up on the strand, though I could not imagine who would use them, for no one lives near.

Michael wanted to explore the far northerly point of the Iron Cape, and so we followed the paved road up the peninsula. The combination of bare hills, bright light and warm winds reminded us of Cape Sagres in Portugal, where the south-western point of Europe projects far out into the Atlantic, although there the cliffs are tremendous and here one is quite close to the sea, in spite of the rugged coastline. The Greek Navy have taken over much of this land, but we hoped that the end of the Cape might be accessible. Twice the road crosses narrow isthmuses which threaten to turn the further hills into islands in time, if this end of Crete continues to sink. But just as we thought we must reach our goal, we came upon a barbed wire fence with a sentry and were forced to turn back.

A few kilometres along the west side of the peninsula we came to the Monastery of Toploú, and stopped a few yards past. An elderly man and his wife were waiting for a bus by the roadside, and the low murmur of their voices with the intermittent clicking of the man's worry beads blended with the humming of bees from the nearby hives. The sun was lower now, and the shadows lengthening as we walked towards the honey-coloured stone buildings. An ancient windmill stands on guard, facing west over the road, ready to grind the monks' grain in season, for Toploú is one of the wealthiest monasteries in all of Greece, and its lands stretch for many miles around. There was no gatekeeper at the entrance, where we noticed modern stainless steel fermentation vats in the open door of an outhouse. On entering the massive stone gate under the Venetian campanile, we were almost overwhelmed by the powerful odour of fermenting wine drifting up from the cellars. We waited in an ancient shaded courtyard, for we could hear the monks chanting their prayers in the church and the reason for the building's apparent desertion became plain. A late-comer hurried through the gate, his dark robes agitated as he walked, his long black hair and beard falling in oiled ringlets on to his shoulders from under his head-dress. He would not speak, but pressed his forefinger to his lips as he hurried on into the chapel. One of the monastery cats regarded us sleepily from a warm corner, evidently resting from his allotted task of keeping down the mice. Simple country people once believed that bats were no more than mice, who had found their way into a church and eaten Christ's body in the sacramental wafers, and so sprouted little angel's wings.

The monastery was built in the fourteenth century on the site of a much older church. Turkish pirates sacked it in 1498 during one of their many attacks on the Cretan coast, and in 1612 the building was destroyed by an earthquake. It was rebuilt in its modern form, with the addition of the great bell tower. In those days, the monks defended it with a cannon, like a castle, no doubt to ensure that no pirate should get the better of them again. The Turks gave the monastery its name, from the Turkish *top*, or cannonball. Toploú is dedicated to the Panayía Akrotíriani, the Virgin of the Cape, who seems a suitable patron for this wild place. This, as so many of the monasteries, was at the forefront of the resistance movement against the Turkish occupation, and actively supported the *andártes* during the Second World War.

The chapel is worth waiting to see, particularly for a remarkable icon painted in 1770 by Ioannis Kornaros, at the age of twenty-five. The style is distinctly Venetian, and this influence had obviously lingered on through more than a hundred years of Turkish rule. The painting is a massive undertaking, illustrating in 61 scenes a prayer written by the Patriarch Sophronion of Jerusalem. The whole is enveloped in a mass of extraordinary detail, embellished with wild animals, sea monsters, cypress trees and the rivers of paradise, sun and moon containing angels. The work is a masterpiece and, one suspects, was almost as much fun to paint as it is for the spectator to explore.

As the sun set, we returned along the Gulf of Mirabéllo, always facing west into the explosion of rich colour in the sky, the moun-tains gradually fading into deeper and more mysterious shades of blue and violet as the night came on. The sunset was so fine and the evening so clear in the hills that it compensated for the last few miles grinding along in the dark behind a line of trucks.

View from the tavérna *at Sitía, languid and romantic*

The campanile of the Moní Toploú

The north-east coast near Cape Sídheros

CHAPTER 22

The Kapsás Monastery

Walking with Malcolm by the sea, early the next morning, the air felt close and humid. Lightning flickered away in the mountains and the rumble of thunder gradually grew louder and closer. As we reached the back door of the hotel, the first heavy drops began to fall, and then suddenly a torrential downpour began, which blotted out the view, turned the terraced gardens into a series of gushing rivulets and started water flooding in beneath the doors. We stood for a while on the covered balcony of our room, watching the forked lightning flash down and speculating as to whether the building was fitted with a conductor system or not.

After breakfast, we drove through the storm to Ierápetra, grateful at least for the water washing the mud from the car. The farmers and tractor drivers we passed were dressed in oilskins and button-down leather caps, hunched against the wind. The weather in Crete, they say, is much like the people, usually very nice, but capable of getting rough quickly. *Kheimónas* or winter, Cretans call this kind of weather, even if it comes in August.

There are two small markets in Ierápetra: one for fish and one for vegetables, but nothing to compare with the big market at Khaniá. A large number of shops are given over to the kind of agricultural hardware which might be expected: rotivators, irrigation pumps, tractors and, of course, the plastic water piping which is strewn over most of the flat areas of Crete. We spent some time talking to an Athenian woman in charge of a draper's shop. She obviously felt herself an exile, and in the sharper, staccatto accent of the capital deplored the higher prices on Crete, due to the need to import so many items by sea. A large, self-service grocery and general store was interesting, with imports from all over the world. English kippers were next to Portuguese salt-cod, canned Japanese squid and Canadian salmon. There was an enormous variety of local jams and

249

conserves, honey of course and fresh, crusted yoghurt, literally by the barrel. Bottles of English Worcester sauce shared a shelf with West Indian chilli relish and Canadian maple syrup. There was an excellent collection of smoked and preserved meats and sausages from all over Europe in the delicatessen section, together with all the different Cretan cheeses – and cheesemaking is a highly regarded art here. Michael and I spent a happy time in a wine merchant's shop, always one of the pleasanter ways to kill time. Armed with a tasting glass each, we worked our way down the hogsheads, asking the owner's advice as we went. Finally, we went on to the old Turkish quarter and sat for a while by the fountain, the rain having stopped for a moment. How incongruous the mosque seems amidst the modern buildings and traffic, as if the Greeks would sooner it simply disappeared, thus expunging the last reminders of the Ottoman Empire.

The road to the east of Ierápetra runs along the coast, past the new hotels and a camping site, a long, desolate route, until it turns north to Sitía by the village of Pilalímata. We turned to the right a little earlier, and kept along the coast on a muddy track. It was raining hard again, driving inland with the wind from the sea, and though there were plantations of tomatoes under the frowning mountainsides, everything seemed poor and deserted. We had passed no eating place since leaving Ierápetra, thirty kilometres before.

Somewhere near Kaló Neró, we came to a long, low building, surrounded by wattled fencing and animal pens with palm-thatched awnings, like a Turkish *khan* or *caravanserai* – indeed perhaps it once was. The wind blew flurries of rain across the muddy yard and odd patches of torn polythene flapped in the fences of nearby gardens. A neglected shutter banged intermittently against the wall. No one was in sight anywhere in this dreary landscape, coloured in shades of grey under a lowering sky. It looked as though nothing ever had and nothing ever would happen there. Without much hope of lunch, we trooped in through a dilapidated porch which had a leathery tuna tail nailed to it, and a doorway shielded by a hanging curtain.

The large concrete room was furnished with green plastic-topped tables and wooden chairs. The usual stove stood on the bare stone floor with a long flue running along the ceiling. A small television set was fixed high in a corner of the wall, and a chrome-topped table by the door with two or three bottles, did service as a bar. There was a row of hooks on the wall for coats, and a couple of old calendars had been tacked up for decoration. The window at the far end of the room, the seaward end, was opaque with encrusted salt.

This may have seemed an unpromising start, but appearances were deceptive. A young girl, very surprised to see us, emerged from the living quarters at the side, and, after checking with her parents, reported that they could manage lunch if we would like some potato omelette. Her mother brought us a delicious meal: light, fluffy omelettes and a fresh, sharply-flavoured wild salad, wholemeal bread, home-made wine and freshly squeezed orange juice. As we drank our coffee, another customer arrived in a gust of wind, and sat down to begin a long card game with the proprietor, sitting unshaven in his shirt-sleeves at a table by the door. We bought them a drink; they sent us a complimentary plate of fresh-peeled cucumbers, that vegetable which in mixed company is usually referred to as "excuse me, cucumbers", due to its phallic shape. We all drank each other's health in *raki*, and time drifted on. As had happened several times already, we caught ourselves referring to Europe as if it were another place, a more pressurised world to which we were soon to return.

Poverty is still close to the surface in some of these villages. The lavatory for the *kafeneíon's* clientele, a concrete-floored affair outside with sacking hung over the open doorway, was also the family's bathroom, with a few washing things: soap, a shaving brush and a tiny cracked mirror on the washstand. The total bill, incidentally, came to less than five English pounds for the five of us, and we would have paid more if it could have been done without giving offence.

The rain had stopped as we bumped on down the track, although the wind blew as hard as ever. The narrow strip of fertile littoral was gradually squeezed out by the encroaching mountains as they crowded up to the sea. At last we were driving along a shelf dynamited out of the cliff face, the water growling and frothing a hundred feet below at the bottom of a boulder-strewn slope. Only the road showed man's influence on this world of rock and water, and nothing but barren treeless cliffs were visible above the foam-streaked sea ahead. Eventually, we rounded a corner to see a small patch of flat ground on which ankle-high thorn bushes struggled to live amongst the stones. A solitary tamarisk tree stood silhouetted against the sea, and intermittently a great plume of white spray rose up in slow motion as the waves hit the rocks behind it. The tamarisk loves the salt and the bitter land of the shore, but it is a tree with no useful fruit. When Christ was taken in Gethsemane, they say, he was left tied to a tamarisk for a few minutes; he struggled to escape, but the tree would not release him and so he cursed it with barrenness for all time.

We walked over the useless stony ground to a dry riverbed, scattered with larger boulders which must have been washed from the mountains by the infrequent floods to spread out here on the shore. There was no trace of water now, for the land had simply soaked up the morning's rain. Nevertheless, a thin dusting of green, feathery grass shoots grew in the lowest part of the washout, and a proper grove of tamarisks clustered about it. The entrance to the gorge was above, a gash in the cliffs cutting the mountains into two blocks, the sides of which towered sheer for a hundred metres on either side. It reminded us of the *fiumara* of Calabria which lie dry and useless for years on end, until the flood rushes dangerously and destructively out to sea, carrying with it the fertile mud which might have nourished crops. On the eastern cliff of the gorge, precariously built into the rock face, the Convent of Kapsás almost melts into the surroundings, the white-painted buildings seeming to crouch and shrink into the grey limestone. Only a couple of cypress trees and a straggle of prickly pear below the walls masks the boundary between the wilderness and this man-made retreat.

The wind was buffeting so hard through the chasm that we had to shout to make ourselves heard. Joan took shelter in the tamarisk grove while we walked and then scrambled up the gorge. We soon found our way encumbered by giant boulders, many of them as large as a house, tumbled and jammed in the passage. It is hard to imagine the kind of spate which could move such weights, but the floods must be infrequent, perhaps at intervals of a decade or more, because in odd pockets of silt grow oleanders and bushes to the height of a man. The canyon winds far into the mountains, and there is a path somewhere up above which runs inland to the village of Perivolákia. But the bed of the gorge makes for painfully slow progress, and in half an hour's clambering we had only made a few hundred yards. From a smooth grey rock, as if perched on the giant body of a slaughtered elephant, I could see through the narrow gap to the dull blue sea with the tamarisk grove just visible under the white horses beyond.

A stone was dislodged above, and we were amazed to see three goats, presumably from the monastery, grazing a tiny patch of thorn bush halfway up the precipice. They had reached this dizzy eyrie by jumping from side to side down the vertical walls of a chimney leading from the top of the cliff. There seemed little point in climbing further until someone sprained an ankle or smashed a camera, and we made our way back to rejoin Joan, before walking up the steep path to the monastery gate. A guard dog was tied up in front of the entrance, near a cave used for penning animals. At the gatehouse, we were greeted by an old woman, dressed in the inevitable black, who seemed to be the only occupant. She left her tiny kitchen to come out and quieten the dog, before conducting us up to the chapel and showing us its treasures. She spoke very rapidly, and I was unable to understand whether the monastery or convent was still in use. She helped Malcolm and Steven to buy and light a candle each, showed me the icons and a holy relic – a skull partially encased in silver – which she indicated that I might kiss if I wished. The chapel was very old and dark, smelling sharply of incense, and it was difficult to make out the smoke-blackened paintings in the gloom. I thanked the gatekeeper for her trouble at the church door, and then, as she seemed to be hovering expectantly, although we had put some money into the offertory box, I handed her a few drachmes. I instantly realised that I had misunderstood and made a grave mistake. She said nothing, but her bleak and stony stare spoke volumes, filling me with embarrassment and consciousness of my own clumsiness. "For the church," I said, indicating the box, but the harm was done and she shuffled back inside.

Once more on the main road, we passed the village of Lithínes, and made our way north through desolate mountains, eventually relieved by sections of elaborately terraced and irrigated green hillside, not of ancient origin, but recently constructed with a bulldozer. In the mountains to the east lies the ancient city of Praisós, believed to have been the remote capital of the Eteocretans or Post-Minoans, long after the rest of Crete was in the hands of the Dorians. There are both Minoan and Hellenistic ruins, and three inscriptions were found, dated at 600-300 BC. The letters are Greek, but the language is not Hellenic, possibly a separate descendant of Linear "A".

Beyond Sitía, I looked back to the east, to see a kestrel hovering over the road, framed by a perfect double rainbow. At the end of a long track leading to the coast lies the Monastery of Faneroméni, on a cape of the same name, famous for its subterranean church and a marvellous view of the Gulf of Mirabéllo. Despite the stormy day, the sunset on the Cretan Riviera was magnificent again: wonderful shadows over the water and a fleeting sight of a little chapel built into the rock which we had never noticed before. There is a mysterious quality about these limewashed shrines on their inaccessible crags, ancient and brooding monasteries seen from far away, black-robed priests and monks riding lonely upland paths as if time had no meaning. These images return later to one's mind in a colder northern climate. The ghost won't be laid until one has returned, perhaps after years, and climbed up to the place. There are so many of these confident statements of unshakeable faith, visible from afar, that surely no one could ever know them all. For me they epitomise the mountains and foothills of Crete.

CHAPTER 23

Spinalónga and Cape Ayios Ioánnis

Breakfast was a subdued affair after packing our bags, for we had to be at the airport by three o'clock. But the day was fine again with clear skies and a warm wind as we drove north along the gulf to Eloúnda. A freighter was anchored in the bay; too large to go alongside the mole at Ayios Nikólaos, it was waiting for the lighters. Beyond Eloúnda and the little fishing village of Pláka, we took the winding road which climbs up into the mountains of Cape Ayios Ioánnis, through the yellow broom and the carob trees. When we stopped for a moment, we could pick out each flat-topped white building of the village far below, spread along the pale ribbon of the coast road. The shingle beach, with a line of tamarisks, has a small boat jetty, while behind the village is a dull green parkland dotted with olive trees.

Across the mouth of the inlet are the Venetian fortifications of Spinalónga island, a business-like and stark sea-castle in the calm waters, looking very like the prison island of Alcatraz in San Francisco Bay. It proved as tough to capture as it appears, for the Turks could not dislodge the Venetians until 1715, forty-six years after Candia and the mainland of Crete had fallen to them. In the nineteenth century, Turkish fishermen used it as a base, until they were made to give it up in 1903. Then Prince George, doubtless appalled by the hideous sight of the lepers at the Lazaretto Gate of Iráklion, requisitioned the island. Lepers and their families from Iráklion, a lepers' village north of Ierápetra, and the caves which they had been forced to inhabit in other parts of Crete, were sent here by the police to form an isolated community among the fine Venetian houses.

Before the last war and the general availability of curative or inhibiting drugs, leprosy was not uncommon in Greece generally. In the early days, there was no doctor on Spinalónga, but nevertheless it was not a place of horror, but a kindly community where lepers were able to live in conditions of cleanliness and self-respect. As time went by and their numbers grew, a clinic with medical staff was established. Each patient received an allowance from the state, clean, laundered clothes, a house and garden. The lepers had their own *tavérna*, their own Church of St Pantaleimon and their own concrete-lined cemetery, although the wood for the coffins had to come from the mainland. By 1931, there were 277 lepers on Spinalónga. Visitors were freely permitted, although healthy people were not allowed to stay overnight. A little building near the landing stage was used to disinfect visitors as they left, using steam and methylated spirits. According to surviving members of the colony, some of the women staff had sexual relationships with lepers, and no contamination took place. There were even weddings on Spinalónga, although the children of these unions were removed to an orphanage in Athens by the authorities. There *were* children here though, for child lepers were sent to Spinalónga too.

During the Second World War the island refuge became a trap, and the inmates starved. But the worst aspect of the war for the lepers was that, for six years, the sulphone-derived drugs which were now available to inhibit the spread of the disease were denied to them. When this became subsequently known, it caused great anger among the inhabitants of Spinalónga.

In 1954, the decision was taken to close the colony and most of the patients had left by 1957, although there were caretakers still on the island in the early 1960s, among the crumbling Venetian palazzi and weed-grown streets. Nowadays, in summer, the island is busy every day as boatloads of tourists arrive to explore the ruins, but in the winter it is left empty. A number of survivors of the Spinalónga colony now live normal lives with their families among the Greek community, grateful for the drug which has permitted their miraculous return to the living.

When we first came here, there was only a dirt road up to the village of Vrouchás, barely passable for a car. The village had seemed desperately poor: no cars to be seen and no one young. The flat-roofed, single-storey houses, typical of eastern Crete, had ancient carved wooden doors, scoured clean by wind and weather, with great internal arches to take the ceiling's weight. The old people, leading their donkeys in from the fields, had stared at us as if we had come from the moon; the young had all emigrated or were working abroad. An elderly couple had smiled and talked to us over the dry stone wall of their tiny courtyard, interested as so often in our fair-haired children. The man had held Steven up to stroke his mule, tethered by the wall; the woman, with that curious Turkish reticence about showing the teeth kept her black shawl wrapped around her mouth and head, fluttering in the strong wind which always blows over this highly exposed cape, surrounded as it is by the Cretan sea on three sides.

Now the road is paved right up to the village, there are television aerials above the roofs and a few cars. A small child was playing on a doorstep. The land still seems to be more rock than soil, and the olives are twisted and stunted by that relentless wind which blows from the sparkling blue sea below the towering cliffs. But in a few short years, with the coming of the road, the whole atmosphere of the village had changed.

There are dry stone walls everywhere on this peninsula, dividing countless tiny fields and forming the sides of ancient cobbled track-ways, the stones of which are now loosened and ankle-wrenching. These roads are just wide enough to lead a loaded packmule between the walls across the low hills from one village to the next, and I have not seen anything like them elsewhere on Crete. Their purpose is obscure, for the labour of building the screening walls would have been considerable, and they are not high enough to offer very much protection from the wind. Perhaps when the little fields were cleared, the stones had to be put somewhere. One theory is that the Venetian garrison of Spinalónga built the trackways, between the fall of Candia and 1715. They would have relied on these nearby villages for provisions, and may have built the roads to protect their mule trains from Turkish attack at harvest time. For their part, the Cretans risked an agonising death on the hooks of the *gaunche*, or by impalement, if the Turks found that they had been in contact with the Venetians.

The land is hard, and yet the brilliant light, the fresh wind which even blows away the heat haze of summer, and the constant background of the sea, so lift the spirits that, for me, this is one of the most beautiful corners of the island – although of little historical importance as far as I know. We left the car by a little shrine at a crossroads, a perfect tiny model of a cruciform church in red, white and blue, set upon a stone block, and began to walk, following one of the mule tracks winding uphill. Some of the ancient trunks and roots of the olive trees are incorporated in the walls, but they may not be so old as olives go. There are trees standing in Attica which are said to have been planted in the third century BC. Olives are a slow business, and the cross-grafting required to keep trees cropping regularly and heavily is highly skilled. When a new tree is planted, it is twelve years before the first fruit appears and, with time, about thirty gallons of oil can be expected every second year. There are more than sixty varieties of tree; the fruit in Crete tends to be small and not particularly good for eating, but table olives are a sideline, the vast majority of production being for oil. Small olives, they say, contain the most oil. Before the last war, Crete was producing an annual 32,000 tons of oil and 2,500 tons of table olives, which represented over a third of the total Greek crop. In recent years production has fallen somewhat, but olives are still popular with the peasants, together with wheat, for these are the traditional crops of the island. Some damage has occurred from a parasite known as the "dacos fly", which lays its eggs on the trees and necessitates protective spraying.

A hoopoe perched on a wall above us for a moment before taking flight. A little later, a weasel snaked over the path before vanishing among the stones. As we climbed higher, we met an old woman, the lower part of her face covered by the black shawl thrown over her shoulder, leading a laden mule downhill. Perhaps she wasn't such an old woman after all, for life here is very hard; constant work and poverty take their toll on the complexion and the teeth. A little further, and we passed a mule tethered to an olive trunk in company with half a dozen sheep. The owners, a man and woman, were working on the trees a few yards away, tapping at the branches with long poles.

High above the olives and carobs, we could look down towards the distant sea over bare meadows still haphazardly divided by the dry stone walls and, on this day, quite white with daisies. It was almost painful to walk across, crushing the flowers among the rocks at every step. Windmills are scattered here, one or two to every field. A few are in good working order with corrugated iron roofs and securely bolted doors, but many are no more than ruined stone towers, the wooden shafts fallen and rotting. We walked into one to find the timbers of the roof half-fallen, but the great apple-wood gearwheels still in place and the worn French millstones left as they had last turned.

"God – his holy name be blessed – gave soil to some, stones to others. Our lot was the stones." (Kazantzakis, *Report to Greco*)

How much grain can one grow on land like this? How can one even plough such rocky terrain? Most of it seems to lie fallow nowadays.

Nearby is a lonely little chapel, enclosed by a wall with a wrought-iron gate. A few cypresses form a windbreak, and beyond is the ruined wall of a much older church. The chapel is a simple, oblong building with tall gables, a single arch above the door supporting the bell and surmounted by a cross. Every inch of the building, even the roof, is limewashed a blinding, pristine white.

They were still building the road here, for there were piles of gravel ready. As we drove to the west, through Séles, Loúmas, Skiniás and Finokaliá – all tiny clusters of houses where faces looked up, surprised to see a vehicle – we came to the end of the paved road, and made our way on the dirt tracks which until recently covered the whole cape. We came across the road surveying team at one point: well-dressed, middle-class Greeks, in contrast to the villagers, working with theodolites and maps. We wondered if they enjoyed their measuring among the arcadian surroundings, or whether time out here was regarded as a penance away from the office in Ayios Nikólaos or Iráklion.

The path became so narrow that the wheels of the car brushed the clusters of wild flowers and bushes encroaching upon it. We had the impression that we were making our way up a private drive, winding through the flowering shrubberies of an English garden, before finally halting in a tiny village, the name of which, like Herodotus, I prefer not to mention. The square single-storey buildings huddled either side of a street just wide enough for the car, or for a pair of mules to pass each other. A crate of empty beer bottles and a faded green sign proclaimed one small building at the beginning of the street to be a *kafeneíon*. There was barely room to park our car off the track by a rough wooden bench against the wall under a notice-board for the Lassíthi Nomós, upon which a number of sun-faded announcements of an agricultural nature had been pinned months or years before. No one was in sight as we looked through the doorway into a small room with a couple of tables and some rickety wooden chairs.

As we emerged, a middle-aged man with a stubbly face came down the street. He correctly identified our nationality at once and spoke English with a strong American accent: "You want a drink? She's not here, but I'll get it for you. What would you like?"

We all had a beer, drinking from the bottles, as the glasses could not be found. We sat outside on the south-facing bench, blinking in the strong sunlight, sadly conscious of the seconds ticking away and the bad roads between this place and the airport. But after a while we began to relax, talking to our new acquaintance who had all the time in the world. Three or four other men joined us on the bench and greeted us warmly, for word seemed to have passed around that there were strangers (or guests, for the Greek word *xénos* is the same) in the village. Quite a party atmosphere developed, but the shrouded women contented themselves with peering curiously around the doorposts further along the street; as far as they were concerned the *kafeneíon* was for men. These lingering prejudices tend to reinforce the old accusation that the Greeks are a people with an oriental mentality in a Western world, although this kind of behaviour becomes rarer with each passing year. Michael fetched his camera from the car, set it up on the wall opposite and, amidst general hilarity, took a group photograph using the automatic timer facility. Travellers in Greece before the last war say that simple country people used to cross themselves and run when they saw the camera, believing that the little box contained the evil eye.

According to Lawrence Durrell, the same pre-war traveller on arriving in such a village as this would be welcomed and seated in the *kafeneíon* in the company of the assembled elders, before being asked with great formality: "And what news of Europe?" (This has never happened to me. Instead they ask: "What do people in England think about the political crisis in Greece?" There invariably is a political crisis, needless to say.)

We asked if tourists often found their way up here. A few, but not many, maybe ten or a dozen a year. We were the first this spring and were asked all the usual questions. We had come from England; where were we staying? Where were we going to? To Ayios Nikólaos, the big town on the Gulf of Mirabéllo? To the little hamlet of Ayios Nikólaos here on the cape? Whatever for – there was only one family living up there now? We tried to explain that it was just a point whimsically picked out on a map. We liked to travel up here because it was so beautiful. This they did understand, for the rural people of Crete appreciate the loveliness of their island in a way the townspeople do not. There is a story about St Peter, the gatekeeper of heaven, who one day felt extremely tired and wished to sleep for a while. He turned to his assistant and asked him to cope with the admissions while he took a few hours off.

"You shouldn't have any problems," said the saint, "for you speak all languages." The assistant replied that he spoke every language except Greek.

"Oh don't worry about the Greeks," said St Peter, "they never come here. Their own land is far too beautiful."

Our friend had travelled and had lived in America for a while, part of the Greek *diasporá* in an attempt to escape poverty, and one of the many who returned. Was he happy living here in Crete now? Of course, he was born in this village. No one ever got rich here though – this with a wry smile. But did we know that the road was coming here? Things would be better then.

The average Cretan peasant farmer owns between twenty and thirty *strémmata* of land, a *strémma* being equal to about a quarter of an acre. In the highlands, where much of his income will be obtained by grazing animals on mountain pastures, this may be considerably less. The problem is that due to generations of complicated sub-dividing in dowries and inheritances, this land will probably be split into a large number of small parcels. In 1963 there were an average of 10.4 separate plots per farm. The same calculation made in 1970 produced an average of 12.7 plots per holding, varying from 10 to 90 minutes' walking distance from the house. Thus the farmer is likely to spend an hour or two of his working day simply in travelling. This sounds very inefficient, but does not actually compare badly with the armies of office workers who commute daily by train into the great cities of the world. The division of land militates against efficient cash crop farming, but where direct subsistence agriculture is involved, as is still sometimes the case here, the existence of large numbers of plots on differing soils, each devoted to a different product, is a good insurance against the natural disasters which tend to affect a single crop. The water rights can be even more complicated than the ownership of land and individual trees, such that the duties of the *agrophýlakas*, the rural guardian, must be extremely onerous. In spite of efforts at land reform, the importance of dowries, inheritances and family unity in general cannot be over-emphasised. There is still a tradition that an eldest son will see all his sisters safely married before he does so himself – sometimes easier said than done.

I have tried to avoid romantic illusions about the grinding poverty of Cretan village life, which, traditionally at least, was narrow, cramped and almost brutish, relieved only by a rich folklore and the natural gaiety of the people. The Greek national statistics of only a few years ago make it plain; in 1961, 47 per cent of households had no mains electricity, 85 per cent no sanitation, and 71 per cent no mains water. To deal specifically with Crete; in 1961, over 80 per cent of rural houses were quite without piped water, relying either on a public tap in the village street, a well or a spring. In 1948, only 2 per cent of villages had electricity. In 1940, even the power station at Iráklion had a capacity of only 1350 kw while Réthymnon's power was generated by a single 100 hp diesel engine. Today, electric power is available almost everywhere.

The dreadful state of Cretan roads in the nineteenth century has already been mentioned. A scheme to metallise the main north coast road (i.e. the "Old Road") began after the First World War, and was complete between Iráklion and Khaniá by 1935. This was of poor quality water-bound tarmacadam and could only take a single line of traffic, with occasional passing places. None of the bridges, either wooden, or antique Turkish stone arches, could support more than seven tons. A car could travel between the two towns in three hours then, but the road became so damaged during the Second World War that subsequently the journey time was extended to five hours for a car and seven hours for a bus. Other roads were improved during the German occupation, but a survey in 1948 found that 50 per cent of Crete's villages could only be reached by mule, and only some third of the total had any kind of bus service. At that time there were 953 motor vehicles on Crete: 64 private cars, 120 taxis and 155 buses, the remainder being lorries and tractors. The economic consequences of these restrictions were enormous. There is little point in growing perishable and easily damaged cash crops such as tomatoes, however perfect the soil and climate, if they can only begin their journey to foreign markets being bruised and jolted for hours on the back of a pack mule. And today, of course, there is a metalled road to the vast majority of villages of any size, often adequate for lorries, or at least pick-up trucks.

Before the last war, rickets and pellagra were not uncommon, malaria was a hazard in low-lying districts and leprosy has already been mentioned. Infant mortality in some areas was at a level now associated with the Third World. Travellers were generally advised that Crete was not a good place to fall ill. Life expectancy then was forty years; today it is sixty-five.

A survey in 1920 found that 52.6 per cent of the adult population were illiterate, although it points out that the census included many adults whose education had been disrupted by the rebellions of 1866 and 1896. In fact, the Turkish administration had made almost no provision for education until the Pact of Khalépa in 1878, when the Cretan Assembly tried to arrange for a standard of schooling similar to that in the free kingdom of Greece. By the 1928 census, a considerable improvement to 43 per cent overall illiteracy had been achieved. This survey gives a division between the sexes – 25.6 per cent male illiteracy as against 59.3 per cent female, which indicates the priority given to the education of boys. There has now been a revolution in education, and every modern Greek child can expect a thorough and broad schooling. Nevertheless, illiteracy is still surprisingly common among the older, rural population, and it is possible that the disruptions of the last war are partly responsible.

I am not trying to present Crete as a backward, deprived community, but rather to emphasise the rapidity with which changes have taken place. In spite of the Litton Corporation fiasco associated with the Colonels' Junta and the collapse of their development scheme for Crete and the Peloponnese, the OECD development plan of 1965 (including Iráklion airport, the enlargement of Iráklion harbour, irrigated agriculture, roads, electricity and many other schemes) was implemented with conspicuous success. It may have occurred with dramatic speed, but Greece, and Crete with it, is in every way a modern European state. It is this rapid modernisation, while odd backwaters such as this village remain relatively unchanged, which provides such a contrast between the haves and have-nots. Life styles and standards of living are being revolutionised in one generation. The most obvious result is that the young are no longer forced to travel abroad to find work, and perhaps the *xenitiá*, the exile which has been the curse of modern Greece, will eventually become a thing of the past.

Half as many Greeks are said to live abroad as in Greece itself. The effect of these expatriate "Greeks of the Dispersal" on the economy has been considerable in the past – in the way that tourism, from which Greece earns a third of its foreign currency, affects it now. It is not uncommon for a sealed coffin to arrive in Crete from Australia or America, at considerable expense, but fulfilling the last wish of the occupant to be buried in his native soil. The songs of exile were always among the most poignant, showing the melancholic, almost neurotic side of the Cretan character:

> To be abroad, to be an orphan, to be sad, to be in love.
> Put them in the scales, and the heaviest is to be abroad.
> The man who is exiled abroad should put on black,
> For his clothes to match the black fire of his heart.
>
> I beg you, my fate, do not send me abroad.
> And if you should send me abroad do not let me die there;
> For I have seen how they bury them abroad
> Without incense and candle, without priest and deacon,
> And far from Church.

> (Trs. Michael Llewellyn Smith, *The Great Island*)

Greek blood is spread far and wide about the world. I once went fishing out of Colombo harbour in Sri Lanka with Otho Constantine Weetakoon, a Sinhalese-Greek seaman, who had been almost everywhere at some time in his life. I can still picture his brown face and grizzled beard, grinning as he thumbed his special mixture of rum-steeped tobacco into his pipe, hanging on to the tiller as the boat slammed into the seas. He was endowed with more than his share of general recklessness, for he thought nothing of taking a home-made open boat about fourteen feet long way out into the Indian Ocean beyond the continental shelf if he thought he could find a fish in the big swell. Perhaps, like Zorba, he always acted as though he were immortal.

"Oh we are mad fellows," he would say, laughing at the suggestion of flares or life jackets. We never saw a marlin, but his stories kept us entertained all day long.

When Pashley travelled in Crete 150 years ago, he was welcomed by a people whose religious observance was so strict that they fasted not only for Lent, but every Friday in memory of the death of Christ, and every Wednesday in mourning for Judas' betrayal. Their women were as totally veiled and secluded as those of any Arab or Turk. They had just emerged from a bloody civil war, for the revolt of 1821–24 was fought as much between Cretan Christians and Cretan Muslims as between Greeks and Turks. The villages were burned and almost every family mourned its dead, yet still a stranger was welcomed with unfailing courtesy. Foreigners of high rank were actually addressed as royalty – "noble" or "kingly" people. "I will tell you how to thank me," a villager said to Pashley who had enjoyed his hospitality for the night, "visit my house again when next you come this way." "In Crete," wrote Kazantzakis, in *Report to Greco*, "the stranger is still the unknown god. Before him all doors and all hearts are opened."

Despite the implacable hatreds, the bloodshed and the cruelty, the people still danced and sang of love as well as war:

> O thou so dearly by me loved!
> Thou'rt like the cypress tall
> And in thy conversation sweet
> The words like honey fall.

> (Robert Pashley, *Travels in Crete*)

The romantic *mantináde* which Pashley recorded in 1833 is matched by a song which William Stanley Moss heard sung by a young *andárte* on guard outside the cave in which they held General Kreipe one night during 1944:

> My ship has the wings of a swan for sails,
> And I'll fly from the sunset into your arms;
> And the kiss of the waves and the kiss of your lips,
> Will carry us, my loved one with a beating of hearts,

With a beating of oars, to my whitest home,
My home in the clouds of the islands,
Where the vines hang low like your hair hangs low
And the cypresses frame your face, my love,
My loved one, my own . . .

(William Stanley Moss, *Ill Met by Moonlight*)

Today, Cretans work in factories, drive lorries and sit at computer terminals in the offices of Iráklion and Khaniá. They have been subjected to a publicity campaign by the Greek Government warning of AIDS, which the annual influx of summer visitors would almost certainly be bringing to their country. Like all Greeks, the young tend sometimes to make fun of the quaint customs and speech of their grandparents. "Village language, village ways", a friend used to say scornfully of everything which was not fashionable in Athens or abroad. The enthusiasm for the fruits of an industrialised Western economy which has so recently arrived, can result in an impatience with what are regarded as embarrassing, peasant superstitions, however interesting tourists may find them. Yet these young Cretans have sprung from extraordinary stock, a quite exceptional race, even among the Greeks, who are themselves a remarkable people. Like Hadzimichalis Daliannis' lost *pallikária*, the "Dew Shades" who stalk through the dawn mists at Frangokástello, their ancestors crowd close behind them, populating the empty landscape of Crete with memories and history.

We got up to leave our new friends, for time was against us, and shook hands all round. "A safe journey," they said to us, "go to the good."

264

Historical Chronology

c.6500 BC   First human settlement in Crete, probably from Asia Minor or North Africa.

c.2600 BC   New settlers join the original Neolithic inhabitants and the "Minoan" culture begins to evolve.

c.2000 BC   The first palaces are built at Phaestós, Mália, Knossós and probably Káto Zákros.

c.1700 BC   First destruction and rebuilding of the palaces.

c.1450 BC   Palaces overwhelmed by unknown catastrophe. Only Knossós rebuilt.

c.1370 BC   Final destruction of Knossós and decline of Minoan power, followed by Dorian settlement.

c.300 BC   Cities of western Crete form the 'Confederation of Oreioi.'

67 BC   Roman conquest.

c.60 AD   St Paul's landing on Crete, eventually followed by the appointment of Titus as Bishop of Górtyna and the spread of Christianity.

395 AD   Division of the Empire, and the beginning of Crete's first Byzantine period.

824 AD   Crete captured by the saracen Arab pirate, Abu Hafs Omar, and Christianity virtually extinguished.

961 AD   Nicephoros Phokas recaptures Crete and the second Byzantine "golden age" begins.

1204 AD   Following the Fourth Crusade's attack on Byzantium, Crete is ceded to the Venetians who fortify and colonise the island in spite of a series of Cretan uprisings.

1453 AD   Constantinople falls to the Turks; much surviving Greek culture reaches Crete, stimulating the "Cretan Renaissance".

1645 AD   The Ottoman Turks capture Khaniá, followed by Réthymnon, and go on to besiege Candia.

1669 AD   Candia falls, and the Venetians are left only with the island fortresses of Gramboúsa, Soúda and Spinalónga.

1770 AD   The Daskaloyiannis uprising in Sfakiá, encouraged by Russia.

1821–4 AD The '21, a general revolt in unison with the uprising on the mainland, eventually suppressed by the Egyptian forces of Ibrahim Pasha, following which the Sultan cedes Crete to Egypt.

1828 AD The Hadzimichalis Daliannis revolt and the suppression of Gramboúsa.

1841 AD Crete returned to Turkish rule.

1866–9 AD The '66 or the "Great Revolt" and the siege of Arkádi. The "Organic Statute" of 1868 promises reform, but the Great Powers reject the idea of *énosis*. Unrest continues.

1878 AD The Pact of Khalépa puts the reforms promised in the Organic Statute into practice and a period of relative peace ensues.

1895–7 AD Increasing unrest, followed by inter-communal violence between Christians and Muslims, results in an occupation by the Great Powers.

1898 AD Turkish troops finally expelled and Crete achieves autonomous status under Prince George as High Commissioner.

1905 AD Revolt of the Cretan liberal opposition, under Eleftherios Venizelos at Thérisso, results in the resignation of Prince George and the appointment of Alexander Zaimis as High Commissioner.

1910 AD Venizelos becomes Prime Minister of Greece and, following the First Balkan War ended by the Treaty of London, 30 May.

1913 AD Union with Greece is finally achieved.

1923 AD The population exchanges following the Treaty of Lausanne result in the remaining Muslims being exchanged for Greek refugees from Smyrna.

1935 AD The Venizelos rebellion generally supported in Crete, resulting in the subsequent enmity of the Metaxas dictatorship.

1941 AD The Battle of Crete, followed by Axis occupation and guerrilla warfare.

1945 AD Liberation of Crete.

1965 AD The OECD development plan for Crete's infrastructure. The planned expansion of tourism begins.

1967 AD The colonel's coup and military dictatorship.

1974 AD The restoration of democracy.

Glossary

acrópolis   citadel or summit

agrími   Cretan ibex

agrophýlakas   country warden or guardian

agorá   market place

amanádes   Turkish love songs

anáskelos   mythical beast: the devil in the shape of a donkey

andárte   resistance fighter or guerrilla

Apocriés   carnival preceding Lent

árchontes,   or *archontópouli* those of noble birth

arsenali   Venetian arsenals or galley-repairing depots

ártos   bread

baklavás   pastry with nuts and honey

barboúnia   red mullet

bastinado   beating of the soles of the feet

bazoúkoi   mandolin with a "jangling" sound, originating in Asia Minor

bougátsa   cheese pastry

bríki   coffee pot

caique   fishing boat or small coasting vessel

capóta   shepherd's cloak

chasmophytes   plants adapted to grow in the dark recesses of gorges

chibouk   long clay pipe

demotiki   popular, everyday modern Greek

diasporá   the dispersal, through emigration, of ethnic Greeks

díctamo   Cretan dittany

dolmádes   vine leaves stuffed with rice

énosis   literally "union", but specifically the joining of Crete to "Mother Greece". A word which, during the twentieth century, came to be associated with Cyprus

epitáphios   the bier on which Christ's body is symbolically laid at Easter

fábrica   olive oil mill or factory

féta   white ewes' milk cheese

fréya   single-axle tractor or cultivator

fustanélla   the traditional kilt of mainland Greece

gléndi   celebration or party

graviéra   Cretan cheese, rather like gruyère, as the name suggests

halvá   sweetmeat made with honey and sesame seeds

hasápiko   the "butcher's dance", performed by a group of men with hands on each other's shoulders

hórta   a salad of wild herbs

iconostásis   the screen in an Orthodox church, usually of carved wood, which separates the sanctuary from the nave, and on which religious pictures, or icons, are hung

isichía   peace, tranquillity

kafeneíon   café, coffeeshop

kaliméra   good morning

kalispéra   good evening

kallikántzaros   a mischievous, Pan-like spirit

kapetánios   captain or leader

kariofílis   a long-barrelled muzzle-loading rifle with an ornate, curved butt

katáchanas   fiend or vampire

katavóthras   a swallow hole, typical of limestone mountains, often draining an upland plain

Kathará Deftéra   "Clean Monday", the first day of Lent

katharévousa   an artificially 'purified' form of modern Greek, purged of foreign words

kefalomándilo   black, fringed headcloth

kharatch   Turkish poll tax

kiatib   Turkish public letter writer

kléphtis   brigand: a word particularly associated with the wild mountaineers of the mainland who rose against the Turks in 1821

kombolóyia   string of worry beads, like a rosary

koúles   tower or fortress

kouloúria   ring-shaped rolls with sesame seeds

koumbáros   best man or godfather

kri-kri   Cretan ibex

levendiá   a difficult word to translate; a combination of gaiety, courage and optimism

loukoúmi   Turkish delight

lúta   Cretan lute or mandolin

lýra   the three-stringed Cretan viol. The strings are of wire and the tune is played only on the outer two, the centre being used as a "drone"

madará   the name given in Western Crete to the high pastures of the White Mountains

mantinádes   satirical rhyming couplets, often improvised on the spot. Popular in Cyprus as well as Crete

Megáli Idéa   the "Great Idea". The concept of expanding Greece's frontiers to include all the ethnically Greek communities once scattered about the Levant and the Black Sea

meltémi   the "honey wind". A cool wind from the north which sometimes causes summer storms in the Aegean *métrio* medium, medium-sweet (of coffee)

mezéthes snacks or hors d'oeuvres

mikanís literally "machine". Motorcycle or three-wheeled pick-up

miralóyia funeral dirge

mitátos shepherd's cheese-making hut

monaxiá loneliness, solitude

moussaká the famous Greek casserole, usually composed of layers of minced lamb and aubergines, topped with a white sauce

myzíthra type of Cretan cheese

nargileh oriental water pipe with flexible stem

nomós prefecture, or administrative department of modern Greece

oikoyeneiaká literally "family problems". Vendetta or blood feud

oká archaic Turkish measure of weight, 1.283 kg

oúzo aniseed flavoured aperitif

pallikáre a brave young man, a warrior

pappás priest

passatémpo sunflower seeds, nibbled to pass the time

paximádia hard dried bread, which has to be soaked before eating

pentozáli the "five steps", an ancient Cretan war dance

perivóli garden or smallholding

philótimo personal honour, pride

philoxenía hospitality toward strangers

phrýgana low growth of thorny plants on otherwise bare mountainsides

polja high fertile plain, characteristic of the limestone Dinaric mountains

portokáli orange

psomí bread

pyrína fuel made from crushed olive stones

rakí fiery liquor made by distilling grape mash left after wine-making

rayah literally "cattle", the subject peoples of the Ottoman Empire

retsína wine with pine resin added

rizítika literally "of the roots" – i.e. of the mountains. Slow mournful ballads of war and death

Romiós another difficult word. Literally "Roman citizen", the word which the Christian Greeks used to describe themselves during and after the age of Byzantium, as opposed to Hellene, with its classical and pagan associations. Now the situation is reversed; modern Greeks describe themselves as Hellenes, and *Romiós* is tending to fall into disuse

Romiosíni quality of essential Greekness. It emphasises all those elements of Greek culture – music, dance, folklore, language – which have developed since the Classical age, and includes the influences of all the races – Arabs, Franks, Venetians, Slavs, Turks – with whom the Greek people came into contact. One might say that *Romiosíni* and Hellenism form the two opposing poles of the modern

Greek character. And one might associate *Romiosíni* with *demotikí*, the exuberant modern language with all its Turkish and Venetian words, while pairing Hellenism with *Katharévousa*, the purified "intellectual's Greek". Patrick Leigh Fermor is very good on this – see his book *Roumeli*

sakoúli knapsack

santoúri stringed instrument struck with small hammers, originally from Macedonia

saríki turban or headcloth

scirócco south wind

semántron curved length of wood or iron, used as a bell in monasteries

skéto plain, unsweetened (of coffee)

soumádha a drink, hot or cold, made from almonds and orange blossom

soúvla stake or skewer

souvlákia spit-roasted meat, "kebabs"

stifádo casserole of meat cooked with onions, bay leaves and red wine

stiniyássas good health to you

strémma measure of land, about a quarter of an acre

sýnteknos gossip, godbrother

sýrtos a graceful circling dance from Asia Minor

tavérna tavern

tespi Turkish rosary

tramountána north wind (Venetian origin)

tsikoudiá word used in Western Crete for *raki*

visinádha a drink made from cherries

vólta the Greek word for the evening promenade which takes place in every Mediterranean town

vrákes enormous and voluminous breeches worn with high boots, a relic of Ottoman days. Still to be seen in Cyprus in their full glory

vrykólakas vampire

xaírete greetings (on arrival or departure)

xenitiá exile

xénos foreigner

Yenicheri the "New Soldiers" or Janissaries. An elite corps of the Ottoman army, originally made up of sons taken in their childhood as tribute from Christian families

Bibliography

Allbough, Leland, *Crete: A case study of an underdeveloped area*, Princeton University Press, 1953.

Bowman, John, *The Traveller's Guide to Crete*, Jonathan Cape, 1985.

Braddock, Joseph, *The Greek Phoenix*, Constable & Co., 1972.

Clark, Alan, *The Fall of Crete*, Anthony Blond, 1962.

Clutton, Elizabeth, and Kenny, André, *Crete*, David & Charles, 1977.

Cuddon, J.A., *The Owl's Watchsong: a study of Istanbul*, Barnie & Rockliff, London, 1960.

Davaras, Costis, *Phaistós*, Editions Hannibal, 1984.

Doren, David MacNeil, *Winds of Crete*, P. Efstathiadis & Sons, 1981.

Durrell, Lawrence, *The Greek Islands*, Faber & Faber, 1978.

Fermor, Patrick Leigh, *Máni*, John Murray, 1958.

Fielding, Xan, *The Stronghold*, Secker & Warburg, 1953.

Grant, Michael, *The Ancient Mediterranean*, Weidenfeld & Nicolson, London, 1965.

Graves, Robert, *The Greek Myths*, Penguin, 1969.

Greece, Naval Intelligence Division Geographical Handbook, Vol. III, August 1945.

Greenhalgh, Peter and Eliopoulos, Edward, *Deep into Mani*, Faber & Faber, 1985.

Hopkins, Adam, *Crete – Its Past, Present and People*, Faber & Faber, 1977.

Huxby A. and Taylor W., *Flowers of Greece and the Aegean*, Chatto & Windus, 1977.

Kazantzakis, Nikos, *Freedom and Death*, Bruno Cassirer, 1956.

_____, *Report to Greco*, Faber & Faber, 1973.

_____, *Zorba the Greek*, Faber & Faber, 1961.

Kubly, H. *Gods and Heroes*, Gollancz, 1970.

Mead, Robin, *Crete*, B.T. Batsford, 1980.

Miller, Henry, *The Colossus of Maroussi*, Secker & Warburg, 1942.

Moss, W. Stanley *Ill Met by Moonlight*, George G. Harrap & Co, 1950.

Pashley, Robert, *Travels in Crete*, Murray, 1837.

Pendlebury, J.D.S., *Knossós: a handbook to the Palace of Minos*, Max Parish & Co., 1933.

Polunin, Oleg, *Flowers of Greece and the Balkans*, Oxford University Press, 1986.

BIBLIOGRAPHY

Powell, Dilys, *The Villa Ariadne*, P. Efstathiadis & Sons, 1982.
Prevelakis, Pandelis, *The Tale of a Town*, Doric Publications, 1976.
Provatakis, Theocharis, *Monastery of Arkádi*, Athens, 1980.
Psychoundakis, George, *The Cretan Runner*, Murray, 1955.
Renault, Mary, *The Bull from the Sea*, Longman, 1976.
Renault, Mary, *The King Must Die*, Longman, 1971.
Simpson, Colin, *Greece – the Unclouded Eye*, Hodder & Stoughton, London, 1969.
Skinner, J.E.H., *Roughing it in Crete in 1867*, London, 1868.
Smith, Michael Llewellyn, *The Great Island*, Longman, 1965.
Spratt, Capt. T.A.B., *Travels and Researches in Crete*, J. Van Voorst, 1865.
Stark, Freya, *Alexander's Path*, John Murray, 1958.
Stillman, W.J., *The Cretan Insurrection of 1866–8*, New York, 1874.
Thomas, W.B., *Dare to be Free*, Pan Books, 1955.
Tournefort, Joseph de, *A Voyage into the Levant*, London, 1718.
Trevor-Battye, Aubyn, *Camping in Crete*, Witherby & Co., 1913.
Woodhouse, C.M., *Modern Greece – a Short History*, Faber & Faber, 1977.

Index